MW00824442

# PRESENTING DATA EFFECTIVELY

## SECOND EDITION

Sara Miller McCune founded SAGE Publishing in 1965 to support the dissemination of usable knowledge and educate a global community. SAGE publishes more than 1000 journals and over 800 new books each year, spanning a wide range of subject areas. Our growing selection of library products includes archives, data, case studies and video. SAGE remains majority owned by our founder and after her lifetime will become owned by a charitable trust that secures the company's continued independence.

Los Angeles | London | New Delhi | Singapore | Washington DC | Melbourne

SKIP

# PRESENTING DATA EFFECTIVELY

## Communicating Your Findings
## for Maximum Impact

**SECOND EDITION**

**Stephanie D. H. Evergreen**

*Evergreen Data & Evaluation, LLC*

Los Angeles | London | New Delhi
Singapore | Washington DC | Melbourne

FOR INFORMATION:

SAGE Publications, Inc.
2455 Teller Road
Thousand Oaks, California 91320
E-mail: order@sagepub.com

SAGE Publications Ltd.
1 Oliver's Yard
55 City Road
London EC1Y 1SP
United Kingdom

SAGE Publications India Pvt. Ltd.
B 1/I 1 Mohan Cooperative Industrial Area
Mathura Road, New Delhi 110 044
India

SAGE Publications Asia-Pacific Pte. Ltd.
3 Church Street
#10-04 Samsung Hub
Singapore 049483

Copyright © 2018 by SAGE Publications, Inc.

All rights reserved. No part of this book may be reproduced or utilized in any form or by any means, electronic or mechanical, including photocopying, recording, or by any information storage and retrieval system, without permission in writing from the publisher.

All trademarks depicted within this book, including trademarks appearing as part of a screenshot, figure, or other image are included solely for the purpose of illustration and are the property of their respective holders. The use of the trademarks in no way indicates any relationship with, or endorsement by, the holders of said trademarks.

Printed in the United States of America

*Library of Congress Cataloging-in-Publication Data*

Names: Evergreen, Stephanie D. H., author.

Title: Presenting data effectively : communicating your findings for maximum impact/Stephanie D. H. Evergreen.

Description: Second Edition. | Thousand Oaks : SAGE Publications, Inc., [2017] | Revised edition of the author's | Includes index.

Identifiers: LCCN 2017001369 | ISBN 9781506353128 (pbk. : alk. paper)

Subjects: LCSH: Visual communication. | Presentation graphics software. | Graphic design (Typography) | Information visualization.

Classification: LCC P93.5 E94 2017 | DDC 001.4/226—dc23
LC record available at https://lccn.loc.gov/2017001369

This book is printed on acid-free paper.

Acquisitions Editor:   Helen Salmon

Editorial Assistant:   Chelsea Neve

Production Editor:   Veronica Stapleton Hooper

Copy Editor:   Judy Selhorst

Typesetter:   C&M Digitals (P) Ltd.

Proofreader:   Dennis W. Webb

Indexer:   Michael Ferreira

Cover Designer:   Rose Storey

Marketing Manager:   Susannah Goldes

eLearning Editor:   John Scappini

18 19 20 21 10 9 8 7 6 5 4 3

# Brief Contents

# Detailed Contents

## 3   Text     76

# 4   Color                 120

# 5   Arrangement     154

# About the Author

 **Stephanie D. H. Evergreen**, PhD, is an internationally recognized speaker, designer, and researcher. She is best known for bringing a research-based approach to helping researchers better communicate their work through more effective graphs, slides, and reports. She holds a doctorate from Western Michigan University in interdisciplinary evaluation, which included a dissertation on the extent of graphic design use in written research reporting. Dr. Evergreen has trained researchers worldwide through keynote presentations and workshops for clients including The World Bank, Verizon, Head Start, American Institutes for Research, the Rockefeller Foundation, the Brookings Institution, and the United Nations. She is the 2015 recipient of the American Evaluation Association's Guttentag Award, given for notable accomplishments early in a career. Dr. Evergreen is coeditor and coauthor of two issues of *New Directions for Evaluation* on data visualization. She writes a popular blog on data presentation at StephanieEvergreen.com. The first edition of this book was published by SAGE in fall 2013, and her second book, *Effective Data Visualization,* was published in spring 2016. Both books hit number one on Amazon best-seller lists.

# Acknowledgments

Deepest gratitude to my elders and mentors who have protected my time and my talent and taught me how to choose where to invest myself.

Thanks to the colleagues who have become my friends, for the inspiration, the laughs, and the belief that I really can sit down again and write another book. My heart grows three sizes whenever we are together.

I'm forever grateful for the opportunities to work with amazing clients, hungry to improve, asking me hard questions so I can keep growing in my answers. Your work is all over these pages, and you didn't have to give me permission but you did anyway, because you are leaders like that.

To my team at SAGE and the patient peer reviewers, thank you.

## Publisher's Acknowledgments

SAGE wishes to acknowledge the valuable contributions of the following reviewers.

Charlotte Baker, Institute of Public Health, Florida A&M University

Nicole Binder, Department of Education, Saint Leo University

Chris Koch, School of Behavioral and Health Sciences, George Fox University

Bianca Montrosse-Moorhead, Department of Educational Psychology, University of Connecticut

Peggy Slota, College of Health and Wellness, Carlow University

Pamela Whitehouse, Department of Education, Midwestern State University

# Preface to the Second Edition

Hi, Rock Stars—

This book walks you through how to use simple strategies from the graphic design world to enhance your reports, slideshows, posters, and graphs so that you are presenting your data effectively. It's as if a communications book and a statistics book had a baby. I teach you about color and text and how those two tools can help you tell your story clearly. I show you how you can add graphics—appropriately—to engage your reader. I illustrate how to arrange all of those things on a page or slide so that it is organized and tidy. This book essentially uproots many of the things we were taught in academia about how to report our data, digging up what may have worked 20 years ago but needs to be adapted for a digital reading culture and applying what the graphic design students are learning. But graphic designers are afraid of data, and we, dear friends, are data nerds.

So, if the first edition of this book was so awesome, why did I write a second?

WE ARE NOW IN FULL COLOR. Hallelujah! That alone is probably enough to justify a second edition, but it isn't the only reason.

Ever since the first edition of this book published, my inbox has been flooded with requests from wonderful data nerds all over the globe, doing their best to present data effectively. I've logged many miles traveling near and far to help. Nearly all these clients have asked hard questions, set their sights on lofty designs, and then asked, "Can Microsoft Office do that?"

They have pushed me to invent more solutions, develop new frameworks for thinking, and create more streamlined techniques. And you, Rock Stars, have pushed yourselves! You've written to me with your own hacks and tricks to make reporting ever better, and I'm thrilled to feature the work of readers and clients throughout this second edition.

Here's the lowdown on the fresh material in each chapter.

## Chapter 1: The Justification for Presenting Data Effectively

In my workshops all over the world, the number one excuse for not making great slides is that the audience will want the slides, so they must have detailed notes, lots of text, and generous bullets. Goodness, no! In the revised Chapter 1, I introduce the simple and beautiful idea of handouts. They will change your life. I also address dashboards, which have continued to rise in popularity since the first edition of this book was published. I show you strong dashboards, and I offer reasons *not* to use them and tell you what you could consider instead.

## Chapter 2: Graphics

Another super-common question I hear from audience members concerns how to choose the right kind of imagery for sticky subjects, like premature babies or the death penalty. In Chapter 2, I discuss how the audience determines our imagery options and how our story helps us select the best options from the field. I also include new content on how graphics help guide readers through material and update the section related to icons, including a new example. I answer the tough question "How many graphics are okay?" and the entire last section on graphs is brand new.

## Chapter 3: The Chapter Formerly Known as "Type"

My editor, Helen Salmon (bright pink hair, can't miss her at the conferences), said that a second edition usually has a lot of minor updates and a handful of really significant ones. I thought full color was going to carry the weight here, so I set about making some minor but important changes to the material itself. And then I got to the chapter formerly known as "Type." I scrapped about half of what was there and added all-new content designed to give you the biggest bang for your buck. I also changed the chapter title from "Type" to "Text" because I get pretty serious about the actual words we use and how they work to tell our story. You'll see some cool examples from recent clients, and I'll persuade you that you have to stop using Calibri.

## Chapter 4: Color

Number one, IT IS IN FULL COLOR! Yahoo! Beyond that, I explain why the stoplight color system doesn't work, addressing aspects of compliance with federal law concerning barriers to information technology access. I also show how you can use color to help readers work their way through your reporting in a digital reading environment. Color is one of our most powerful tools for storytelling inside graphs, so in that section I show you several ways you can apply color to your data.

## Chapter 5: Arrangement

This chapter got a serious overhaul. I provide grid structures to use for both reports and slides or posters so that your content is organized and you look like the pro that you are. Chapter 5 introduces you to an unsung hero of reporting—sidebars. They are powerful organizing tools that also contributes to white space. And I detail the wrong kind of white space I've seen in my clients' old reporting, the stuff we shouldn't be using in the 21st century. Hint: "This Page Intentionally Left Blank" must die a quick death, and I explain why in Chapter 5. I also launch us into modern-day reporting by providing a framework for rethinking the order in which we share our research, whether in a report, poster, or presentation. Finally, the section on graphs here is all new, including a structure for deciding when it is okay to change the scale on your y-axis, perhaps one of the hottest debates in the data visualization community.

## Chapter 6: Making It Easy

This chapter has always been about how to make reporting more efficient, especially considering that your audience and I are asking you to do so much more. Well, my own design practice is always pushing me to find new ways to be better, and in the new version of Chapter 6 I share a new strategy for faster high-impact reporting. You'll love it.

## Appendices

Along with the Report Layout Checklist in Appendix A, a second checklist has been added to this edition, this one focused exclusively on data visualization. Coauthored with my friend Ann Emery, the Data Visualization Checklist is our compilation of the best that's out there about how to create a graph that tells your story. It is detailed. It deals with the nitty-gritty. We wade into the weeds. You'll see the nuts and bolts of how to format every little bit of your graph so your data can shine. In each chapter, I refer to relevant guidelines in the Data Visualization Checklist and show you what you're aiming for with your design skills.

## Digital Resources

Visit the open-access companion website that accompanies this text!
study.sagepub.com/evergreen2e

So, while a second edition is usually a decent evolution, the world of presenting data effectively changes so fast that this second edition is a pretty major overhaul. Which means, come to think of it, that there will probably be a third edition down the road, too. Good thing this topic is so critical to our work and that we like each other so much.

*Stephanie Evergreen*
*Kalamazoo, Michigan, USA, and at Large*

# CHAPTER ONE

# THE JUSTIFICATION FOR PRESENTING DATA EFFECTIVELY

## LEARNING OBJECTIVES

**After reading this chapter, you will be able to:**

- Contrast weak and effective data presentation
- Articulate the basic steps of how the brain retains information
- Pinpoint where in that process the graphic design cues are useful
- Position data presentation within the web of related fields

W hen you need to convince your colleagues that their data presentations need a bit of sprucing up, this is the chapter to surreptitiously place in their mailboxes. This chapter discusses why it is so critically important for us to learn about better data presentation. You probably already know some of this intuitively. For example, you were bored during a presentation as the speaker read the text off his slides, or you struggled to keep alert while dragging through a report and peeked ahead at how many more pages of narrative awaited you, or you wasted time trying to decode a cluttered graph and your eyes glazed over.

For a speaker and author, the eye glaze is like the kiss of death. When you see it happening to members of your audience, you know that you have 3 . . . 2 . . . 1 . . . yes—an audience checking their email messages. Whichever end of the exchange you are on, you understand the importance and necessity of a presentation that attracts and maintains interest.

## Dissertation in a Nutshell

I looked at the extent of graphic design use in evaluation reports, which I gathered from a national repository. With an extensive literature review of cognition-based design theory and the iterative input of a panel of graphic design experts, I pulled together a checklist of graphic design best practices, as applied to the context of evaluation and research reports. A version of the checklist can be found in Appendix A of this book and is downloadable in the online companion.

I trained a group of raters and then asked them to apply the checklist to a culled sample of the evaluation reports. The results probably will not surprise you too much. The reports scored high on those checklist items that are default settings found in most word-processing programs.

The reports scored lowest on the presence of graphics. Graphics, in this case, refers to pictures, diagrams, charts, and graphs. Yes, some reports had no graphs at all. Others that continued to rely on default settings produced cluttered and miscolored graphs that caused confusion for readers.

In fairness, there were actually several reports whose authors really got it right and produced engaging materials that lured readers to scroll through, regardless of report length.

*(Continued)*

(Continued)

So, those were the main findings of the study, but in the process of conducting it we discovered something else: We used interrater reliability to look at how closely the trained raters matched my scoring of the sampled reports. The score was high. In other words, with some training and maybe a splash of predisposed interest, people can learn what great (and not-so-great) data presentations look like. Some folks like to claim that I have some innate talent or creativity, but I do not think that is true. Creating great data presentations is a skill that can be learned. You can do it, too.

How is it that most of us can relate to the irritation of sitting through weak data presentations, but there is still so much weak data presentation in the world? Well, old habits are hard to break. Many of us who have come up through an academic pipeline have been drilled with our departments' required style manuals, which seemed to point toward pages and pages of prose, or the painful construction and formatting of graphs and figures. In turn, some of us found our way to government positions where PowerPoint templates and colors were mandated, and clearance departments had the final say in the look of all reports. And most of us are better at critiquing bad design than we are at envisioning what an effective data presentation looks like. This book is your new style guide, your step-by-step resource on how to make your work more memorable. But don't worry—these steps are still aligned with the major academic style guides and with the U.S. government's guidelines around universal accessibility. We're good to go. So, let's go.

## What Does Effective Data Presentation Look Like?

It seems that it is always easier to spot weak presentations than to organically develop effective data presentation. It may be useful to walk through a few examples.

### Reports

Familiar, isn't it? If you haven't guessed, we are looking at the first two pages of a report. Indeed, the first page is pulled exactly from my dissertation. I followed the university's dissertation formatting guidelines with precision—and if you have ever been in a similar situation you know that at times the guidelines can appear more

**Figures 1.1 and 1.2    Cover and second page of a weak report**

DEATH BY BOREDOM: THE ROLE OF VISUAL PROCESSING THEORY IN WRITTEN
EVALUATION COMMUNICATION

Stephanie D. H. Evergreen, Ph.D.

Western Michigan University, 2011

Evaluation reporting is an educational act and, as such, should be communicated using principles that support cognition. This study drew upon visual processing theory and theory-based graphic design principles to develop the Evaluation Report Layout Checklist intended to guide report development and support cognition in the readers of evaluation reports. It was then reviewed by an expert panel and applied by a group of raters to a set of evaluation reports obtained from the Informal Science Education evaluation website with maximum variability sampling. Results showed fairly high exact percent agreement and strong to very strong correlation with the author's ratings. Ratings revealed a low level of theory-based report formatting in use of graphics and some aspects of type, alignment, and color among evaluation reports in the sample.

TABLE OF CONTENTS

**Figures 1.3 and 1.4    Cover and second page of an effective report**

# Death by Boredom
The Role of Visual Processing Theory In
Written Evaluation Communication

Stephanie D. H. Evergreen, Ph.D.
Western University
Winter 2011

© iStockphoto.com/Mari

# Foreword

Evaluation reporting is an educational act and, as such, should be communicated using principles that support cognition. This study drew upon visual processing theory and theory-based graphic design principles to develop the Evaluation Report Layout Checklist intended to guide report development and support cognition in the readers of evaluation reports. It was then reviewed by an expert panel and applied by a group of raters to a set of evaluation reports with maximum variability sampling. Results showed fairly high exact percent agreement and strong to very strong correlation with the author's ratings. Ratings revealed a low level of theory-based report formatting in use of graphics and some aspects of type, alignment, and color among evaluation reports in the sample.

In short, the study showed that we still have fairly extensive and pleasant work ahead of us. Yet we also have inspiration on our side as well as the open minds of our audiences, waiting to engage.

Stephanie Evergreen, Ph.D.
Western University

mysterious than the study itself. On examination, there are several elements that actively prevent a reader from engaging with the text. The title, for example, is set in all caps, which makes it difficult to read at length (and aren't they all lengthy?). The centered alignment adds another layer of reading difficulty. Then when the reader whips past the first page to get to the content, she is met with, well, the table of contents (pages of them, in my case). Page numbers are misaligned. It is a mess. With just these first two pages, the reader now understands that if she chooses to continue to read, making any sense or meaning out of the report is going to take work. Ultimately, this type of reporting does not engage the reader. It is weak. Now, let's contrast that a bit.

Notice any changes? Of course you do! While I left some of the healthy white space on the cover page of the weaker version, I added a photograph of a bored child. At a glance, the photograph is interesting, engaging to a viewer, relatable, and works hard to communicate the author's point. Now, I understand that a graduate college never allows a dissertation submission with a photograph on the cover. But then again, few people outside the graduate college, and an applicant's advisers, ever read the dissertation in the condition it is submitted. For outside audiences, you should adopt the flexibility to repackage your study to make it more appealing, interesting, and memorable. As we discuss later on, graphics are a great way to do just that.

Notice that the title is larger rather than in all caps. It stands out as the most important text on the page and is now more legible. The subtitle is bumped down to its own line. On the second page, I replaced the table of contents with a slightly more intriguing foreword. It is short, increasing the likelihood that people will read it, and it contains the personal touch of my picture.

If you had the choice to flip through either of these reports on your lunch break, I feel certain that you would pick the effective one.

## Slideshows

Of course, this range of quality in data presentation exists in all dissemination formats. Home slides like this one are pretty common fare.

It is likely that you instantly recognize this design as a slide template, one of the default options that come preloaded in slide software programs like PowerPoint. Communicating "default" is probably not what we seek when we are trying to engage an audience with our work. On close inspection, you'll notice that there is also a bit of uneven spacing happening in the chunk of text at the bottom of the cover slide. The company logo is somewhat plastered in the upper right corner. The font, as we discuss later, is inappropriate for slide projection.

**Figures 1.5 and 1.6    First and second slides from a weak slideshow**

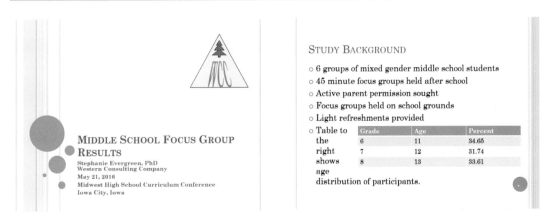

On the interior slide, shown on the right, there is simply too much text. The table is full of numbers that take a lot of cognitive processing to understand. The alternating banded rows further interfere with legibility. Imagine trying to weed through this slide while the speaker is reiterating the points verbally. This is a great way to lose an audience by just the second slide of a talk. How could these slides work better?

**Figures 1.7 and 1.8    First and second slides from an effective slideshow**

© iStockphoto.com/kalig

In this version, a large, relatable image draws in the viewer on the home slide. It gives a much clearer indication of the subject of the presentation to audience members who may be milling around the room before they find their seats. Obvious information (like the name of the conference and the date of the presentation) is removed to declutter the slide. The font is larger, and the sans serif style is much easier on the eyes, particularly when projected.

The interior slide now visualizes the logistical description that had been text based in the weak slide. The diagram communicates in an instant what the table did not. At this point it looks as if critical details, such as the fact that the focus groups were mixed gender and that we served snacks, are gone, but they really are not. It is just that those details come from the speaker, who is the proper center of attention. Effective data presentation with a deck of slides means that the visuals are a support tool, not a replacement for the speaker.

And this is why rad presenters never give out their slides. The thing is, if the presenter has done a great job, you really don't want the slides. No, really, you don't.

A long long time ago, Garr Reynolds taught me that if someone can look at your slideshow and tell all the things you are going to say, there's no need for you, the speaker. The content and value of the talk should come from the presenter's mouth, not the projector. The slides by themselves will be pretty useless. Here's a screenshot of a current slide deck, in slide sorter mode:

**Figure 1.9   Slide sorter view shows many slides at once**

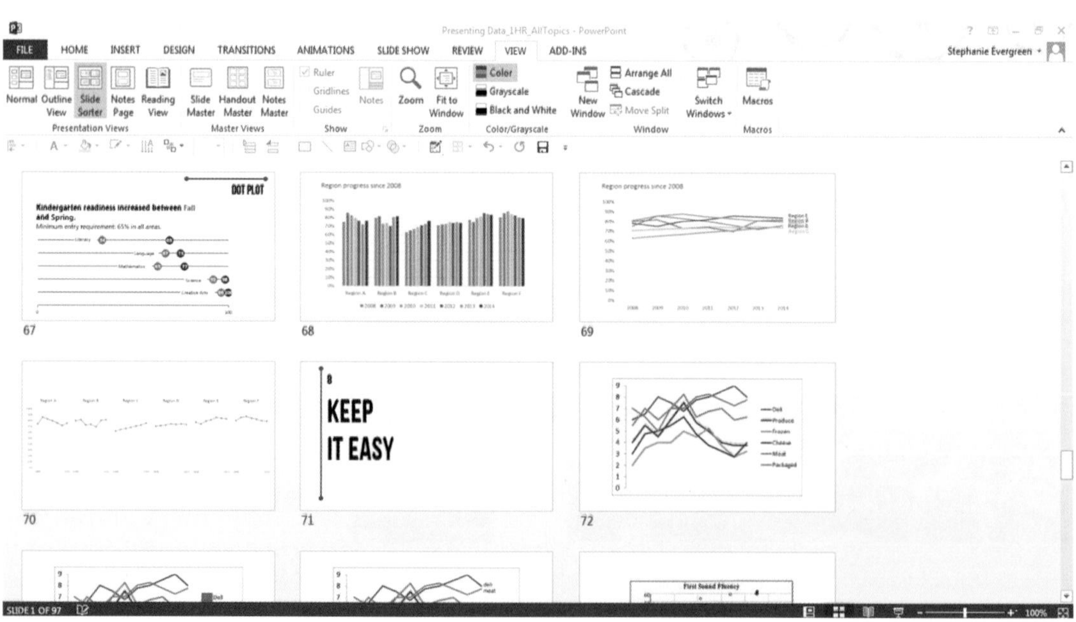

Doesn't provide much value, does it? That's the idea! I need to be there, as the speaker and the value giver, in order for the slides to make sense.

Moreover, I often have slideshows with 300+ slides in them. I go through them so quickly an audience member would never know how thick my deck is. But that's another reason you really don't want to print out my slides.

I hear you talking back to this page right now, saying something like "But I want a reminder of what you said to jog my memory when I get back to my office." Of *course*, darling! I'm not going to leave you hanging. Any speaker worth her salt will have a handout that accompanies the talk.

## Handouts

A handout is a short, condensed version of all the key points, URLs, and references mentioned in the slideshow. It may even have tiny visuals that match the slideshow to visually cue the audience member's memory. The handout is a useful support for viewers' efforts to put in place the things they learned in the talk. Here's a current handout that belongs with the slide deck above:

**Figure 1.10    A handout is a useful summary of a talk**

Audiences like handouts because they are, well, handy. They summarize the key points, free up the audience to listen, and look really great pinned to an office wall.

You have a few choices when it comes to the kind of handout you distribute.

Option A is a detailed handout where you have pasted in the key points from your notes.

**Figure 1.11    A detailed handout contains your notes**

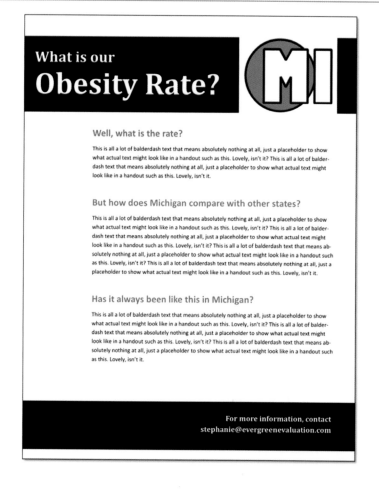

You'll tell the audience, "You are welcome to take notes but I have a handout for you with all of my key points that I will pass out as you exit." Why as they exit? So that your audience members do not read your handout instead of listening to you speak.

Option B is a semiblank handout where you have pasted in just your main topic areas, leaving plenty of empty space for audience members to take their own notes.

Figure 1.12    **With a blank handout, audience members construct their own takeaway points**

You will want to include in the handout any URLs, references, or resources—anything you wouldn't want the audience to have to copy from a slide. But the rest of the handout leaves each audience member the room to construct a document that will be most helpful after the workshop. This handout works best when you know each person will take away different lessons from your presentation.

Sometimes I'll create a hybrid of these two options, leaving the handout fairly empty but typing in some of my key points.

Your choice between these two handout options will hinge a bit on your audience needs. A CEO, for example, probably does not want to create her own handout. She wants you to give her one that already has all the detail. On the other hand, certain groups can't just sit and listen. Teachers are a great example of this kind of crowd (I know, I used to be

**Figure 1.13    Put dense material on a handout**

## 5 Impact Areas

|  | National | Michigan | Site 1 | Site 2 | Site 3 | Site 4 |
|---|---|---|---|---|---|---|
| **Obesity** | 62.3% | **64.7%** | 65.1% | 68.1% | 59.9% | 63.8% |
| **Graduation** | 60.3% | **71.3%** | 66.9% | 78.2% | 61.4% | 75.6% |
| **Home Ownership** | 21.1 | **20** | 20.9 | 22.9 | 20.7 | 22.3 |
| **College Aspirations** | 75.7% | **74.2%** | 78.5% | 82.3% | 80.4% | 77.5% |
| **Art Show Attendance** | 38.0% | **36.0%** | 44.3% | 39.7% | 39.2% | 46.0% |

For more information
stephanie@evergreenevaluation.com

one). They have to be multitasking. They'll be in a professional development meeting, knitting while they listen. This group would benefit from keeping their hands busy and creating their own handout.

One more option to consider: Whenever you have something dense, like a table or a complicated diagram, put it in a handout.

No one wants to look at that thing on a big screen. Pass it around so each person can examine it up close, take notes, and refer to it later.

Your goal here is to deliver to your audience members an easily accessible document that contains a high-level overview and gives them a resource for getting more information if they need it. You should aim for something that they will want to hang on their walls.

Or refrigerators. I know this isn't exactly a presentation handout, but I think it illustrates my point. This flyer came from my kid's school. It probably looks pretty similar to what you retrieve from your kids' backpacks too.

**Figures 1.14 and 1.15    Weak handout**

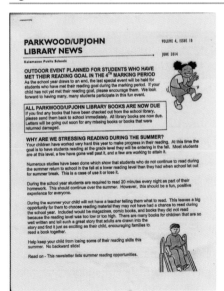
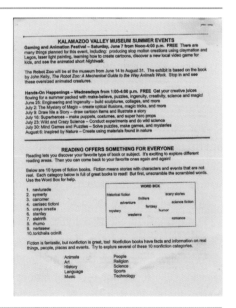

*Source:* Kalamazoo Public Schools.

On the back of the newsletter, you can see that the story at the top is about the events happening at the local museum over the summer. That same day, we also received the museum's flyer.

**Figure 1.16    Effective handout**

*Source:* Kalamazoo Valley Museum. Image of little girl with painted hands © iStockphoto .com/hannamonika.

One of these landed on my refrigerator and one of them went into my recycling bin. I'm sure you can see the differences that make a difference. While both use images of children, the school's flyer uses cheap-looking clip art while the museum's has an actual photograph that looks fun and engaging. Both handouts use color. The school's handout is printed on blue paper, probably under the assumption that the paper color would make it stand out from all of the other junk that comes home with my kid. The museum flyer uses one color as an organizing tool. It sections off different events and structures the page so it is more readable. The real distinction here is not money or time (the museum is free—it has no large graphic design department) or even software (you can make effective handouts in Publisher or even PowerPoint). No, the real distinction is that someone at the museum learned the nitty-gritty about how to present information effectively.

Handouts are a way to meet people where they are with however much information they need from us at that time. The few people in the audience who are hungry for more can follow a URL in the handout to obtain the full report. But for the majority of our audience, the handout will be their next step in our presentation adventure.

## Posters

I would wager that once or twice you've wandered the aisles of a conference poster exhibit and spotted some posters similar to the example below.

**Figure 1.17   Weak research poster**

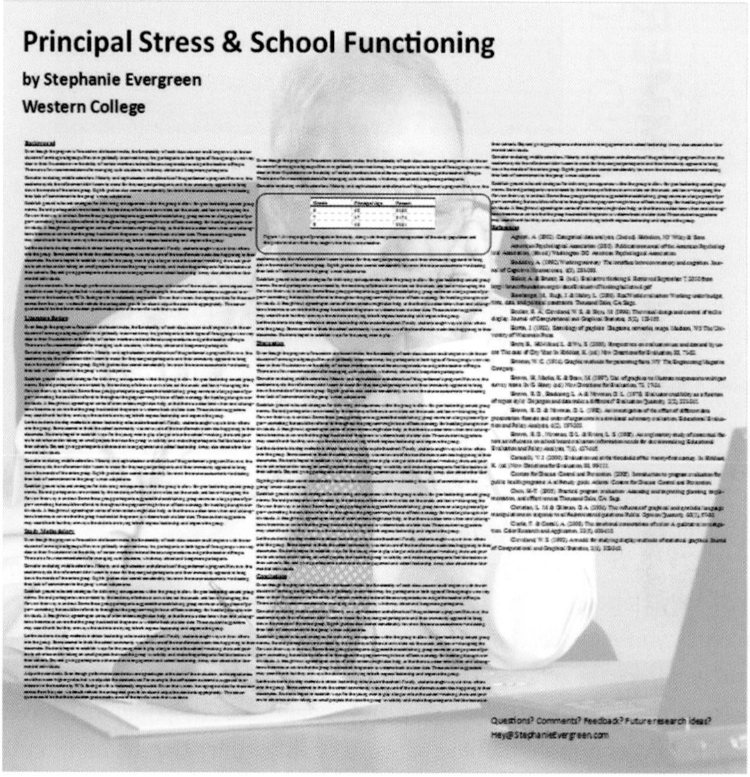

© iStockphoto.com/SteveLuker

Research posters are usually at least 3.5 feet wide and 3.5 feet tall. The poster shown here has been shrunk to the extent that you can't read the text. But you are familiar with the general layout of a poster where narrative text is used to explain the background, literature review, methods, analysis, and discussion of a study. Posters are usually intended to stand alone and to deliver the entire message without a speaker to elaborate. Yet this poster cannot explain the study because it is impeding efforts to engage and communicate.

While relevant to the topic, the background picture obscures the text and renders it somewhat illegible. Imagine trying to read the text that rests on top of the principal's patterned tie. Yikes! The average conference-goer will not even bother. The table covering the principal's face is also oddly placed, and with its white background, it is a literal bright spot to a viewer, sticking out more than anything else on the poster. The table's encapsulation inside a box further contributes to its prominence. With this level of emphasis, whatever is in that table better be the key take-home message.

**Figure 1.18    Effective research poster**

© iStockphoto.com/SteveLuker

Research posters are difficult to master. Poster designers often have to balance the competing needs of large text that is readable at a distance and up close. The poster size itself allows for much more space than we are used to in a research paper, and thus compels a desire to add some visual interest. At play are also poster guidelines dictated by the conference, such as a minimum font size. Now, mix in the tendency to want to detail the entire contents of the related research paper, and that is how we end up with posters like Figure 1.17. Still, it is possible to work within all of those parameters to develop a more effective data presentation.

Creating a more effective version of the poster required very few changes. It uses the same fonts, font sizes, and photograph of a disheartened principal, yet it conveys the key message more clearly. Good poster design can and should incorporate some visual imagery; it just should not hide behind text. Here, it is off to one side, resulting in a better view of both the photograph and the text. Rather than a table, which feels a bit like it is just more text, the revised poster includes a graph of the key findings. However, the sizes of the photograph and the graph mean that some of the poster's space is no longer available for the study narrative. That's okay—there is still plenty of space to relay most necessary details for an onlooker to comprehend the study procedures.

## Data Displays

Let's look at data displays, since they tend to make an appearance in each of the methods of presentation addressed above.

If you've been anywhere near the discussions around data visualization in the past few years, then you know that pie charts are a bit of a flash point. Some people think that there is no better way to express parts of a whole. Other people assert that pie charts are fairly useless because humans are pretty terrible at judging angles. Of course, that specific problem is compounded when the pie chart is rendered in three dimensions, as in Figure 1.19. Research in this area is quite clear— three-dimensional data displays slow down interpretation and often lead to inaccurate comprehension. In addition, this display uses the default color scheme of Microsoft Excel, where each

**Figure 1.19    Weak data display (3-D pie chart)**

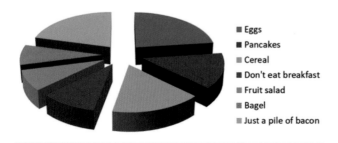

**Attendee Breakfast Preferences**

- Eggs
- Pancakes
- Cereal
- Don't eat breakfast
- Fruit salad
- Bagel
- Just a pile of bacon

*Source:* © 2012. Reprinted with permission from the American Evaluation Association.

slice of the pie is assigned a different color. How well will the distinctive colors hold up when the display is reproduced in black and white? Many organizations save on costs by printing in black and white (and yes, many people still print!), which means that we have to devise more effective data presentation methods.

Several adjustments make the display of these same data more effective. In Figure 1.20, the data are represented by a bar chart instead of a pie chart, because humans are much better at roughly assessing length than they are at perceiving angle. Bar charts are easier to decode. Also, the bars are ordered from the greatest to the least to make that decoding process even more straightforward. The graph now has a more descriptive title and an explanatory subtitle. In a sense, the study authors have taken a stance on the analysis in the study—created a story to tell. Previously, in the weak example, the data were simply presented. Even if the authors had an opinion, it was left up to the viewer to interpret the data and decide what was important. The problem with presenting data in that manner is that it assumes that the average viewer takes the time to engage with the data and has the mind-reading ability to pull out the most pertinent elements that relate to the author's points. Those are quite large assumptions. Communication with stakeholders is clearer and more effective when the graph's key points are highlighted. The viewer can always disagree, and all the data are there with which to do so; nothing is hidden. This format just respects the time and energy of the audience and relays the data directly. In the effective example, the key message is both stated in the title and made obvious by the changes in the bar colors such that the less important points are a light gray and the point that illustrates the message pops out the most.

**Figure 1.20    Effective data display (bar chart ordered greatest to least)**

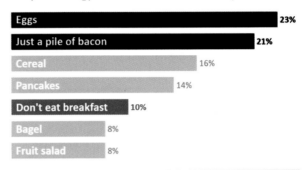

*Source:* © 2012. Reprinted with permission from the American Evaluation Association.

## Dashboards (and Dashboard Reports)

Dashboards are intended to give the 30,000-foot view of an organization's key performance indicators on one page full of data displays, for fast assessment by CEOs and directors. The idea is that the decision makers have the data they need at their fingertips. One-pagers sure are nice, as just discussed in the context of handouts, and there's a lot of pressure to get all the important data onto a one-page dashboard.

Dashboards are so hot these days they'll burn you. I mean it. I've consulted with dozens and dozens of clients on dashboards, and through all of that experience, I've discovered that dashboards can actually undermine good decision making.

Don't get me wrong. I understand the need for a succinct compilation of performance data on key indicators. It sure beats a 200-page slide deck. But in the race away from the lengthy tomes of the past, I think the pendulum has swung too far. These days, the dashboard trend is to try to cram everything important onto a single page. I've done it for clients! Here's one:

**Figure 1.21    A possibly perfectly fine data dashboard**

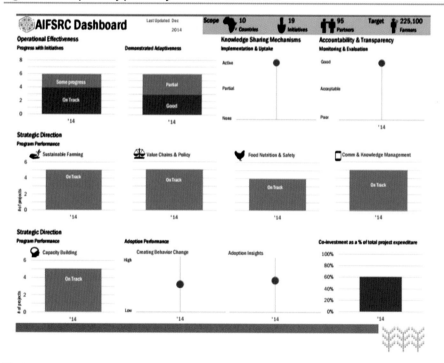

*Source:* Reprinted with permission from the Australian Centre for International Agricultural Research.

As far as I know this client is operating perfectly well with this dashboard. I have taken many, many clients to this place. And they generally feel good about the design. But sometimes I'll get the quietly concerned email from the people in my tribe, my fellow research nerds: "Um, Stephanie? This looks elegant, but we had major data collection issues in Q3 and that's not obvious in the dashboard and I'm concerned that if the Board sees this they aren't going understand the caveats." These are legitimate concerns.

People are driven primarily by their eyeballs. People want to look at the graphs and, if the graphs are strong on design and readily understood, be able to take actions based on the graphs. And this is when the research team freaks out. What about the context? What about how the measurement on this metric changed three times? Yikes, please don't make decisions off of this quite yet.

But the modern conceptualization of a dashboard leaves little room for those extremely important narrative points of interest. This is the downfall.

As opposed to a single-page dashboard, let's loosen up to a dashboard report. A while ago I edited a journal article written by my friend Veronica Smith (2013), in which she outlines the difference. Where a dashboard is a single page of visualized metrics, a dashboard report is a multipage document with one or two visualized metrics per page and healthy room for narrative. It's the pendulum swinging back toward the middle, but not nearly so far as those 200-page text-heavy doorstop reports. Here's one page from a dashboard report I produced with some long-term clients, the Oregon Health Authority:

**Figure 1.22    One page from a possibly more effective dashboard report**

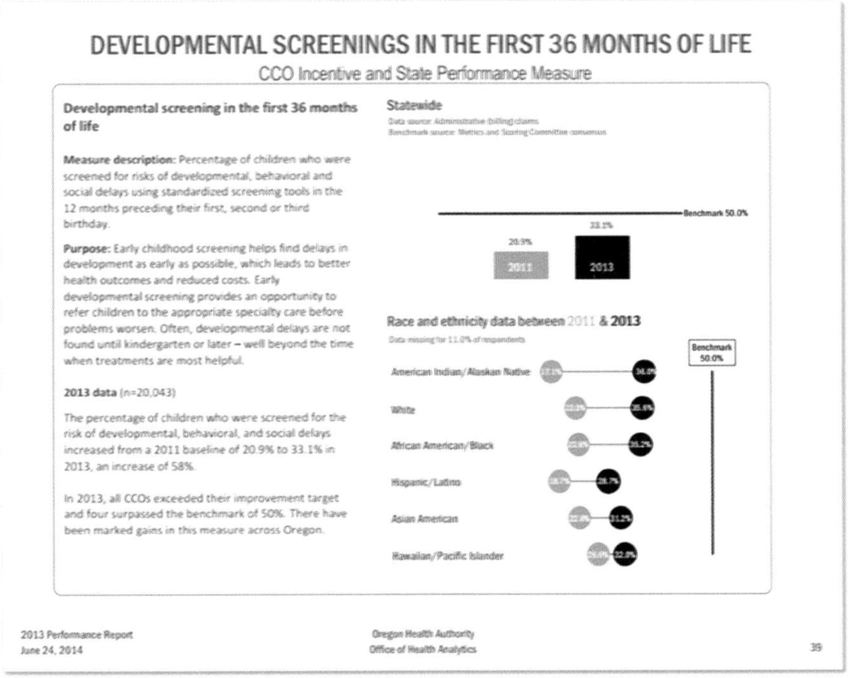

*Source:* © 2013. Reprinted with permission from the Oregon Health Authority.

You can see we are reporting two metrics here, and they are accompanied by a text box that holds helpful explanation. It isn't a burdensome amount to read; it doesn't even fill up the left-hand side of the page. But it gives the research team enough space to say their piece and feel comfortable sending the data off to the decision makers. Dashboard reports balance out high-quality visualizations and a tiny bit of narrative so everyone can sleep well at night.

Regardless of our fields, positions, or geographic locations, we are all in the business of presentation. The way we package our words and our data is reflected in our audiences' perceptions of our quality, credibility, and trustworthiness. These sets of examples reflect the obvious differences and stark contrast between weak and effective data presentation. Everyone is tired of the current models of data presentation precisely because they are weaker and do not engage viewers or increase the likelihood that they'll be able to recall the information presented. Effective data presentation creates a shortcut to audience comprehension.

## What Makes Data Presentation *Effective?*

This section may be the most important part of the entire book. I am going to devote some space here to describing the science of communication. Often, my workshop participants, full of excitement and inspiration, try to take fresh ideas back to their home organizations and universities, only to find that no one listens; someone says something like "We don't have time to worry about making things pretty." One workshop attendee who worked in academia said that if a faculty member does not use bullet points and text-heavy slides, she is seen as unprofessional and unscientific. By far, this resistance from the uninitiated is one of the most common areas of concern for my workshop participants. Our strongest justification for evolving our reporting is based in being aligned with how the human brain operates and how people retain information. If our hard work is to draw attention, make an impact, and convince others to take action (e.g., award funding), then communication can no longer be presented in the weak style of the status quo. An effective data presentation may look pretty, but the true goal is to support audience cognition.

Visual processing theory describes the way the brain perceives and interprets what the eyes see. Graphic design incorporates the science of visual perception in creating designs that better attract viewer attention. What follows is a supremely oversimplified primer on visual processing theory, how information ultimately gets retained in the mind of an audience member, and how effective data presentation assists in that retention process.

## Pictorial Superiority Effect

Rather than delay the suspense, let's jump right to the main point: We get our information about the world primarily through our eyes. Certainly, we have other sensory organs that feed information to our brains. But the reality is that vision dominates. Today's researchers refer to this as the *pictorial superiority effect,* a term so difficult to work into a conversation that it clearly comes from academia. The pictorial superiority effect essentially reminds us that what the eyes see always wins, even if we intentionally try to confuse our senses. Large parts of our brain and brain activity are devoted to visual processing (Stenberg, 2006).

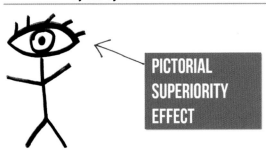

**Figure 1.23   The pictorial superiority effect essentially means our brains are led by our eyes**

PICTORIAL SUPERIORITY EFFECT

Apparently I knew at an early age what I wanted to be when I grew up because I actually studied this topic when I was in fourth grade. We had to devise an experiment for our school science fair. I ran a taste-test experiment, where I poured three identical glasses of cola. I left one glass as is, dropped red food coloring into the second glass to give it a red tint, and added green food coloring to the third glass. Then I called my friends over and made them taste each glass (this was before concerns about the potential germ proliferation caused by sharing glasses). Across the board, my friends thought that the red cola was cherry flavored and the green cola was disgusting. What the eyes see always wins, even though scent and taste should have made the experiment obvious.

This example is not just fourth-grade foolishness, either. In his book *Brain Rules* (2008), John Medina retells how French researchers at the University of Bordeaux conducted a similar experiment on a more sophisticated set of subjects, wine sommeliers, which must be the best job in the whole world. Wine sommeliers are the people who judge wine competitions. However, it is not easy to become a wine sommelier. There are dense textbooks to study and challenging tests to pass that assess learned knowledge about wine and wine history and determine the extent of the sensitivity of the tester's palate. Wine sommeliers have extremely well-refined smell and taste abilities. These people can detect that a peach orchard was growing 200 years before the vineyard was planted on the same grounds. They can actually pick up the peach flavor and aroma in the wine. As an acknowledgment of their talents, they wear a special pin on their lapels identifying their superhuman powers. It's amazing. Anyway, back to the study where the researchers at the University of Bordeaux (right!) obtained white wine and tinted it red with dyes and food coloring. Then they gave it to the wine sommeliers. You can probably guess what happened. When the wine sommeliers were asked to describe the wine to the researchers, even though their noses and mouths were screaming "White wine! White wine!" they used the language of red wine in their descriptions. Vision wins.

The pictorial superiority effect is exactly what we can use to our advantage in effective data presentation. This effect is what allows us to move information along the memory continuum to catch the reader's eye, focus the reader's attention, and affix in the reader's memory. Let's talk about how the pictorial superiority effect works in three stages along the memory continuum.

**Figure 1.24    We have always had the pictorial superiority effect**

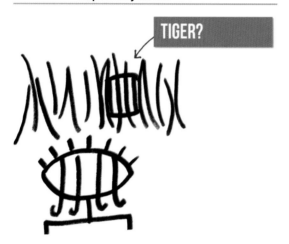

**Figure 1.25    We can apply the pictorial superiority effect to our research reporting**

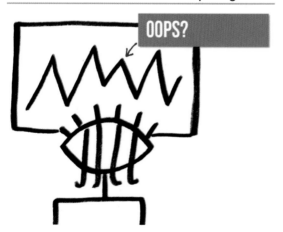

## Early Attention

As far as anyone knows, this visual dominance has always been a human trait (except, of course, in cases of individuals who are blind at birth). To a large extent, it is this effect that has advanced our survival as a species to date. Humans are naturally skilled at scanning the horizon, looking for food, or mates, or danger. We are adept at noticing patterns in our environment and spotting abnormalities in those patterns.

In fact, we are so awesome at using our eyes to take in information, our brains do not even have to be cognitively engaged for the process to work. When something just catches our eye, it is tapping into our earliest stages of attention, an activity that is so subtle that some researchers call this stage **pre**attention (Callaghan, 1989; Ware, 2013). This process occurs without focused energy on the part of the viewer.

Effective data presentation makes use of this early attention function.

A lot of graphic design operates in this stage. Emphasis techniques like color, alignment, motion, orientation, and size grab a viewer's early attention. Visual cognition research reveals that capitalizing on the pictorial superiority effect boosts the audience's ability to recall information. However, in order for information to be available for recall, it must be stored in the brain's long-term memory, which is Stage 3. Information moves from Stage 1, early attention, to Stage 3, long-term memory, along a path that can be a bit tricky, but graphic design helps it get there.

## Working Memory

Now to discuss the tricky part of that path—working memory.

Working memory is what we use when something has caught our eye and we decide to bring it into mental focus, to contemplate it, and to engage our cognitive energy. Working memory is where we wrestle with information to understand and process it so that it can eventually be assimilated into long-term memory. But the problem is that working memory is like a sieve. It is weak, can't wrestle for long, and can't wrestle with much. Research shows we hold only three to five chunks of information in working memory at any one time, and even that number varies depending on the environmental context (Baddeley, 1992; Cowan, 2000; Xu & Chun, 2006). If a subject is in a stressful or distracting atmosphere, even three chunks of information cannot be handled at once. When a viewer's working memory is overloaded, it drops some chunks of information, and then misunderstanding or frustration results (Woodman, Vecera, & Luck, 2003).

Enter graphic design. Although working memory has limits on its cognitive load, graphic elements can reduce the overload by doing some of the thinking for the reader. By visually organizing and emphasizing information, graphic design makes it more accessible, increasing the reader's capacity to engage with the words and data.

By virtue of this process, richer chunks of information are actually created, which in turn enables the viewer to essentially handle a larger cognitive load at one time (Shah, Mayer, & Hegarty, 1999). By paying attention to format, color, and font

**Figure 1.26  Avoiding the overload of working memory is a key tenet behind effective design choices**

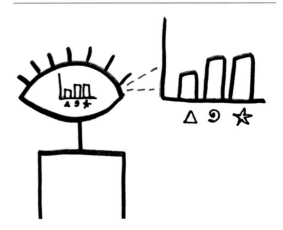

**Figure 1.27  Organizing information makes it easier to comprehend**

choices, we assist readers in encoding our information and grappling with it; this is how comprehension occurs. The more engagement, the more that passes through the working memory checkpoint, the more information that stays in long-term memory.

## Long-Term Memory

The last stage is long-term memory. When information is received into long-term memory, it can be recalled later on, retold to others, and combined with other ideas— to evolve into something even more amazing.

In order for new information to be encoded in the brain, it must be incorporated into existing schemas. If you're like me, you probably haven't heard the phrase "existing schemas" since high school biology class. This phrase refers to our mental models or our belief systems about how the world works. Again, effective data presentation assists this process because graphics are particularly good at activating those existing schemas. When we add visuals to verbal explanations, readers generate an increase of 65 percentage points in creative transfers and applications of knowledge (Mayer, 1997). That is why so many of us are better at remembering faces than names, and at navigating using landmarks rather than street names. We are visual beings.

Now, there are a host of other factors that help us retain information for the long haul. We have probably all been in situations where we remembered something for two days only to forget it after two months. Individual experiences, culture, emotion, and even exercise can play into the health of our brain's storage capacities (Medina, 2008). As students, researchers, and data presenters, we do not have complete control over those aspects for each of our audience members, but we can own our part in this recall process. Effective data presentation, where we use graphic visualization to emphasize information, speeds the acquisition of that information and reduces the opportunity for misinterpretation (Johnson, 2014; Stenberg, 2006). Because it is so important, here is that statement again: When we adopt the principles discussed in this book, we help our audiences to engage with our work more quickly, and we reduce their errors. These end results are precisely what we want to encourage among those stakeholders listening to or reading our findings.

**Figure 1.28    Effective data presentation is retained in long-term memory**

Even though some elements of this discussion of visual processing theory have been linearized and oversimplified, the time and effort expended on intentional data presentation are justified. With the research cited above leading the way, we can make clear to our colleagues, professors, supervisors, and clearance departments that our energies are not wasted. The end result is increased audience understanding. If we are not working toward that end, why are we engaged in our work in the first place? The true waste of our own effort, our funding sponsorship, and our audience's time and attention occurs when we retreat back to weak status quo communication, because the audience will choose to mentally check out (or check their email).

## What Do I Need to Develop Effective Data Presentation?

The research-based principles I detail in this book can move us from the weak presentation to the effective. Additionally, they can elevate the effective presentation to the beautiful, useful, and inspiring. I present the tools and ideas you need to achieve these wonderful goals, supported by the required tools of your good cheer and open-minded disposition.

However, it is important that you know what this book does not address: your content. It does not discuss how you write reports, how well you have designed your study, or the strength of your references; I assume you have all of that under control. Instead, it does discuss how your information gets used by your audiences. In *Utilization-Focused Evaluation* (2008), legendary evaluator Michael Quinn Patton points out a set of findings produced in 1995 by the U.S. General Accounting Office (now the Government Accountability Office) on what happens to evaluation reports. The GAO examined the dissemination paths of several major federally funded program evaluations in its study *Program Evaluation: Improving the Flow of Information to the Congress.* This study probably doesn't sound like a nail-biter, but Patton notes that the report's main finding was that evaluation information does not get very far, despite the significant funding poured into evaluations and the high profile of many of the programs under scrutiny. His point is that we can take strides to make evaluation ultimately more useful by engaging stakeholders throughout the process of the study, ensuring the study examines aspects of importance, and delivering the report to decision makers in time for them to use the information as evidence. But let us tack on to this list of utilization strategies the role of effective data presentation. That same GAO report has these details buried inside: "Lack of information does not appear to be the main problem. Rather the problem seems to be that the available information is not organized and communicated effectively." It goes on to say, "Information did not reach the right people, or it did, but it was in a form that was difficult to digest" (p. 39). So you see, this book is not about the quality of your content; you are the expert in that area. This book is about organizing that content and communicating it in more digestible and effective ways. Here is what you need.

## A Disciplinary Positioning

In addition to learning some concepts around visual processing theory, you should also know how this book fits in with its larger field of study. Knowing this is important to your development as an effective data presenter, because it will tell you where to look for new research and opportunities. And this way, you have more tidbits to share at the next cocktail party when people ask you what you are reading. Data presentation sits at the intersection of closely related fields like usability testing, user interface design, graphic design, journalism, and document design. All of these areas fall under the broad umbrella of information design.

Figure 1.29   **Stephanie's classification of the fields influencing data presentation, all of which could be referred to as information design**

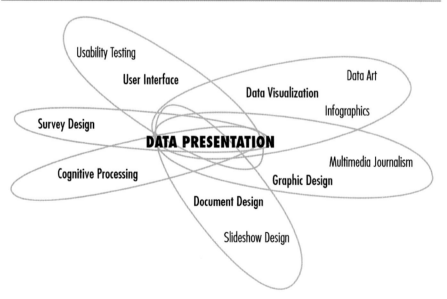

Without a doubt, even more information design subdisciplines will evolve into legitimacy in the years to come. Here, for the purposes of this book, we focus on data presentation, which encompasses both the layout of our written descriptions of data and the graphic displays of them using data visualizations as well as research-based effective practices from other areas under the information design field. Data visualization has already split into two fields: data visualization that is used for analysis and that which is used for presentation, which is the focus of this book. (As of this writing there is a slight resurgence in discussion among thought leaders trying to clarify this divide—see Gelman & Unwin, 2012.) The illustration in Figure 1.29 helps diagram these relationships, as I see them intersecting around data presentation.

The ideas from the hybrid zone of data presentation apply to many dissemination formats. In fact, each chapter in the remainder of this book introduces effective practices and applies them to a span of dissemination products you normally use—reports, research posters, slideshows, and the like—and each chapter includes a section that overlays those same principles on data displays themselves.

Shouldn't these topics be split into two volumes—one on reports and one on data visualization? Definitely not. In my studies of evaluation reports, I have often come across published tomes in which all of the graphs and tables are grouped into the appendices. So even if we have engaging, inspiring data visualizations, they cannot be very effective unless we also address reporting as a whole. As I will illustrate, the same basic principles apply to the reporting medium and the graphs it contains. Thus, we borrow bits and scraps from many other sources to bear on the work we present in higher education, nonprofits, government offices, and wherever and whatever your location. Information design may not be your main field, but in this process you will become a bit of an interdisciplinarian (that is the 50-cent word to throw around at cocktail parties).

## Necessary Software

If it is not obvious already, this book is not written for graphic designers, as they would probably find this discussion boring very quickly. If you have a degree in art, you would likely enjoy arguing over the nuances of some of my points (and we can do that, but you have to buy me a coffee first). What you need to know is that this book was developed as a support tool and reference guide for the student scrambling to make a good impression, the social worker engaged in street intervention, the community college faculty member teaching students how to build wind turbines, and the nonprofit executive saving the world with long hours and a tiny budget. People like you. I wrote this book to help my friends and colleagues, who hold down day jobs (which often extend into the night) and know that kicking their presentations up a notch is going to be a game changer.

That is why all of the examples and demonstrations included in these chapters use software and tools most people already own and can navigate fairly well. You don't have to know any new tools to apply the principles discussed here. I mainly work in Microsoft Office (and while I wish I were getting some paid product placement for telling you that, instead I am just being honest). In the online companion to the book, Open Office and Google Drive are also included, as many people, especially those on very small budgets, are moving to these free platforms. I do not work very often with sophisticated graphic design software, because the learning curve is usually too high and the files are not easily opened by my peers, colleagues, supervisors, and clients. This book illustrates how to use the tools you already own in more effective ways. You probably will not be able to quit your day job to become a professional graphic designer, but you will be able to make a more compelling case out of your work.

My intention is to help you use the tools you already have to make more compelling data presentations so that you can better convince your stakeholders of the worth of your work, secure more attention and funding, and make the world a better place. Please contact me and let me know about your victories after you have implemented the many suggestions included here.

## How Do I Navigate This Book?

Chapters 2 through 5 represent the four practical groups of graphic design principles that emerged from my research. Chapter 2 starts us out where my research showed we are the weakest—graphics. This chapter discusses how to locate great graphics, how to tell if they are actually great, how to think about the different types of graphics needed for research and what each communicates to the reader. Chapter 3 introduces the main varieties of typefaces and outlines when the use of each variety is appropriate. The chapter specifically reviews how type can help organize your data presentation and ease engagement for a reader. Chapter 4 is about the proper use of color for legibility, decoration, and spotlighting critical information, including how to locate effective color palettes and then alter the color settings in your software. Chapter 5 illustrates how to arrange the different components (e.g., your text, photos, graphs) into a cohesive unit. It also details how to justify text, how wide columns should be, and even why deleting the legend in your graph increases impact. In Chapter 6, I pull everything together and share some tips on how to make data presentation design more efficient. I also rearticulate the justification that underpins our efforts to communicate effectively. Throughout, the guiding ideas shaping each chapter are applied to reports, slideshows, handouts, research posters, dashboards, and data visualizations. And at the end of each chapter are lists of some of my favorite online resources and activities to help extend your thinking even further.

## What Is the Bottom Line?

The three phases of visual processing guide the choices of graphic designers so that their work has a greater likelihood of being encoded in long-term memory. For the rest of us, these skills better clarify our data presentations and support subsequent audience understanding.

The eyes win. People read much faster than they speak. Simultaneous listening and reading, which is common in slideshow presentations, overloads working memory. In the end, this means that the audience does not comprehend the content very well, because their brains are trying to do too many things at once. Presenters often further exacerbate the distractions by adding cartwheeling animation to their slides. This method of presentation literally interrupts the audience's attempts to make meaning.

That is not the only place where we get in our own way. As you might have suspected when I was talking about assimilating new information into existing schemas, the more hard-and-fast our existing schemas, the more new information struggles to find a home in long-term memory. In addition to the steep learning curve, this struggle is another good reason for us to be wary about the use of visualization tools that can make fancy, artistic diagrams. The research in this area repeatedly shows that when the viewer (young or old) is unfamiliar with the type of display, she spends cognitive energy just trying to understand the display rather than decoding the data it is attempting to communicate (Chen & Yu, 2000; Shah et al., 1999). Interpretation slows. Accuracy wanes. The result is that viewers just give up. Super data nerds like me are drawn to curious displays, but in those cases we are more interested in the novelty than we are in the data. Those types of displays tend to showcase the programming expertise of the graph maker

*(Continued)*

(Continued)

in place of supporting audience cognition. Viewers and their brains far prefer simpler displays (Robertson, Fernandez, Fisher, Lee, & Stasko, 2008). This book is not designed to teach you how to make your data look like a sunflower or a cracked windshield; rather, it discusses in depth how to make better use of the tools and displays you already know well.

At their core, the techniques in this book can be summarized into two basic strategies: simplification and emphasis. Moving from weak to effective data presentation involves stripping out nonessential information and then adding back in selective emphasis to bring attention to meaning. In the presentation examples earlier in this chapter, the weak varieties had several things in common. They were cluttered, too full of trivial details, and contained unrelated graphic splash. The effective presentation examples were pared down to the critical information, with key graphic elements in place to support the reader's attention.

Presenting data effectively involves combining the strong content you already possess, the software and Internet access you already own, the willingness to be understood and useful (I am confident you have that, too), and the adoption of the accessible strategies contained in the rest of these pages. However, I want to give you fair warning: What this book shows you, you can't unsee—begin thinking about presentations in this way, and you cannot go back. You still have the option of returning this book to its shelf right now. But this is your last chance. After this, you will always notice weak presentation and know how to make it better. Are you prepared for that inevitable outcome? Are you ready? Me, too.

## Key Points to Remember

The desire is not just to look good. Looking good is the natural outcome of communicating data in line with the way people think about and retain information.

- Information uptake occurs in three phases: early attention, working memory, and long-term memory.
- Graphic design elements and techniques draw attention, help a viewer digest information, and boost the viewer's recall of that information later on.
- Effective data presentation uses design principles built around graphics, typeface, color, and arrangement to support engagement with our research products.

## How Can I Extend This?

The exercises below involve websites and activities that can reinforce the concepts presented in this chapter. Do keep in mind that the Internet sources listed can change at a moment's notice. If the URL provided here is not functional, try searching on the keywords to find related material or the website's new location.

### Check Out

The International Institute on Information Design's website (**http://www.iiid.net**) has helpful and authoritative definitions for the bevy of jargon floating around and tons of free user-friendly white papers and books. Download for offline geek-out sessions. Also, take a peek at the list of skills and competencies that information designers need. You'll be surprised to find that you probably already possess these qualities.

The debate around what is data art and what is useful for communication began with the 2008 blog post "5 Best Data Visualization Projects of the Year," by Nathan Yau (**http://flowingdata.com/2008/12/19/5-best-data-visualization-projects-of-the-year**). Andrew Gelman, more of a statistician, disagreed with Yau's picks, saying they were not functional for many and were too artistic in their display. Several years later, the discussion is still alive, with Gelman and Unwin's (2012) paper on the difference between what they call "information visualization" and statistical graphs. It is healthy and normal to debate such ideas when a field is under rapid development. Read up on both sides to help you figure out where you stand.

Stephen Few's thoughtful discussion "Data Art vs. Data Visualization: Why Does a Distinction Matter?" (**http://www.perceptualedge.com/blog/?p=1245**) is also a must-read. His point is that data visualization's purpose is to communicate. While I often daydream about making a 6-foot column chart out of clay, our goal in visualizing data should be to support the audience's attention to make meaning from our work. Thus, the types of data displays in this book are not art.

Chris Lysy's cartoons (**http://freshspectrum.com**) are also worth checking out. Chris is a visual designer and consultant and his cartoons are about engaging stakeholders, presenting data, and more. Hand-drawn on his iPad, they encapsulate the organic, familiar feel that illustrations of that type tend to communicate.

*(Continued)*

(Continued)

**Try This**

A sincere thank-you to the anonymous person who sent me a preview copy of Don Moyer's *Napkin Sketch Workbook*. In it, he depicts the importance of working with our strong visual literacy skills and walks the reader through how to make simple hand-drawn sketches. The sketches that appear throughout this chapter are inspired by Moyer's lessons. Try this example from his book: Illustrate the organizational structure of your department, using little stick figures as necessary. Then use circles or some other technique to demarcate the people clustered in various working groups or miniprojects. Notice how the illustration is much more concise (despite how messy you might believe it to be) than the narrative text it would take to explain that diagram and the mental processing energy required to understand such a paragraph.

As I did with the cola experiment I conducted in fourth grade, you can illustrate the dominance of vision among a group of colleagues or classmates using a classic experiment that demonstrates what is known as the *Stroop effect*. In this test, the subject reads off the names of different colors that are listed on the screen, but the words are cast in colors that are different from the colors named. Go to **http://faculty.washington.edu/chudler/words .html** to take the Stroop effect test or print out the cards to test and time others. It is harder than you think!

## Where Can I Go for More Information?

Baddeley, A. (1992). Working memory: The interface between memory and cognition. *Journal of Cognitive Neuroscience, 4*(3), 281–288.

Callaghan, T. C. (1989). Interference and dominance in texture segregation: Hue, geometric form, and line orientation. *Perception & Psychophysics, 46*(4), 299–311.

Chen, C., & Yu, Y. (2000). Empirical studies of information visualization: A meta-analysis. *International Journal of Human-Computer Studies, 53*(5), 851–866.

Cowan, N. (2000). The magical number 4 in short-term memory: A reconsideration of mental storage capacity. *Behavioral and Brain Sciences, 24*, 87–185.

Gelman, A., & Unwin, A. (2012). *Infovis and statistical graphics: Different goals, different looks.* Retrieved from **http://www.stat.columbia .edu/~gelman/research/published/vis14.pdf**

General Accounting Office. (1995). *Program evaluation: Improving the flow of information to the Congress* (GAO/PEMD-95-1). Washington, DC:

Author. Retrieved from **http://www.gao.gov/products/PEMD-95-1**

Johnson, J. (2014). *Designing with the mind in mind: Simple guide to understanding user interface design guidelines* (2nd ed.). Waltham, MA: Morgan Kaufmann.

Mayer, R. E. (1997). Multimedia learning: Are we asking the right questions? *Educational Psychologist, 32*(1), 1–19.

Medina, J. (2008). *Brain rules.* Seattle, WA: Pear Press.

Patton, M. Q. (2008). *Utilization-focused evaluation* (4th ed.). Thousand Oaks, CA: Sage.

Robertson, G., Fernandez, R., Fisher, D., Lee, B., & Stasko, J. (2008). Effectiveness of animation in trend visualization. *IEEE Transactions on Visualization and Computer Graphics, 14*(6), 1325–1332.

Shah, P., Mayer, R. E., & Hegarty, M. (1999). Graphs as aids to knowledge construction: Signaling techniques for guiding the process of graph comprehension. *Journal of Educational Psychology, 91*(4), 690–702.

Smith, V. S. (2013). Data dashboard as evaluation and research communication tool. *New Directions in Evaluation, 2013*(140), 21–45.

Stenberg, G. (2006). Conceptual and perceptual factors in the picture superiority effect. *European Journal of Cognitive Psychology, 18*, 813–847.

U.S. Department of Health and Human Services. (2006). *The research-based web design and usability guidelines* (enlarged/expanded ed.). Washington, DC: Government Printing Office.

Ware, C. (2013). *Information visualization: Perception for design* (3rd ed.). Waltham, MA: Morgan Kaufmann.

Woodman, G. F., Vecera, S. P., & Luck, S. J. (2003). Perceptual organization influences visual working memory. *Psychonomic Bulletin & Review, 10*(1), 80–87.

Xu, Y., & Chun, M. M. (2006). Dissociable neural mechanisms supporting visual short-term memory for objects. *Nature, 440*, 91–95.

# CHAPTER
# TWO

# GRAPHICS

## LEARNING OBJECTIVES

**After reading this chapter, you will be able to:**

- Locate high-quality graphics for inclusion in your reports, slideshows, and posters

- Identify the proper size for a graphic

- Place a graphic so that it has impact and supports the related text

- Blend a graphic with its background or surrounding elements

- Build a visual theme

- Decide among methods to increase efficiency of graphic production

- Develop different types of icons quickly

- Handle large file sizes

- Simplify data displays

One of the most effective ways to draw attention to and emphasize content in your reporting is through the use of imagery. In addition to catching the early-attentive eye, images, when they are used well, are good at making their way through working memory to get stored for the long term. Let me tell you a little story about the use of imagery.

I was researching the effectiveness of a jail diversion program for a local county government. Like most counties around the United States, this one was strapped for cash. The diversion program was a way to relieve jail overcrowding (and the cost of extended jail stays) by releasing low-level offenders into the hands of community organizations. To enter the program, offenders underwent screening by program staff that included serious and sensitive questions about drug use history, sexual abuse history, income, and so on. These interviews took place in a room where three other staff members might all be screening other potential participants at the same time, in a space that was about 6 feet by 15 feet, which is smaller than the smallest campus office I have ever seen, with more people inside. Can you imagine what happens when offenders overhear such personal information about one another? And the room had to hold the staff members' computers and the files on everyone they had ever screened. You can probably see what I wanted to tell the program funders in our dissemination meeting. Here is an example of a kind of slide commonly used at those types of meetings.

And if I were a common presenter, I would stand at the front of the room reading off the bullet points one by one. The problem with slides of this type again comes back to

**Guiding Ideas**

Pictures/graphics are present

Graphics direct toward text

Size corresponds to changes in meaning

Visual theme is evident

Graphics are simple

Graphics are near associated text

Figure 2.1   **Typical slide with too much text, difficult to read on a textured background**

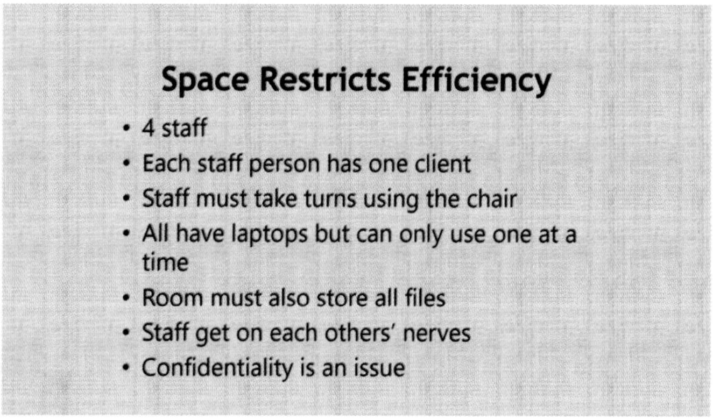

**Space Restricts Efficiency**
- 4 staff
- Each staff person has one client
- Staff must take turns using the chair
- All have laptops but can only use one at a time
- Room must also store all files
- Staff get on each others' nerves
- Confidentiality is an issue

how our brains receive and react to data. Rates vary, but normal reading speed is two to three times faster than normal speaking speed. In other words, the audience can finish reading the entire list while I am still explaining Bullet 2, but their comprehension is impaired because their brains are trying to do too many things at once. The brain actually does a better job of retaining visual information when it is also paired with verbal information. In fact, a good pairing of these two elements increases retention to 75% (Mayer, 1997). But in this setting where the visual information is all text—the same as is spoken—something is slipping out of working memory.

So, as I told the county commissioners about the situation inside their diversion screening room, I showed them the slide in Figure 2.2.

They erupted into laughter. Shortly thereafter, they commissioned a study of the jail to find ways to better utilize their current space (at a time when spending money was a rare activity for county governments); they hired me on for further work, and they chuckled about this slide long after our dissemination meeting was over.

The use of the image highlighted my message. Images stick with people when words do not.

**Figure 2.2   Clearer slide with fewer words and impactful image**

## Space restricts efficiency

And this reality is also true for presentations, brochures, even technical reports. Whatever method you are using to talk about your research, people tend to read in depth only if something has caught their eye. As one designer said to me, we live in a "high-concept" society; we have about three seconds to capture attention, which is hardly enough time to read text. So use an image to help.

## How Do I Use Images in Effective Ways?

The presence of graphic elements with associated text results in greater information recall and retention. When used well in data presentations, graphic elements actually help the reader more effectively comprehend our words and our data. There are five ways to use images for effective impact. Images should be

1.  present (seems obvious, but it isn't)
2.  emotional
3.  placed for high impact
4.  quick at communicating
5.  repeated

## Images Are Present

Imagery tends to be the weakest area of research reporting (Evergreen, 2011). In my dissertation study, the examined research reports contained sparse use of images, and some reports contained no images at all, not even graphs. Therefore, simply the use of images is the first way to be effective at data presentation.

Imagery does not necessarily mean photographs. Graphics can also include charts and diagrams, arrows and other attentional cues, and even lines or blocks of color. The style manual for the American Psychological Association (2010; called the APA Guide from here on) uses *figures* as the umbrella term rather than *graphics* and includes as figures anything discussed here except tables. Either way, inclusion of these elements leads to greater credibility and increases audience willingness to engage with the material. Graphics and visual imagery are helpful—they are better than words alone at making it through the precarious memory path to stick in long-term memory, right where we want our data to go.

As discussed in Chapter 1, our working memory is prone to cognitive overload, and getting past that hindrance is the tricky part of teaching and presentation. To reduce the risk of overload, a researcher can predigest some of the information. Think of the way a graph represents some mental processing that would have had to take place in the viewer's brain if she was simply reading the information as gray text. Since working memory can only hold roughly four chunks of information at one time, the designer "prechunks," essentially allowing more, richer information into working memory than is otherwise possible.

### Guiding Idea

Pictures/graphics are present

Pairing an image with a few keywords on a slide, or with a few summary sentences in a report or research poster, serves to create a chunk of information mentally processed as one unit. Presenting the combined image-idea pair replaces lengthy narrative, speeds up the pace at which people engage with the material, and generates more interest. Visuals are powerful presentation tools for researchers.

## Images Are Emotional

Imagery is emotional when viewers feel they can relate. Sometimes this is achieved through empathy, for example, when international development organizations depict their underresourced beneficiaries in their donor appeal letters. But if the goal is to draw an emotional response, the imagery does not always have to be sad or based in power relationships. Emotional imagery can induce pride, the way a university includes images of students at a football game in its promotional materials. With discretion and moderate use, good graphics can evoke delight by being humorous or novel. Emotion can even be stirred through the use of visual metaphors for a topic if it is more abstract in nature. By making the content more relevant, the metaphor can create powerful and compelling emotion. The effective use of graphics can make readers feel a sense of familiarity and connection (I will discuss later in this chapter how that idea applies to graphs). Here is an example of emotive graphic use inserted into a proposal.

I wanted to partner with a program focused on girl empowerment, so I needed to construct a proposal to present my ideas. To make my cover page, I searched through stock photos on the website iStockphoto.com using the keyword "empowerment" and found one great, relevant photo.

I believed that the client would really connect with this photo in an emotional way, because these girls are exemplifying the sisterhood and confidence that the

**Figure 2.3    Photograph of girls, arms uplifted, from stock photo website**

© iStockphoto.com/aldomurillo

program hoped to produce as well. At the time, I think this photo cost about US$5. To make it fit on a piece of paper, I combined it with a black box so it would take up the whole page and added text boxes with the title and contact information. This is the completed cover page of the proposal.

**Figure 2.4    Front cover of proposal using stock photo**

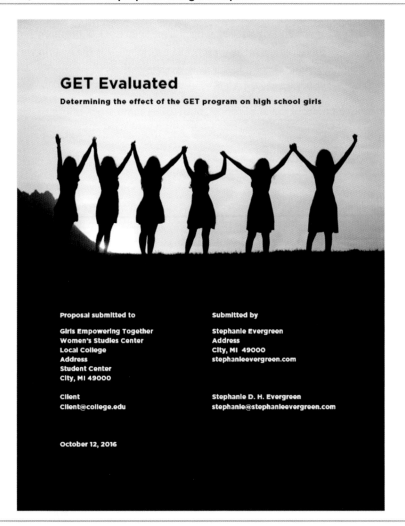

*Source:* © 2009. Reprinted with permission from Susan Haworth-Hoeppner. Photo © iStockphoto .com/aldomurillo.

After the project commenced, I repeated the same image in the background of my logic model, on the cover of the final report, and in the opening and closing slides of my presentations.

Note that I did not say I pasted the picture on every slide or every page of the report, because that would oversaturate my audience probably to the point where they would lose their ability to even notice the picture. However, using the image for the introduction and conclusion helped create a brand for me and this particular project. Additionally, all of my work was now easily recognizable to the client, who could quickly distinguish the materials among the multiple piles and folders on her desk (similar to the best professors' offices). I achieved brand recognition, which made me and my work more memorable, and in a very quick and visual way, it helped me keep track of my many projects as well. Nevertheless, more than just the presence of the image, it is the emotion evoked by this particular image choice that makes it work so well.

**Figures 2.5 and 2.6    Logic model and front cover of report, both using same stock photo**

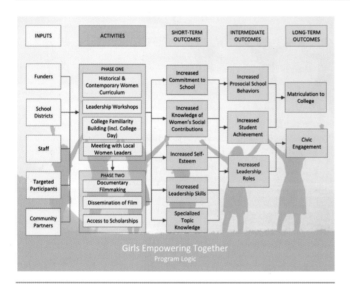

*Source:* © 2010. Reprinted with permission from Susan Haworth-Hoeppner. Photo © iStockphoto.com/aldomurillo.

*Source:* © 2009. Reprinted with permission from Susan Haworth-Hoeppner. Photo © iStockphoto.com/aldomurillo.

The emotional response summoned by imagery is weakened when hackneyed pictures are used. A current trend at the time of this writing is the use of faceless, bare, alien-like creatures holding various objects, such as a target or a pencil. These alien figures lack emotion and relevance and should be avoided. Likewise, the handshake image is so overused that it is glossed over, as is the image of people of various ethnicities holding hands while standing around a picture of the Earth. These images are tired and clichéd, so try to push your thinking a little further. The judgments our audiences make about our graphics (Generic! Overdone!) get associated right back to us as the speakers and the organizations we represent. And our game is not cliché.

Relatedly, even if the picture would typically bring about some emotion, if it is unrelated to the content or discussion at hand, it doesn't work. I was once speaking with a group of environmentalists who cursed the use of pictures of adorable sea turtles on slides that communicated something completely unrelated, like total grant funding. In the next sections, I'll talk more about where to put these emotional pictures so they have a strong impact. But before we head there, let's get slightly more nuanced about emotional imagery.

What kind of imagery do you use when talking about the death penalty?

**Figure 2.7**  **If you are anti–death penalty, you probably want to highlight the life a prisoner could have if spared, so good picture choices might be a prisoner and her family in the visiting room, or the prisoner being productive making license plates**

**Figure 2.8**  **If you are pro–death penalty, you might want to focus on justice, with imagery of gavels, or on low-crime communities, with pictures of kids playing in parks**

**Figure 2.10**  **If you want to talk about the people involved in that system, perhaps you'd do well with stock photos of their uniforms—a prison jumpsuit, a judge's robe, a nurse's scrubs**

**Figure 2.9**  **If you want more humane death penalty options, how about pictures of the tools used, like an empty electric chair, or a syringe, which tap into the painful part of this issue**

I was working with an awesome client a few months ago. In the past, I had pressured them to use graphics in their reports and slides. And they did! Only the pictures they chose were images of government buildings—like, a report on teacher quality would have a picture of the state department of education building. Yeah, not exactly compelling, right?

So Graphics Level 2 was about picking out relevant, relatable, moving graphics that connect the audience to their topic. The amazing part of my work with them was that as soon as we started talking, they quickly generated heaps of ideas for most of their topics.

Then they said, "Stephanie, this is sweet and all but what do we put on the cover of our report about the death penalty?"

[sound of crickets chirping]

Not a simple answer! I chewed on this for a while.

It depends on the message you want to convey to the audience.

On the previous page I share some super-basic sketches—the kind of thing you should be doing while you think about your topic so as to save a mountain of time when you go online to search the stock photo site.

If you are just reporting facts and have to stay neutral, like my client, think about not including any pictures per se. But still include graphic elements, such as big blocks of color or simple shapes, so the report is engaging and professional without swaying emotion one way or the other.

Lots of options, eh? So the question isn't as simple as "What emotional graphic do we pop on the report cover?" It's actually "What's the emotional message we are trying to get across here?" *Please* do not just start searching on "death penalty" at your favorite stock photo site. While those sites can be super-powerful, they can't predict your message. Start off with sketches, like I did, to hone your emotional appeal.

## Images Have Impactful Placement

Graphics and images are effective at catching the eye, right? So why does their placement matter? The visual impact of your research products increases if the images are large, well blended with the background, and positioned to support the text. You can achieve all of these elements by using simple word-processing software.

### Large and Bleeding

Figure 2.11 is a recommendation slide from the presentation discussed at the start of this chapter. I was pointing out that program staff needed to do a better job of hooking up the ex-offenders with community organizations on their way out of jail so that rehabilitation would be more successful.

What makes this slide work so well is that the picture of the paperclip and chains takes up the whole slide. It is very large, which is called a full bleed in graphic design world.

Figure 2.12 is a really poor execution of the same slide.

Do not use clip art; actual photography of real images communicates credibility and legitimacy to the viewer (Samara, 2007), even when those images are manipulated with a program like Photoshop. Hand-drawn images, which I love to use, communicate genuineness, directness, and warmth, whereas clip art communicates amateurism. This example of high-quality digital renderings can also work in some situations.

Figure 2.13 is how the image looked when I purchased it from the stock photo site, but it was not quite making the desired visual impact. I increased the visual impact by expanding the photo so that it consumed the entire slide.

Figure 2.11    **Recommendation slide expressing a weak link in the program**

**Connect with resources**

Figure 2.12    **Slide containing clip art**

To achieve this effect in Microsoft PowerPoint, click on one of the dots at the corner of the photo and drag it all the way to the corner of the slide. Of course, the image then looked upside down in this case, so I also rotated the image by clicking on the green circle sticking out of the top center and dragging the whole photo 180 degrees. By rotating the image, I made the direction flow better—from nearby in the upper left to away in the lower right. Expanding the image to fill the screen (bleeding it) taps into the Gestalt theory of closure (for an overview of Gestalt principles in media design, see Graham, 2008). This principle says that our eyes naturally continue the picture off the edges of the screen and into the real world—a good thing when we are trying to make connections from our findings to our audience's circumstances.

Figure 2.13    **Slide with image as originally purchased from stock photo website**

Notice how the effect is not quite the same if we stop short of a full bleed, such as in Figure 2.14, or if the image is squished. That is why it is critical to enlarge the image by using the sizing circles at the corners and to expand it fully to the edge of the slide or page—or even off the edge. If it appears that your picture is changing its aspect ratio, right-click on it and choose the *Position* function, then lock the aspect ratio.

Sometimes your materials need to contain more words, don't they? And at other times, the picture is just not sized to completely fit a full slide or page, therefore a full-bleed picture is not always feasible. Partial bleed is also a good option. In a partial-bleed arrangement, the picture takes up a portion of the page, hanging off the edge, while the rest of the page contains words.

Figures 2.14, 2.15, and 2.16   **From left to right, slides that are almost bleeding, fully bleeding, and fully bleeding with text**

**Connect with resources**

Figure 2.17   **Only two of the image's four sides touch the sides of the report page—this is a partial bleed**

This is the sample interior page of a research report. This is the sample interior page of a research report. This is the sample interior page of a research report. This is the sample interior page of a research report. This is the sample interior page of a research report. This is the sample interior page of a research report.

This is the sample interior page of a research report. We are reading about design. This is the sample interior page of a research report. We are reading about design. This is the sample interior page of a research report. We are reading about design. This is the sample interior page of a research report. We are reading about design. Design pushes us ahead in our field. This is the sample interior page of a research report. We are reading about design. This is the sample interior page of a research report. We are reading about design. This is the sample interior page of a research report. We are reading about design.

This is the sample interior page of a research report. We are reading about design. This is the sample interior page of a research report. We are reading about design. We love design. This is the sample interior page of a research report. We are reading about design. This is the sample interior page of a research report. We are reading about design. This is the sample interior page of a research report. We are reading about design.

This is the sample interior page of a research report. We are reading about design. This is the sample interior page of a research report. We are reading about design. Design makes us professional. This is the sample interior page of a research report. We are reading about design. This is the sample interior page of a research report. We are reading about design. Design shows off our attention to detail. This is the sample interior page of a research report. Reading research can be awesome. We are reading about design. This is the sample interior page of a research report. We are reading about design. This is the sample interior page of a research report. We are reading about design. This is the sample interior page of a research report. We are reading about design.

This is the sample interior page of a research report. We are reading about design. This is the sample interior page of a research report. We are reading about design. This is the sample interior page of a research report. We are reading about design. This is the sample interior page of a research report. We are reading about design. This is the sample interior page of a research report. We are reading about design. This is the sample interior page of a research report. We are reading about design. This is the sample interior page of a research report. We are reading about design. This is the sample interior page of a research report. We are reading about design.

©iStockphoto.com/oriba

Images are easier to manipulate in slideshow software and software like InDesign and Microsoft Publisher that is specifically designed for page layout.

To place an image in Microsoft Word, choose the *Tight* option under the *Wrap Text* tab first. Also under the *Wrap Text* option is the ability to *Edit Wrap Points*. The *Edit*

*Wrap Points* procedure customizes how the words wrap around the image. When this option is selected, it changes the lines around the picture to red, and clicking anywhere along the red lines lets you create and drag new corners.

**Figure 2.18    Adjusting the wrap points lets the text flow around the image**

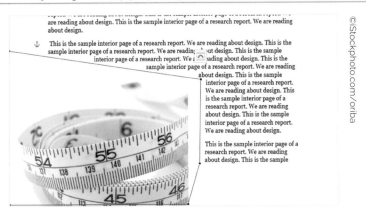

©iStockphoto.com/oriba

Notice how wrapping points does not work very well in this example because the beginnings of the first few lines are staggered. This is not visually appealing and can be annoying and difficult for the reader. Wrapping text points works better when the image is on the right.

In this example, the wrap feature still staggers the ends of the lines, but people are used to reading text lines with varying ends (more on that in Chapter 5).

**Figure 2.19    Moving the image and wrapping its points makes it fit better with the text**

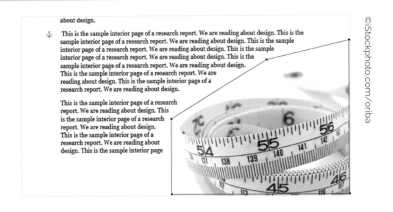

©iStockphoto.com/oriba

## Organizational Logos

It is significant to note that there is one type of image missing from nearly every case illustration in this chapter—a company logo. In most cases, adding a logo to each slide or on the report cover detracts from the impact of the imagery. Departmental or organizational logos are appropriate if they appear in one or two places at most—perhaps on the inside cover of the report or on the thank-you slide at the end of a presentation. Think of it this way: If a document is filled with great content and presented in a memorable way, the audience will not forget who you represent.

### Matching Background

As you will learn in the chapter on color, the optimal condition for reading is when black or very dark text is placed on a white background. Often the high-quality graphics found on online stock photo sites are isolated on white backgrounds, which makes it easier to match a white page for partial bleed in your document.

Of course, there are situations where you want the background color to be something other than white. Placing a white-isolated picture looks a bit odd. Usually, you can solve this problem by making the picture's background transparent:

**Figure 2.20  Screenshot of how to set the transparent color in an image**

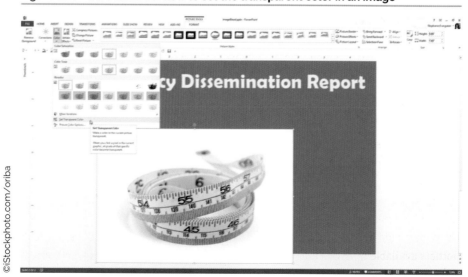

©iStockphoto.com/oriba

In Word on a PC, clicking on the picture activates a pink tab called *Picture Tools.* In the dropdown menu under *Color,* you can select the option *Set Transparent Color.* This option turns the pointer into a pencil. Move the pencil to the white background of the picture and click on it. Every part of the image matching the color where you clicked becomes transparent, which then shows the background color of your document. When using the transparency option, most of the time the end result looks just fine. Sometimes, however, depending on the quality of the isolation in the picture you purchased, some white still shows.

Figure 2.21    **Shadows in the stock photo left distracting white areas around the image**

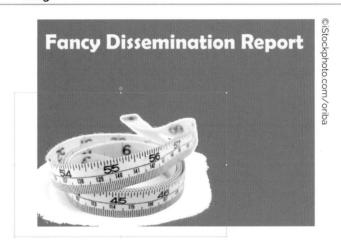

People with access to software like Photoshop or Illustrator can adjust the image so that the white areas no longer appear. But this takes time, skill, and access to software that many researchers and graduate students do not have. The simple solution is to use a white background for your document. Another option is to crop the photo in order to minimize the remaining white areas. If neither of those options works, consider a part-color, part-white background.

To produce this type of background, I inserted a square, enlarged it to the size of the part of the slide I wanted to cover, and made it gray. Then I put the text box with the words on top of the gray square. Such an arrangement affords minimal image manipulation.

One more option is to shrink the picture and put it in a border. This procedure takes back some of the impact of the full-bleed imagery, but it can work in some cases, particularly if people are the subject of the image. However, most of the default borders available in Office and other software packages are not suitable for research dissemination purposes, because they can overmanipulate the image. I often use a

**Figure 2.22**   White sections of the slide accommodate stock photos isolated on white backgrounds

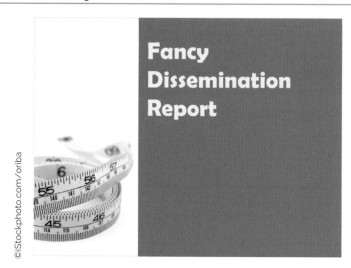

stock photo of a Polaroid picture frame. I purchased the stock photo once and have used it dozens of times, to frame real photographs of real people.

**Figure 2.23**   Real photograph in poster was positioned inside purchased Polaroid stock photo

I crop down the photograph of the people or enlarge the Polaroid frame to make them fit one another. To layer them appropriately, I click on the people photograph and use the *Send Backward* option.

## Guiding Idea

Graphics direct toward text

### Facing Text

Let's talk about the power of the eye gaze when it comes to working with photos of people. Effective use of eye gaze is a powerful way to direct the viewer's eyes toward the text (Reynolds, 2010). For my dissertation study, I reviewed what felt like a billion research reports on human interactions with museum exhibits. Several of the reports integrated actual photos of people engaged with the exhibits, yet in nearly all the selections, the people were positioned with their backs turned to the report's text. Ideally, the report authors should have flipped the photos so that the subjects faced the report narrative. Why does this matter? Humans have a tendency to follow the eye gaze of the subject. In a classroom, if a professor gazes out the window midlecture, the chances are high that the students paying attention will also turn their gaze out the window. The same is true with data reports. We want to place the image so that the reader's eyes follow the gaze of the photo subject, toward the text. Compare the impacts of the eye gaze and photo placement in these two layouts.

**Figures 2.24 and 2.25    The better layout positions the eyes of the model toward the text**

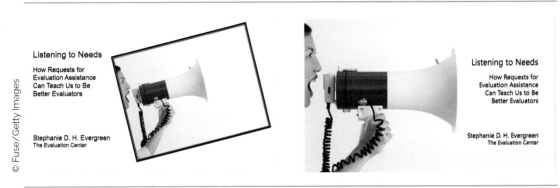

*Source:* © 2009. Reprinted with permission from EvaluATE.

The effect is so beautifully subtle that it is barely noticed in Figure 2.25. However, in Figure 2.24, when the eye gaze is not tracking properly, the viewer senses something is wrong. As shown on the next page, the correct eye gaze placement also increases the visual impact of the posters.

**Figures 2.26 and 2.27**    Even if the eyes are not looking directly at the text, it is still a more powerful placement of the graphic

**Figure 2.28**    The image of the fish points toward the text

*Source:* © 2012. Reprinted with permission from the Environmental Protection Agency.

The sense of directionality imposed by the eye gaze works for other, nonhuman subjects as well. Everyday objects also have naturally implied directionality that we can use to guide attention. In turn, that direction dictates the placement of the words. Note the placement of the graphic in this Ad Council advertisement.

Yes, I suppose there is eye gaze in the image of this fish, but it is really the position of the tail that directs the eyes toward the text. Associatively, it draws some emotion out of the viewer as well. Quite compelling.

## Images Quickly Communicate

Graphic elements are useful guides, leading the reader through the organization of a report or slideshow. By identifying and consistently using graphics, symbol sets, or icons in our documents, we increase the structure of the information, making it easier and quicker for readers to interact with our work. Here are a few types of graphic elements that act as quick visual communication tools.

### Photographs

Intentional placement of photographs doesn't stop with the ideas covered above about how to place them on slides or posters. Photographs can and should be used as navigation markers, like signposts in a report or slideshow, indicating that something new is happening.

Figure 2.29    **Images mark where new sections begin**

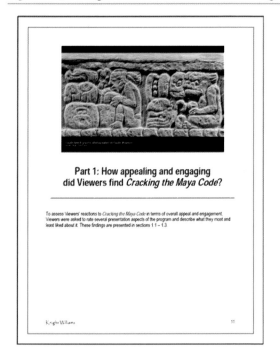
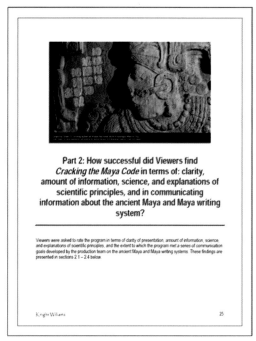

*Source:* © 2008. Reprinted with permission from Knight-Williams Research Communication.

This figure does not show two consecutive pages of a report; rather, these are two section-opening pages. While the text on these two pages isn't perfect, the author has done something really helpful for readers by using a large, awesome image to mark the start of each new section. This means that if a reader is interested only in Part 2, she can hit her scroll wheel until she sees the next really big picture. This is one way to make report navigation more reader-friendly in a digital reading culture.

## Guiding Idea

Size corresponds to changes in meaning

Here's another great example of using photographs to structure a report. Figures 2.30 and 2.31 show parts of a Greenpeace report on climate change.

I pulled these images from the middle of the report to highlight how Greenpeace uses almost full-page pictures to identify the openings of new sections. Corresponding tiny corner images are used to mark each section's interior pages. The sizes of the images mark meaningful changes for the reader. Such organization speeds up the pace at which readers can navigate through the material and more readily reveals the author's mental structure for the report.

**Figures 2.30 and 2.31    Two pages from a Greenpeace report**

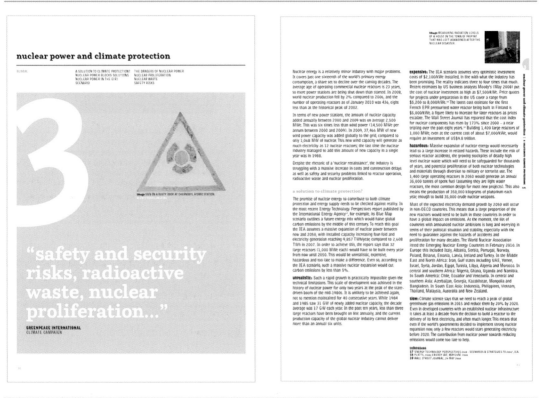

*Source:* © 2010. Reprinted with permission from One Hemisphere/Greenpeace.

Consider how you can intentionally place pictures throughout your longer documents, such as reports and slideshows, to quickly communicate to the audience that you are shifting gears.

## Reference Icons

Reference icons or symbols provide an easy way to organize information throughout a report. When I say "easy," what I really mean is their use makes it easier for the reader. Reference icon sets provide the reader with a mental organizational structure, even if they require more work for the report author. It can be difficult to find a set of symbols through stock image sites that adequately conveys the information in the report.

You can procure icons at the sites listed below; some of them are free, and some come in sets that look like they belong together:

theelearningcoach.com/resources/icon-collection

www.nounproject.com

www.flaticon.com

You can quickly see that the number of possible icons can be overwhelming. Just as when searching for good images, it often takes more time than it is worth to find a good match for your reporting needs. So, here is a quick way to make your own icons.

I made these state-based reference icons myself in about five minutes using Microsoft Word 2010 on a PC.

**Figure 2.32    Reference icons for states included in hypothetical study**

I started by inserting a text box and typing the two-letter state abbreviations in a cool font (this is Gill Sans Condensed). I made the font size large, in this case 72 points.

Then (and this exact procedure varies depending on your software program) I used *Text Fill* and selected white and *Text Outline* and selected black. This creates a black outline with white fill. I made the text box itself transparent, or no fill. Easy enough to get the cute outline letters, yes?

For the shape, I just inserted a circle and used *Shape Fill* and *Shape Outline*.

Then I dragged the text box with the letters onto the circle I had created and grouped them so that they would be easier to move around together. Pay close attention to the placement of each letter set in relation to its circle—you want the letters to appear in pretty much the same spot on each circle. If the letters are centered on one circle and clearly off to the right on another circle, the icons look sloppy. It is okay to use your eyes to judge, but break out the ruler and hold it up to your computer screen if you need to.

**Figure 2.33    Screenshot of how to change the fill color of text**

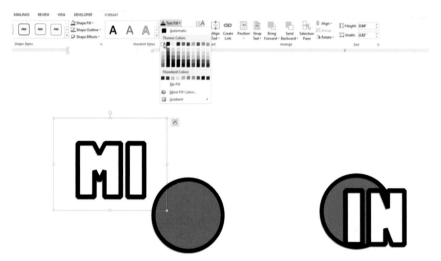

**Figure 2.34    Screenshot of how to change the fill color of a shape**

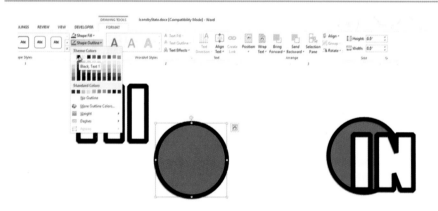

**Figure 2.35    Icon for Michigan**

If I want to make it a little more professional, I can add the state shape behind each abbreviation.

I modified a set of state shapes that I downloaded from the Presentation Magazine website (presentationmagazine.com). The unique shapes also help with quick identification, but it is especially effective to include the abbreviation as well in a case like states (after all, who is able to recognize Wyoming solely by its shape? No offense, Wyomingites).

The similarity in shape and font really gives these icons the feel of a set. Now, this set adds impact and structure to my report. In this example, I am trying to compare key indicators (rates of graduation, obesity, and home ownership) between Michigan; our nemesis to the south, Indiana; and the national average. (All numbers in the example are totally fictitious.) Figure 2.36 shows how a typical table looks, and Figure 2.37 illustrates how the addition of the reference icons begins to give it more visual interest.

**Figures 2.36 and 2.37   Same table, with and without reference icons**

| | Michigan | Indiana | National |
|---|---|---|---|
| Graduation | 76.3 | 74.1 | 74.9 |
| Obesity | 30.5 | 29.1 | 33.8 |
| Home Ownership | 73.1 | 71.7 | 67.4 |

| | **MI** | **IN** | **US** |
|---|---|---|---|
| Graduation | 76.3 | 74.1 | 74.9 |
| Obesity | 30.5 | 29.1 | 33.8 |
| Home Ownership | 73.1 | 71.7 | 67.4 |

Obviously, I know that adding icons to one table doesn't do much to enhance the report. However, when I use the icon system in each data display throughout the report, I build a predictable organizational structure that speeds recognition and aids comprehension.

**Figures 2.38 and 2.39   Data displays that capitalize on the introduction of reference icons**

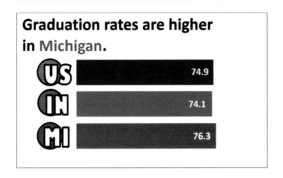

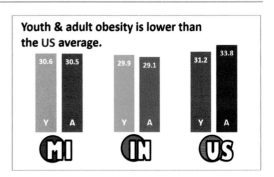

In this next example, Paul from Community Partners wanted to contrast the classic way organizations operate with the networked way of operating. His original presentation of the concepts is shown in Figures 2.40 and 2.41 (p. 54).

Pretty typical, right? I redesigned this talk with Paul to introduce visual depictions of classic and network organizations through the use of reference icons. First, we introduced the two types of organizations (Figure 2.42, p. 54).

Then, we repeated the use of those icons when referencing more of their corresponding details (Figures 2.43 and 2.44, p. 55). Using reference icons in this manner helps viewers better organize the presented information. Audience members automatically connect one part of the presentation to the next in a visual way.

**Figures 2.40 and 2.41 Two slides from the deck Paul was originally using**

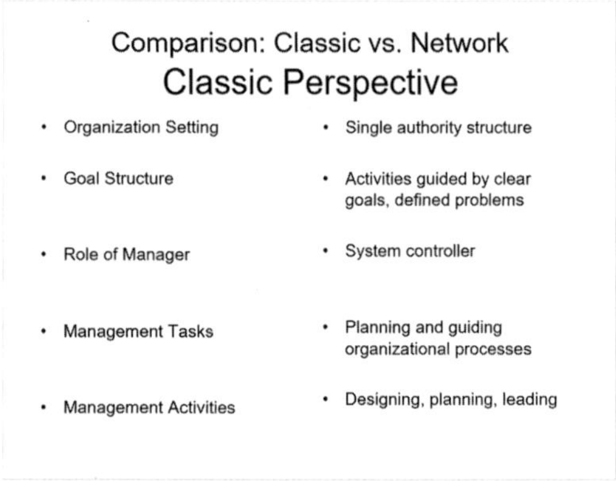

Comparison: Classic vs. Network
## Classic Perspective

- Organization Setting
- Goal Structure
- Role of Manager
- Management Tasks
- Management Activities

- Single authority structure
- Activities guided by clear goals, defined problems
- System controller
- Planning and guiding organizational processes
- Designing, planning, leading

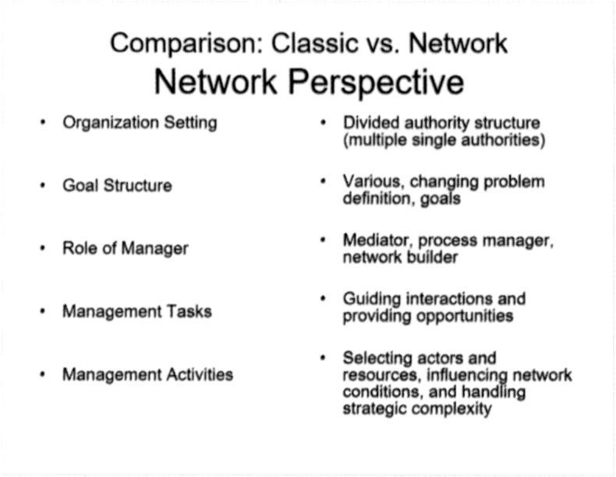

Comparison: Classic vs. Network
## Network Perspective

- Organization Setting
- Goal Structure
- Role of Manager
- Management Tasks
- Management Activities

- Divided authority structure (multiple single authorities)
- Various, changing problem definition, goals
- Mediator, process manager, network builder
- Guiding interactions and providing opportunities
- Selecting actors and resources, influencing network conditions, and handling strategic complexity

*Source:* © 2011. *Networks That Work*, http://www.communitypartners.org. Reprinted with permission from Paul Vandeventer.

**Figure 2.42 Introduction of reference icons for classic and network**

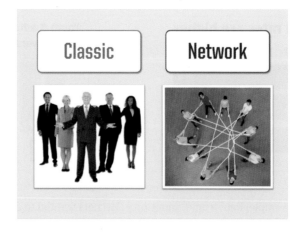

*Source:* © 2011. *Networks That Work*, http://www.communitypartners.org. Reprinted with permission from Paul Vandeventer.

One more example. You know how when you are presenting your findings, the people in the audience who don't like what they see will start questioning your methods? How about we stop that conversation in its tracks and put the method next to the finding with an icon! That's what Sheila Robinson did in Figure 2.45.

**Figures 2.43 and 2.44**   Subsequent explanatory slides with reference icons in corner

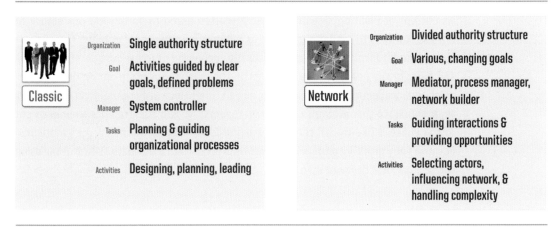

*Source:* © 2011. *Networks That Work,* http://www.communitypartners.org. Reprinted with permission from Paul Vandeventer.

**Figure 2.45**   Add an icon to give information on your data collection methods if they will be easily confused or questioned

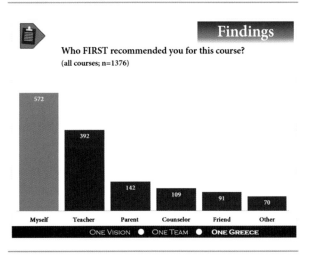

*Source:* © 2016. Reprinted with permission from Sheila Robinson.

Working within her organization's mandated fonts and color schemes, Sheila created some quick icons to represent each of her survey data collection methods—paper, online, and phone. Then she put the appropriate icon in the upper left of each Findings slide to remind the audience where the data came from, in case they forgot or had questions.

## Judgmental Icons

As current or budding researchers, we are often asked to go beyond our ability to crunch numbers to render our advice or judgment on the topic at hand. Our professional standards in research validity usually encourage us to use very careful wording and defer to the need for future studies on the matter. But often our readers, particularly nonacademic audiences, prefer more straightforward communication. Rather than obfuscate that attempt in our own readers, we can use graphics to help us cut to the chase. I like to call these *judgmental icons* (clearly distinct from emoticons) because they quickly communicate our interpretation of our data. You can make up the set that best fits your own work.

**Figure 2.46**    **Judgmental icons for high, medium, and low from Angie Ficek**

*Source:* © 2011. Reprinted with permission from the Invitation Health Institute.

Angie Ficek sent me this report to share in which she used judgmental icons to quickly present which aspects of her client's work were most effective. She devised a simple high/medium/low categorization and developed the icons to match.

In her report, of course, she elaborated, detailing each aspect of her client's efforts that worked or did not work, providing the evidence and describing the impact to support her interpretations. Then, she affixed the appropriate icon to the top of each page so that the bottom line of her research findings was obvious at a glance. She even organized the report in ascending order of effort effectiveness.

Figure 2.47   Sample report page with judgmental icon in corner

### Peer Influence Programs   H

| | |
|---|---|
| **Summary** | Peer norms are a strong influence on youth behavior. Some peer influence programs are identified as evidence-based strategies. |
| **Description** | Peer influence programs are based on the knowledge that peer norms are one of the strongest factors in youth ATOD use. These programs aim to counter negative peer norms by identifying or recruiting drug-free youth leaders and assisting them to actively serve as role models for same-aged or younger people. |
| **Existing Data** | Peer influence programs are very popular and many youth go on to play key roles in their communities' ATOD prevention efforts. Examples of effective peer influence programs include Challenging College Alcohol Abuse, Project Northland, and Lions Quest Skills for Adolescence. |
| **Sustained Impact** | Research indicates that peer influence toward ATOD use is one of the strongest correlates with use among youth. The Substance Abuse and Mental Health Services Administration (SAMHSA) has identified the aforementioned programs as evidence-based and included them in their national registry. Such programs have been shown to improve self-efficacy, reduce the number of adolescents using alcohol, and reduce binge drinking in college-aged students. |
| **In Our Community** | For more information on the peer influence programs mentioned above, go to www.nrepp.samhsa.gov and search by program name. |

4

*Source:* © 2011. Reprinted with permission from the Invitation Health Institute.

Figure 2.48 shows some other options for judgmental icons. To create most of these, you can follow the same construction method outlined earlier.

We will talk more about color later, but for now I want to mention that you should avoid using color as the only factor distinguishing the icons in your set from one another. The stoplight colors (red, yellow, and green in most of the United States) are often used, but they are not such a great idea when used exclusively. They are

Figure 2.48    **Just some of the possible sets of judgmental icons**

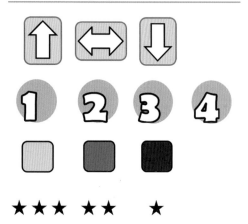

difficult to distinguish for people with certain types of color blindness, and they lose their distinction when printed in black and white (and then copied and faxed, as my reports tend to be disseminated after I deliver them to clients). It is perfectly okay to use color, just be certain to also use some other method of differentiation, such as shape.

## Images Are Repeated

We gain a visual theme when we use repetition. Repetition occurs when we take a few key graphic elements that support our message and sprinkle them (or variations on them) throughout the document group.

In other cases, partial-bleed images create the visual theme. When we develop a visual theme, we build a system of organization throughout our presentation avenues. Just as with the image of the girls at the start of this chapter, a visual theme works best when it is interwoven in all documents related to the project without being overused. However, it can be repeated in a slideshow where some interior slides feature a cropped-down slice of the original image, as in Figures 2.49 and 2.50.

Figures 2.49 and 2.50    **Pieces of cover image are repeated on later slides**

*Source:* © 2009. Reprinted with permission from Susan Haworth-Hoeppner. Photo © iStockphoto.com/aldomurillo.

## Guiding Idea

Visual theme is evident

The same image slice can appear on the related handout and on some interior pages of the accompanying report, marking the start of new sections. In this way, the graphics create a theme that brings cohesiveness to all the products stemming from one project.

# How Many Graphics Are Okay?

Most of the time, and especially with slides and posters, you need one focal image—one big, emotional, relevant graphic that serves as your anchor. But it is still okay to have other graphics, smaller, particularly if we are talking about data visualizations. Beyond one big anchor image, I don't really place a hard limit on the number of graphics. It's really more about how well they fit together and how their arrangement makes them work.

**Figure 2.51    Too many graphics? Or is it their quality and arrangement?**

*Source:* © 2015. Reprinted with permission from Michael Quinn Patton.

This figure was graciously provided by a dear friend, Michael Quinn Patton, who is so established in his career that he can afford to showcase his terrible slides. In real life, the eyeball on this slide was animated to blink. *To blink!* We might be tempted to say that there are too many graphics on the slide. In fact, Michael was trying to convey the idea of sensory overload, so he was actually effective in bringing about the feeling he wanted in his audience. However, I think that if the graphics had a similar look and feel, he could have achieved the same outcome with a better-looking slide that didn't make people cringe. You'll see several examples in Chapter 5, on arrangement, where slides and posters have as many graphics. The main difference I discuss there is that they are arranged in some way that feels organized.

So having more than one image on your poster is just fine, as long as you keep reading the rest of this book to see how to do it right!

# How Do I Efficiently Locate High-Quality Images?

Perhaps the most common remark made by researchers who begin to incorporate graphic images into their work is "But I spend hours just looking through pages and pages of photos. I don't have that sort of time!" No kidding! Let's talk about a few ways to make the job easier: investing in a little conceptual time, using the right stock photo sites, and working with a professional graphic designer.

## Invest in Visual Thinking Before Browsing Sites

Perhaps the best way to cut down the time it takes to find high-quality images is to spend some time refining what you want before you begin to search. Here is my process: I open PowerPoint and duplicate the initial blank slide so that I have a total of six blank slides. Then I print a page or two so that all six slides fit on one page. It looks like this:

**Figure 2.52    Print a page of rectangles so you can sketch**

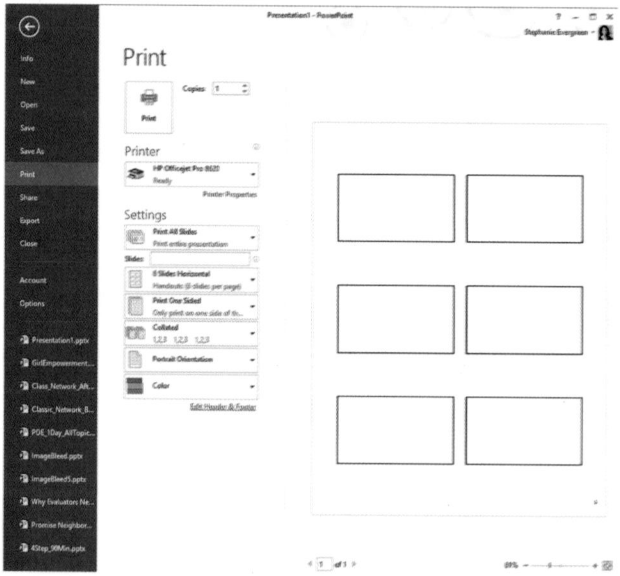

Then I turn off the computer and step away. I sit down with a pencil (and an eraser) and start sketching some ideas. I begin by thinking about the images I tend to associate with the topic at hand. I invest about 15 minutes and engage in some free association, where I basically let my mind wander and my hand doodle as I test out some visual metaphors. Sometimes, if I am stuck, I grab a colleague to ask what comes to mind when I say the topic name. I might also use a thesaurus or quickly search Google Images to get my juices flowing. The goal during this time is to derive several image possibilities and sketch them into the printed PowerPoint rectangles. Also, I scribble a few words to express the main idea of each slide and maybe a phrase or sentence underneath the rectangle to note what the speaker would be saying at that point. The same process works for developing the template pages for a report: just turn the paper sideways so the rectangles are in portrait orientation and sketch a couple of page layout options.

My sketches are not good—mainly stick figures and lines. But the idea is not to make final artwork, just to get a series of images that tie together to support your main points. For example, let's say I am creating a report for my department chair on a faculty network we have developed. If I simply sit at my computer and search on "network," I get back thousands of images, including many related to topics like computer networks, television networks, and nets. But by thinking a bit and jotting down some visual ideas before I search, I might conclude that my department chair will be more convinced of the value of the network if I include images that humanize the project. So, I begin sketching images of people interacting, a teacher and a student connecting, a group of happy students.

Then searching sites can be quicker work because I already have a rough idea of what to look for. To continue the network example, I can refine my search parameters to include keywords like "people," "collaboration," "student," "teacher," and "education."

Aside from greater precision in your search terms, you should also take advantage of the advanced search functions of stock photo sites. Google Images, iStockphoto, and other image sites let you add search specifications such as file size and even color in the photo. This is a pretty handy way to narrow down the search results in order to spend less time sorting through images. Investing 15 minutes in gathering your visual ideas and 5 minutes in setting up your search parameters can save you an hour or more of digging through the results.

## Shop Stock Photo Sites

I am often asked how I found the fishbowl image used at the start of this chapter. I searched "cramped" on iStockphoto.com, working with the feelings I experienced when I was in the program office. For the images used in the classic and network organization reference icons, I searched on "hierarchy" and "teamwork," respectively. I typically work with professional stock photo websites and pay a small amount for each photo I use; I build the stock photo price into my project budget.

The generous Internet universe also provides us with several sites that hold free stock photos. Currently, Creative Commons, stock.xchg, morguefile, and Google Images are popular options. Google Images can seem like a great idea until you search. I searched on "teamwork" and got about 37,400,000 results. Wow! Also, you need to be careful—most of the images you find in a simple Google search are owned by someone else, and it is illegal to just copy and paste them into your own report. Google's search technology is getting better at helping us locate available photos we can use for free. Use the advanced search function in Google Images (at the time of this writing I clicked on a little gear icon and then clicked *Advanced Search*). Then specify the usage rights and elect to view only those images that are available to use, share, and/or modify for free. When I searched again on "teamwork" after specifying usage rights that allow for commercial reuse (the usage required if I want to, say, put the image in a department brochure), Google returned just 65 images. Thus, I had fewer images to sort, and I could be more confident of copyright law compliance.

Despite the time spent, searching on free photo sites like Google Images and stock.xchg can often return options that just do not work. On Google in particular, many of the images are personal photos. Some are too casual—they look like they were taken by someone like me (an amateur rather than a real photographer). The lighting is poor, the composition is cluttered. Imagine if I took a photo of a Little League baseball team. The photo would probably be just a bit too casual and messy—telephone wires cutting across the image, too much fence and not enough team, a mom mid-bite on her hot dog. Perhaps that realism is exactly right for your project. It often is—I have read research reports where it definitely makes sense to have real photos, of real people, really interacting. But for many dissemination settings, you might want cleaner, more professional images. On paid stock photo sites, the great majority of the images are just that—clean and simple. Often, they are taken in controlled environments with no backgrounds that add clutter or "noise" to your page or poster. The search results are almost always restricted to high-quality images, which reduces the amount of sorting you have to do and saves you precious time.

## Guiding Idea

Graphics are simple

Many stock photo sites make the work of locating a relevant, emotional, high-quality image much easier. Before you invest in a photo, though, be certain you are purchasing the size that fits your dissemination. Typically, size is specified in a few different ways. The default way of describing size is often in pixel dimensions; if that's the case, pick something close to the resolution of the screen where you will be displaying the image. The location of the information on monitor resolution varies from computer to computer. On mine, I right-click on my desktop and choose *Properties*. I use two monitors, and the *Properties* window tells me that on Monitor 1, my resolution is 1366 × 768. Therefore, for full-screen graphics I want pixel dimensions that are very similar.

Projectors generally use a standard resolution: 1024 × 768. Even if your computer screen resolution is higher, when you plug it into most projectors, the resolution will downgrade. So if you are planning to use the images in a slideshow that will be shown with a standard projector, save yourself a little bit of cash and go for 1024 × 768. Fancy newer projectors can handle higher resolution and produce crisper displays, so you may want to check ahead about what equipment will be available for you.

Now, pixel dimensions are for screen display. To use the same images on paper, you will need more information. On the photo site, look for details about image dpi, or dots per inch. Low dpi is one of the components that leads to fuzzy graphics, which occurs when the report designer tries to overenlarge too few dots per inch. If you are using the graphic for paper printing, you need to purchase 300 dpi.

Finally, look at the dimensions in inches. Even if you have the right dpi for your dissemination purpose, if you purchase a photo that is only 3 by 5 inches, it will look blurry and unprofessional if you try to stretch it to fill your report cover page. For a report cover, purchase something nearer to 8½ by 11 inches (the standard U.S. paper size). A better but pricier option is to search for and purchase vector versions of your favorite images, which are infinitely resizable. Stock photo sites are generally quite easy options for obtaining high-quality photos. You need to learn a little bit of decoding to understand these sites' pricing schemes, but doing so can save your project budget some major cash.

## Hire a Graphic Designer

The ability to recognize and apply great design can be learned. If you are reading this book, you are showing sufficient interest in this topic to be able to develop your own amazing information design skills. When the stakes are high, when the project will produce a great deal of documentation and you will be in front of important audiences, I am confident that the strategies presented throughout this book will enable you to shine. However, despite a high skill level, data folks are often a very busy crowd, running from classes to meetings to office hours and back again. Those of us in such a position may be better off working with a professional graphic designer who can refine existing products and develop templates for future work.

In one of my projects, we received a large four-year grant in which we promised to produce mountains of printed material, including research resources, newsletters, slideshows, and handouts. Thus, we sat down with a graphic designer in our very early days and spent about two hours discussing the types of templates we wanted, the software available in-house, and the image we wanted to project through our logo. For about US$5,000, the designer returned a whole branded package that we then used throughout the grant.

Even so, as the client of a graphic designer, you will still need to prepare imagery ideas, color scheme possibilities, and thoughts about your own presenting style so that the graphic designer can be most efficient. The APA Guide recommends that authors share the guidelines in its section on figures when working with contracted professional designers. Still, you need to be able to judge whether the design represents your work well and meets your needs. In other words, whether you choose to outsource your design work or build it yourself, the material in this book will help you become a more informed design consumer and a better client.

## What if My File Size Becomes too Large?

Adding high-quality images definitely increases the size of files. For some, this may make it difficult to send or receive the files as email attachments. Here are four ways to deal with large files:

Delete cropped areas of pictures. If you have been working with graphics, you have probably cropped, sliced, and diced some down to the right size, but the cropped areas just stay hidden rather than being deleted, keeping the file size large.

To delete the cropped areas, after inserting the first picture, click on the picture so it is activated and then click on the *Picture Tools* menu that appears (in Office 2010 on a PC, this shows up as a pink tab). Navigate over to *Compress Pictures* and click to open the options there.

Be certain that *Delete cropped area of pictures* is checked. Do not check *Apply only to this picture,* so you only have to enact this procedure once. In this options menu, you can change the quality of the picture as well, which also adjusts the file size. By following this process, I was able to decrease the total file size of my 25-slide PowerPoint file with large pictures on each slide by about one-quarter.

**Figure 2.53    Screenshot of how to delete cropped areas of pictures**

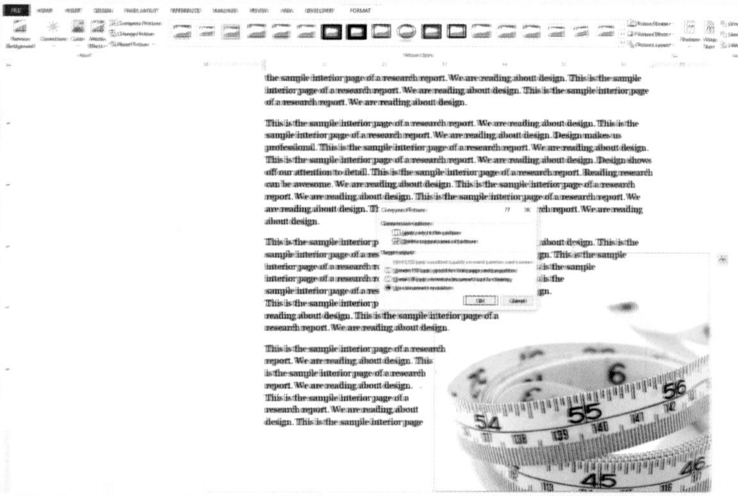

©iStockphoto.com/oriba

We are not into the font chapter yet, but another option is to unembed fonts. On the same slideshow just mentioned, this process saved me about 10% more space. In Office 2016 on a PC (not available in Office 2016 for Macs), click on *Save As.* Before

**Figure 2.54    Screenshot of how to unembed fonts**

*(Continued)*

(Continued)

saving the file, click the arrow just to the left of the *Save* button and choose *Save Options* from the dropdown menu.

Check out the options under *Embed Fonts.* If your document consists only of the most common fonts (Times New Roman, Calibri), you can probably just uncheck the main box for the maximum file size decrease. Other options there also minimize file size. Unembedding fonts can be risky, however, as I demonstrate in Chapter 3.

Saving in PDF format also decreases file size. Often, slideshow navigation can still be preserved as a PDF. If you also want to show the notes in a slideshow, save your notes through the printing function. In the printing options, select *Notes Pages* and then print to PDF. PDF is not always ideal, particularly in circumstances where you need to collaborate, but it can work in many situations.

Finally, if none of the previous suggestions are sufficient, use a cloud service to transfer files. Dropbox and other file transfer services are free to use and contain enough space to hold large, image-heavy documents. Simply sharing a link with others allows access to the documents for download.

**Figure 2.55**   **The bottom of one page, containing narrative, and the top of the following page, with the graph**

## Where Should Graphs Go?

Finally, let's take care of one of the most common mistakes I see in research reporting. Typically, once the main report narrative starts, it just runs on, page after page. As such, a graph is sometimes split from its accompanying narrative text, for example in Figure 2.55.

Here we are looking at the bottom of one page, where the narrative is located, and the top of the next, where the reader finds the associated graph. Sometimes, I even see research reports where all of the graphs are grouped in an appendix, pages and pages away from their corresponding text. But even if the graph is just on the next page, any flipping back and forth between pages to try to cohere the two blocks of information impairs readers' ability to comprehend; we lose them when they have to flip. It is better to isolate one idea per page or at least to start the idea on the page where the graph is located. Just use the *Page Break* option in your word-processing software at the start of a new idea. In Figure 2.56 the narrative and the graph are grouped together, immediately easing comprehension.

## How Do I Apply These Ideas to Graphs?

Visualizing data in graphs and charts is one of the primary ways we present our work, and thankfully many of the same principles that guide good practice in the entire report, slideshow, or poster also apply to data visualizations themselves. Because our readers put so much value into our data visualizations, I have developed the Data Visualization Checklist in Appendix B. This checklist will walk you through each piece of a visualization and help you tweak what's necessary so that it best supports the story you are trying to tell.

## Graph Highlights Significant Finding or Conclusion

Two parts of the "Overall" section of the Data Visualization Checklist are relevant for this chapter on graphics. Probably the biggest deal is that the graph highlights something significant. Meaning, we don't graph the stuff that isn't important. As we've learned throughout the book so far, people are driven by their eyeballs. So if we crowd their field of vision with a bunch of graphs of relatively unimportant data, we confuse them and teach them that the visuals may or may not be worth their attention.

I used to do this all the time when I was a researcher. We would run a survey, and because we were good survey methodologists, we'd be sure to ask the demographic questions first. Then when it came time to report, we would create one graph per survey question, in the same order as the questions were asked to our respondents. This created a situation where our readers had to get through 10 pages of pie charts

**Figure 2.56    Narrative and graph now coexist on a single page**

## Guiding Idea

Graphics are near associated text

for every demographic question, and by the time they got to a graph with data that actually held a significant finding, we'd lost them. So let's reserve the power of the visual and create visuals only for the things that matter.

## The Type of Graph Is Appropriate for Data

You'll also see in the "Overall" section of the Data Visualization Checklist that a big part of getting the data visualization right is choosing the best graph type—the one that appeals to your audience's sensibilities, is easy enough to interpret with accuracy, and highlights your story. For example, humans are good at judging length and bad at judging angle—which means bar and line charts are often good options, or at least better options than pie charts, which are full of angles.

We are also really bad at judging area. Remember how size should correspond to meaning? I've reproduced here something I have seen several times in research reports, a graphic intended to show the response percentages for a Likert-type scale. But in many of the versions I've seen, the sizes of the circles do not accurately or proportionately represent that data. In this example, the circle representing "Agree" is not really 61 times the size of the circle representing "Strongly Disagree."

**Figure 2.57   Typical bubble graph that is difficult to interpret accurately**

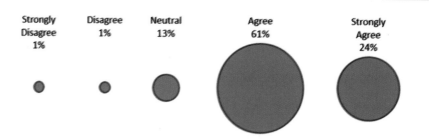

There is some debate in the data visualization field as to whether circles should be sized by area or by diameter. And if the graph designers are still trying to figure out the best way to display circles, then imagine the confusion for an average viewer. This graph would be better as a bar, a stacked bar, a diverging stacked bar, a lollipop, or—well, you have lots of graph options that would showcase these data more effectively. This topic is covered to an extreme depth in my book *Effective Data Visualization* (2016). Use it to figure out the best chart type to use, when, and how to make it in Excel.

## Gridlines, if Present, Are Muted

The "Lines" section of the Data Visualization Checklist will help you to enhance reader interpretability by handling a lot of the junk, or what Edward Tufte (2001, p. 105) calls the "noise," in the graph. By "noise," I mean all the parts of a graph that don't actually display data or assist reader cognition. At this point, let's focus on creating more readability by dealing with unnecessary lines.

In the example in Figure 2.58, the default chart, on the left, has black gridlines. These stand out quite a bit because of how well black contrasts with the white chart background. But the gridlines shouldn't be standing out so much, because they are not the most important part of the graph (the data is! Or the data are! Wherever you stand on the is/are debate, I still love you).

**Figure 2.58   Same graph, with default dark and then light gray gridlines**

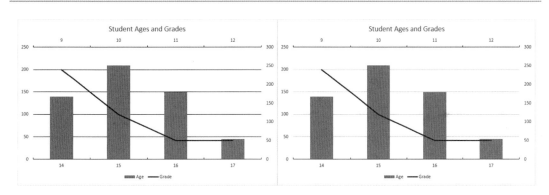

The revised graph, on the right, is more appropriate. I changed the gridline color to light gray. The gridlines are still visible, to help the viewer interpret the values of the data, but the gray color relegates them to the background, playing a supporting role, where they belong. We'll talk later about deleting gridlines entirely, but if you want them in, just make them a light gray.

## Graph Does Not Have a Border Line

Excel will automatically add a border around your graph. This might make it easier to see the graph inside Excel, but usually you will be plopping the graph into something else, like a report page, a slide, or a poster. Data visualizations appear more integrated with the larger reporting document when we remove the boxes and let the white spaces just blend.

**Figure 2.59    Same graph, with default border and then no border**

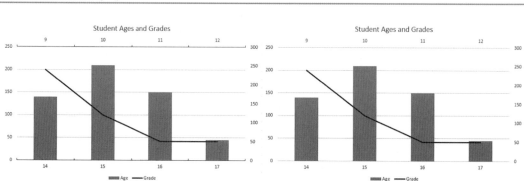

To remove a graph's border, right-click on it, select *Format Chart Area,* and in the *Border* section, click *No Line.*

## Axes Do Not Have Unnecessary Tick Marks or Axis Lines

We are getting better, but we aren't all the way there yet. Changing the gridline color left two lines that were still dark black. Those are the axis lines. And each of them has those tiny little tick marks. Sometimes showing tick marks make sense, such as when data in a line graph fall really far away from the axis, because they help the eye travel. But in this case, the tick marks are just separating the categories, which is pretty useless. They are just cluttering up the joint. We can get rid of the tick marks and the axis lines in one fell swoop.

**Figure 2.60    Same graph, with and without tick marks and axis lines**

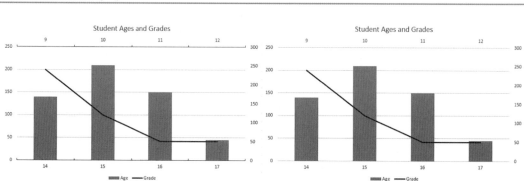

To do this in Excel, right-click on an axis and select *Format Axis,* then choose *No line* from the list of options for *Line.* This will eliminate both the tick marks and the axis line. (Note: The APA Guide asks for tick marks, but if the document is not being submitted to an APA journal, you can do without them.)

## Graph Has One Horizontal and One Vertical Axis

I know, I know: The most annoying thing about this example graph is that it attempts to plot age and grade in the same space! There are two horizontal axes in the graph— one for age and one for grade—and both of those have their own y-axes, which are on two different scales. What goes with what? So confusing. Yet so common! People usually end up here because they want to show the relationship between two variables, but this actually adds more confusion even though the graph authors think it's an attempt at clarity. Often a better option is to show both variables, just side by side.

Figure 2.61  **Same data, one as a graph with double axes and one as a set of independent graphs**

Breaking the data apart makes it easier to interpret each variable, puts them both in appropriate graph types, and still allows for some basic comparisons.

By choosing the right chart type and eliminating all of the noise from the data display, you can create graphics that clearly show the story in your data set. In later chapters, we'll tackle other items from the Data Visualization Checklist that add even more oomph to the storytelling power of graphs.

Research has repeatedly shown that simpler visualizations are interpreted more efficiently and lead to better recall (Tractinsky, 1997). Clean, simple, beautiful visualizations keep viewers interested and engaged for longer periods of time; viewers are more likely to skip visualizations that are cluttered, confusing, or elaborate (yet there is still some debate—see the 2010 study by Bateman and colleagues, which suggests that strong imagery around standard graph types can improve memorability via the pictorial superiority effect). Generally, the cleaner the basic structure of the graph, the greater your audience's ability to engage.

## What Is the Bottom Line?

Many of us involved in research are accustomed to descriptive, academic report writing. We explain. Metaphors, especially visual ones, have rarely had a place in our data presentation, to the detriment of our audiences. Consider this is your license to allow room for creative thinking. For effective presentations, you need to name your key messages succinctly and identify visual images or metaphors that extend and elaborate on them. I know of a few situations in which a researcher handed off the development of visuals to a research assistant or a receptionist. In almost every case, this did not work out well. It is not that a research assistant or secretary lacks the skill to create nice graphics—everyone can achieve that skill if needed. It is just that the development of good visuals takes a more intimate knowledge of the data, the main findings, and the key message the audience should take away. I know and appreciate that everything I discuss in this chapter requires you to invest your time, and maybe even a bit of your money, and you are busy. But the payoff is huge: increased audience engagement, interpretation, and understanding.

## Key Points to Remember

High-quality graphics increase the impact of your data presentations.

- High-quality graphics have minimal clutter. In terms of photographs, stock photo sites are one solid option for finding professional-level graphics. In terms of data displays, nonessential gridlines, axis labels, and tick marks can be removed.

- Whether free or for a fee, images should be procured at the right size so they are crisp when presented. Check pixel dimensions, dpi, and size in inches.

- Simplified graphics can be altered to draw attention to key areas through the use of selective emphasis techniques.

- A strong visual theme is built when graphic elements, such as portions of the same picture, the same color, or the same shapes, are repeated throughout the data presentation suite.

# How Can I Extend This?

## Check Out

Presentation Magazine (**http://www.presentationmagazine.com/editable-maps**): This site is filled with free downloadable material, including the editable map files I used to create the state shapes I talked about earlier. Do not use the downloads directly, because they are recognizable as templates; instead, modify them to make them your own.

Creative Commons (**http://search.creativecommons.org**): Creative Commons licenses release images for public consumption and come in a variety of styles, some of which allow for commercial use and modification of the original image. Searching for images in the Creative Commons is a good way to narrow your results to those that are reusable. Be certain to become familiar with the various license categories.

Slideshare (**http://www.slideshare.net**): Browse this site for imagery inspiration. Type your subject area into the search field and explore the results. Much of the material posted here is aligned with the guiding ideas presented in this book. Consider uploading your own awesome slideshow to inspire others.

## Try This

Gather a small group of three to four people, and take turns sharing your topics (in a word or two) and letting the others brainstorm synonyms or visual metaphors using free association. Make a list of all the ideas (try not to dismiss anything at this point) and then move on to the next activity suggested here.

Download my Slidedeck Planning Sheet at **http://stephanieevergreen.com/slidedeck-planning-sheet** and invest in some visual thinking and sketching of the synonyms and metaphors you just brainstormed before you crack open your computer (it's okay if your sketches are really bad). Add a quick note about the main point you want to make on each slide that corresponds to the imagery. Working these ideas out now, on paper, will save you loads of time inside PowerPoint.

Review your last report or paper and identify at least two places where a stronger visual metaphor would help support your point.

Find a research report online in your disciplinary area and identify where graphics could be added or taken away. Graphics are dramatic and attract attention, so they should be used judiciously. Graphing the responses to every survey question, for example, dilutes the impact. Reserve graphics for your most important points.

# Where Can I Go for More Information?

American Psychological Association. (2010). *Publication manual of the American Psychological Association* (6th ed.). Washington, DC: Author.

Bateman, S., Mandryk, R. L., Gutwin, C., Genest, A., McDine, D., & Brooks, C. (2010). Useful junk? The effects of visual embellishment on comprehension and memorability of charts. In *CHI '10: Proceedings of the SIGCHI Conference on Human Factors in Computing Systems* (pp. 2573–2582). New York: ACM.

Evergreen, S. D. H. (2011). *Death by boredom: The role of visual processing theory in written evaluation communication* (Unpublished doctoral dissertation). Western Michigan University, Kalamazoo.

Evergreen, S. D. H. (2016). *Effective data visualization*. Thousand Oaks, CA: Sage.

Graham, L. (2008). Gestalt theory in interactive media design. *Journal of Humanities & Social Sciences, 2*(1), 1–12.

Lusk, E. J., & Kersnick, M. (1979). The effect of cognitive style and report format on task performance: The misdesign consequences. *Management Science, 25*(8), 787–798.

Mayer, R. E. (1997). Multimedia learning: Are we asking the right questions? *Educational Psychologist, 32*(1), 1–19.

Reynolds, G. (2010). *Presentation Zen design: Simple design principles and techniques to enhance your presentations*. Berkeley, CA: New Riders.

Robins, D., Holmes, J., & Stansbury, M. (2010). Consumer health information on the web: The relationship of visual design and perceptions of credibility. *Journal of the American Society for Information Science and Technology, 61*(1), 13–29.

Samara, T. (2007). *Design elements: A graphic style manual*. Beverly, MA: Rockport.

Tractinsky, N. (1997). Aesthetics and apparent usability: Empirically assessing cultural and methodological issues. In S. Pemberton (Ed.), *CHI '97: Human factors in computing systems; Conference proceedings* (pp. 115–122). New York: ACM.

Tufte, E. R. (2001). *The visual display of quantitative information* (2nd ed.). Cheshire, CT: Graphics Press.

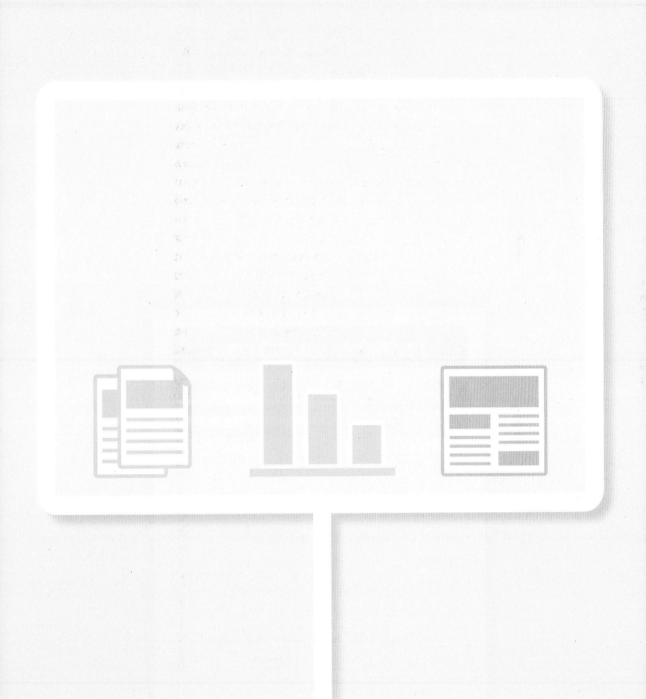

# CHAPTER THREE

## TEXT

### LEARNING OBJECTIVES

**After reading this chapter, you will be able to:**

- Distinguish between different categories of fonts

- Identify the proper application of those different categories

- Appreciate font "personalities"

- Make informed choices about type size

- Calculate appropriate line spacing

- Maximize the few bits of text in a graph

- Know what text to remove from a graph

As I give one last look at a report for work, my usual process is probably similar to yours. I spend an afternoon fussing with the layout and putting a polish on the report before sending it off to my boss for final review. I did just that with a report page similar to the one shown here in Figure 3.1.

I am using this page as my example because it is probably where I spent the most time. It was important to me (and now I am really letting on how far I am willing to go) that this table contained rows of equal height. This required some nudging, squishing, and testing until the table was just right. Then I emailed it to my boss and asked him to give it a last inspection before I shipped it out to the client.

## Guiding Ideas

Text fonts are used for narrative text

Headings and callouts are emphasized

Long reading is in 9- to 11-point size

Line spacing is 11 to 13 points

No more than three fonts are used

Body text has stylistic uniformity

Bullets are slightly less thick than text

**Figure 3.1    A painstakingly formatted report page**

### Appendix

The table below shows demographic composition over the duration of the initiative. Ultimately the changes show that the initiative's primary target population has grown older, more female, and more racially diverse.

**Race (by percent)**

| | 2010-11 | 2011-12 | 2012-13 | Overall Change (in percentage points) |
|---|---|---|---|---|
| American Indian or Alaska Native | 2 | 4 | 2 | 0 |
| Asian | 8 | 10 | 9 | +1 |
| Black or African American | 12 | 13 | 14 | +2 |
| Hispanic/Latino | 8 | 6 | 11 | +3 |
| Middle Eastern | 0 | 2 | 4 | +4 |
| Multiracial | 5 | 7 | 10 | +5 |
| Native Hawaiian or Other Pacific Islander | 0 | 0 | 0 | 0 |
| White | 65 | 58 | 50 | -15 |

As you can see from the table, the initiative has yet to attract any Native Hawaiian or Other Pacific Islanders, despite their representation in the larger organization population.

As we stated in the report, while it appears that the initiative attracted and then lost some who were American Indian or Alaska Native, in reality those participants were a part of one division that was purchased by another organization in late 2012.

Finally, while it may appear from the percentages that the white population decreased, their raw numbers were steady while participation increased from other racial groups.

Instead of sending it back to me, he saved me a step and passed the report directly to our client. I am an easygoing person. I was not bothered by his actions, but I did want an approved and finalized copy of the report for my own records, so I opened up his attachment, and a version similar to Figure 3.2 was what I saw.

At that point, I freaked out. Now, if you aren't a bit of a nerd about these things, which I admit I am, you may not immediately notice the differences between these two versions of the report. First of all, the perfect spacing in the table was ruined in the second version, in that one of the rows grew in height when a word in the first column (Islander) jumped down to a third line. Second, the heading and narrative fonts both look different. And, to add insult to injury, the last paragraph on my original page walked the plank in the version in Figure 3.2.

**Figure 3.2    How the report page looked to the recipient**

## Appendix

The table below shows demographic composition over the duration of the initiative. Ultimately the changes show that the initiative's primary target population has grown older, more female, and more racially diverse.

Race (by percent)

| | 2010-11 | 2011-12 | 2012-13 | Overall Change (in percentage points) |
|---|---|---|---|---|
| American Indian or Alaska Native | 2 | 4 | 2 | 0 |
| Asian | 8 | 10 | 9 | +1 |
| Black or African American | 12 | 13 | 14 | +2 |
| Hispanic/Latino | 8 | 6 | 11 | +3 |
| Middle Eastern | 0 | 2 | 4 | +4 |
| Multiracial | 5 | 7 | 10 | +5 |
| Native Hawaiian or Other Pacific Islander | 0 | 0 | 0 | 0 |
| White | 65 | 58 | 50 | -15 |

As you can see from the table, the initiative has yet to attract any Native Hawaiian or Other Pacific Islanders, despite their representation in the larger organization population.

As we stated in the report, while it appears that the initiative attracted and then lost some who were American Indian or Alaska Native, in reality those participants were a part of one division that was purchased by another organization in late 2012.

Our report was struck by a very annoying phenomenon called font substitution. I am sure it has happened to you, too. You email your poster to your copresenter and when she receives it, the formatting is wacky. You plug your flash drive into the conference session room laptop only to discover it does not look at all how you intended. You upload your slides to the webinar platform and nothing looks right. By the end of this chapter, you will have several strategies on hand to ensure that you are not plagued by these same issues.

## What Is Type?

The term *type* refers to the shapes of individual letters and to the stylistic variations that contribute to legibility in different contexts. I love to think about how there is a type designer sitting in a foundry somewhere in the world, crafting a new lowercase letter *t* to improve on the 13 *t*'s I already used in this sentence. For most of us, at first glance the differences in the angle of the curvature at the top of a *t* do not seem like a big deal. Yet we happily and usually unknowingly are on the receiving end of such careful thought all around us, every day. We do not need to worry ourselves too much with the specifics of creating letter shapes. We just need to know how to use them well in order to present data effectively.

Most of us refer to this topic area using the word *font.* I do. During my dissertation study, when I developed the four main topic areas that are now sections of this book, the graphic designers on my review panel disagreed. The conversation went like this:

Me:     So, I'll break out these principles into Graphics, Color, Font, and Arrangement.

Peter:   You can't call it font. It's called typeface.

Me:     Typeface? Who says that? Everybody I know calls it font.

Peter:   Fine, well, then just call it type. This is very different from font.

Me:     Call it type?! Don't you know that in the real world there are lots of different meanings for the word *type?* I'm calling it font.

Peter:   Font is what you see. Typeface is what you design with.

Me:     . . .

If you relate Peter's comments to your graphic design friends, they will be impressed by how smart you are. However, for the rest of us and throughout this book, the words *font, type,* and *typeface* are used pretty much interchangeably. Don't tell Peter. And we are going to go far beyond just type to talk about text in general and how we can work it to tell our story.

## How Do I Tell These Typefaces Apart?

There are two basic types, or categories, of type: serif and sans serif.

### Serif

The first class of fonts is serif. The top option in Figure 3.3 is Baskerville Old Face. Now, this may sound silly, but font nerds like me enjoy a feisty discussion about how fonts have personalities. For example, the properties of Baskerville Old Face are said to reflect a professional, serious, focused, yet comfortable personality.

The next serif down the line is Georgia. Georgia's personality is known as friendly and intimate. Do you see those personality traits when you compare Georgia to Baskerville Old Face? Georgia is an effective choice for tiny print because it is highly legible, even at small sizes.

**Figure 3.3**  Serif fonts are one of the major font categories (from top to bottom: Baskerville Old Face, Georgia, Times New Roman)

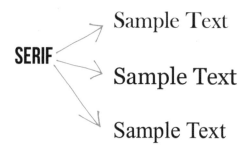

The third serif example shown is Times New Roman. Times New Roman has a reputation. It is seen as sturdy and classic. But it is a bit of a flash point for type nerds. Times New Roman is commonly used in newspapers because it is so easily read at a small size. It also was the default typeface in Microsoft Word for a very long time. For those reasons, some say it is overused, past its prime, and even a little cold.

So while these three examples are all a bit different from one another, what they have in common is that they are serif fonts.

*Serif* is a Latin word that means "little feet." See the little feet at the bottoms of the letters? Those feet help create an almost continual line along the bottom of a length of text, smoothing the reading process. Serif typefaces make reading more fluid (Song & Schwartz, 2008). Research consistently shows that fonts with serifs are easier to read, especially in lengthy smaller print. The APA Guide (2010) advises that serif fonts are preferred. In its style book, the Modern Language Association of America (MLA, 2009) says that the font used should be "easily readable" (p. 116) and suggests Times New Roman.

## Guiding Idea

Text fonts are used for narrative text

You should probably pick a serif font for at least the body text of a written report, where you expect an audience to engage in sustained, narrative reading. In a "Guiding Idea" sidebar here, these are referred to as "text fonts" instead of "serif fonts." I promise that I am not intentionally throwing more jargon into the mix. My rationale for this will become apparent in just a few more pages.

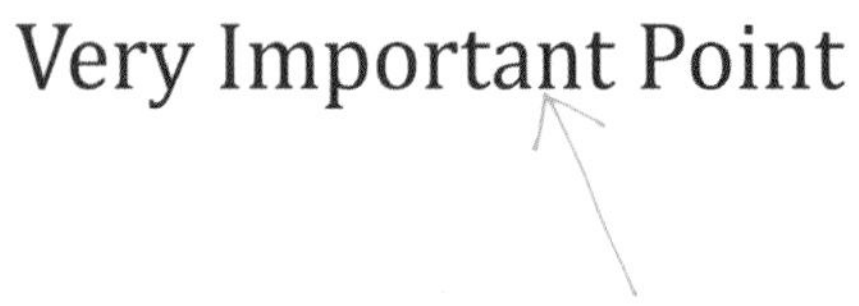

## Sans Serif

Titles, headings, and callouts may be a good place to change things up, especially since these are bound to be a larger size and shorter bursts of text. It is perfectly appropriate to choose a sans serif, or "no little feet," font in those places.

**Figure 3.4** All serif fonts have little feet at the ends of the lines that make up the letters

Very Important Point

Guiding Idea

Headings and callouts are emphasized

**Figure 3.5** Sans serif fonts are the other major category of type—no little feet here (from top to bottom: Baskerville Old Face, Open Sans, and Jokerman)

Sample Text

Sample Text

SANS SERIF

Sample Text

Here again is our focused friend Baskerville Old Face, starting us off at the top. It is a serif font, the first category of type.

The next one down is called Open Sans. Do you notice how it feels more open and modern? This feeling of openness and modernity comes from the fact that Open Sans is a sans serif font. Notice how its ends do not taper into smooth feet. The letter shapes cut off cleanly when the letters are sufficiently formed. Now that you are looking closely, you can see how these two types contrast.

This last font is sure fun. It is also a sans serif, called Jokerman. To me, its personality says *Fajitas Tonight,* and there may be situations where that reflection is exactly appropriate and fits your topic, your client, or your project very well. But you clearly do not want to use it on anything longer than just a couple of words. It is way too annoying to read at any considerable length and would likely lead to abandonment, which is when readers simply give up on reading and move on to something else.

## Slab Serif

So, I may have told you a small white lie earlier. There are more than two types of type. Lots more. Ask your favorite font nerd. For our purposes, we stick to the basics here, but I think you can handle the introduction of one more type of type, now that you are familiar with the first two.

**Figure 3.6   Slab serif fonts have thick, blocky feet (from top to bottom: Baskerville Old Face, Open Sans, and Rockwell)**

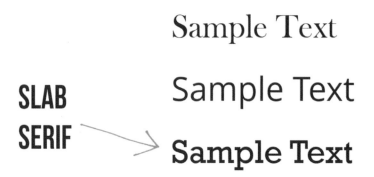

The font at the bottom is known as a slab serif. This particular slab serif is called Rockwell. As points of comparison, I've carried over the serif Baskerville Old Face and the sans serif Open Sans from earlier. Rockwell is similar to Baskerville Old Face in that it has those little feet—well, actually, those feet are quite large. They do not gradually narrow to a graceful finish like the serifs in Baskerville Old Face. The feet on a slab serif are thick and squared off. Rockwell, the slab serif, is also similar to Open Sans in that the lines making up the letters are of an even thickness. According to these characteristics, slab serifs are really their own type of type. How would you use Rockwell? Is it suitable for reading at length like the serif fonts? Or is it better on a heading, where more freedom and shorter passages are standard? Here's a quick behind-the-scenes way to answer those questions within your own computer.

# What Am I Looking at Here?

To illustrate, this book uses two fonts: a serif called PTSerif Regular set in 9-point size for the narrative text, and a sans serif called Raleway set in 14-point size for the first-level headings and 13-point size for the second-level headings. The decorative font used on the front cover is also Raleway, but larger.

Every computer has a *Fonts* folder, but the paths to get there and the details that appear may vary. This example is what the folder looks like on my PC, running Windows 10.

**Figure 3.7    Screenshot of the details for each installed font**

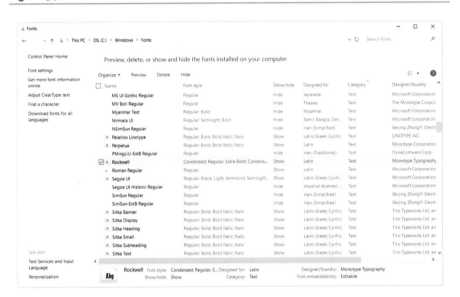

At the top you can see my navigational path. I opened my *C* drive, then my *Windows* folder, and then the *Fonts* folder. Usually the fonts in the *Fonts* folder are presented as little icons. Change the setting using the dropdown arrow in the upper right to specify the *Details* setting. So many cool details! There are the names of the foundries like the one I've envisioned, where someone is sitting at a desk playing with the curvatures on lowercase *t*'s! See the column called *Category?* Here, the operating system indicates the foundry's recommendation for the best use for each typeface.

This screenshot shows some of the text fonts (I told you it would make sense later)—these are the ones suitable for long narrative reading, and there is Rockwell. Scrolling down a bit reveals other categories, including one called *display*.

Display fonts are those fonts created to be used as titles, headings, and other report elements of that nature. You should make sans serif headings very different from the serif body font so that the headings pop right out, making report navigation easier. Display fonts are also suitable for use in slideshows, where the text is somewhat sparse and heading-like. Checking the *Fonts* folder is an immediate way to diagnose proper font usage.

In general, graphic designers suggest you pick two or maybe three fonts for your entire piece of work. Every operating system contains bunches of fonts, many of which you will probably never need in your professional reporting. There are font categories called *script* and *decorative*. On occasion these types of type might be appropriate for a single letter or one or two words in a title, but generally it's best to err on the side of legibility.

## What Works for Paper and What Works for Screen?

Aside from being a useful way to add visual interest to a written page, sans serif fonts are critical for electronic projection, whether on a computer screen or a slide projector.

Serif fonts like Baskerville Old Face do not work well with an electronic screen. Go back and check out Figure 3.6. Notice how Baskerville Old Face shows variation within the line of each letter? Look at the *m* in *Sample*. The line is much thinner at the top of the bumps. That thick-thin line variation makes it very difficult to read serif fonts on the screen. The thin parts of the letters almost disappear, even when the type is greatly enlarged. For electronic screens, use sans serif fonts, which tend to have lines of even thickness. Compare the *m* in the Open Sans example to that in Baskerville Old Face—the thick-thin line variation is gone. Now, check out Rockwell, the third font shown. Slab serifs also do not have that thick-thin line variation, so they are easier to read on a screen.

Therefore, when writing a report that will be read only on computer screens (this is more and more common as companies go paperless), use a sans serif or slab serif font. On-screen legibility tests suggest that Franklin Gothic, Cambria, Verdana, and Consolas are good choices, because they produce fewer errors in character recognition (Chaparro, Shaikh, Chaparro, & Merkle, 2010). Character recognition matters when you need to distinguish a zero from an uppercase *O,* for example, or a numeral 1 from an uppercase *I* or a lowercase *1.*

Slideshow templates do not always follow these guidelines. At this moment, almost a quarter of the default font choices preloaded into the templates on my computer identify serif fonts for the main slide headings, but I think these fonts have too much thick-thin line variation to maintain legibility. If you choose to use a slide template, remember that you are in control of it. You can change the font choices, make the fonts larger, and manipulate them so that the template provides a clearer package for your data.

Changing up the font choice to match the dissemination method is how we arrive at the recommendation of using three fonts per project. The slideshow usually has two—a sans or slab serif for the headings and a different sans or slab serif for the little bits of other content on the slides. But the handout that you distribute to your audience members containing your key points should include a serif font (the third font in your package) for the narrative text.

The headings or callout points on your handout can be set in the slab or sans serif used in your slides. Using the same heading font, plus the repetition of other elements, such as color and graphics, makes it obvious that your materials belong together, represents you as a polished professional, and helps your audience engage with your content. Now that you know the basic rules about typeface, you are equipped to make informed decisions about which types of type to use where and when.

## What About Stuff That Will Be on Both Screen and Paper?

Some of you are in situations where your reports or posters will be printed as well as posted online. What font should you use then? You'll need to look for a hybrid font. Calibri is one. Once people started getting more comfortable reading on-screen, they realized how bad the old Microsoft Office default font—Times New Roman—was for screen reading, so Microsoft switched it up, replacing the default with Calibri, which works well on both screen and paper.

But you can't use Calibri. Friends, Calibri screams default. It says, I just use whatever is put in front of me and don't think outside the box too much. And that's not the image you are trying to project. So keep looking for other good hybrid fonts. Georgia, for example, is a serif with thick lines, making it easily readable on-screen. That's the kind of characteristic you're looking for.

## Did You Just Say I Can't Use Calibri?

Yep. Sorry, folks. Default fonts are the equivalent of using Excel default colors in your data visualizations. Everyone recognizes them as default and then makes judgments about the quality of your work. "She clearly doesn't even care." That's definitely not going to help you sell your ideas! You can and most certainly should branch out beyond the default fonts already installed on your laptop (and everyone else's). One of my favorite places to find new fonts is Font Squirrel (https://www.fontsquirrel.com). I love this site because the fonts are all free and 100% okay to use for commercial purposes. Lately I've also been using Google Fonts (https://fonts.google.com), which is additionally lovely because it suggests font pairings so you can easily snag a heading font and a well-matched text font.

You'll need to download your new font from one of those sites and then distribute it to any coauthors or teammates. Follow these steps (and perhaps check in with your IT department if you get hung up anywhere).

## When the Receiving Computer Is a PC

Open your *Fonts* folder and drag the files into your email to your colleague. (Hint: Trying to attach a font from inside my email system wouldn't work; I was told that I didn't have administrator access—incorrect, Windows Help menu, incorrect.)

Your colleague will download the file as she normally would any email attachment. It's usually a zip file that looks like this:

**Figure 3.8    This zip file contains the license agreement and the font files**

You might as well read that license agreement while you're in there. We know these fonts are all free for commercial use, but close inspection of this agreement reveals that the creator doesn't mind donations.

Then double-click on one file. It'll look like this:

**Figure 3.9 This window shows how the font will look—hit the *Install* button**

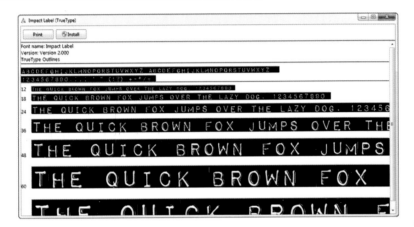

Just click the *Install* button, and it'll do its thing.

Then, when you open PowerPoint (and note—you'll want to close it and reopen before looking for the new font), the downloaded font will appear in your regular font list:

**Figure 3.10 Reopen your software to see the newly installed font**

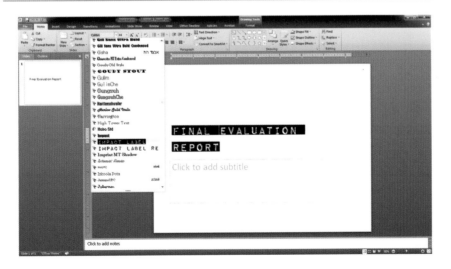

Note that the process works the same regardless of whether the sending computer is a PC or a Mac.

## When the Receiving Computer Is a Mac

The sender goes through the same process—attach the downloaded font files to an email and send.

The receiver opens the email attachment. On my Mac, it opened into my *Downloads* folder:

**Figure 3.11    Download the font file**

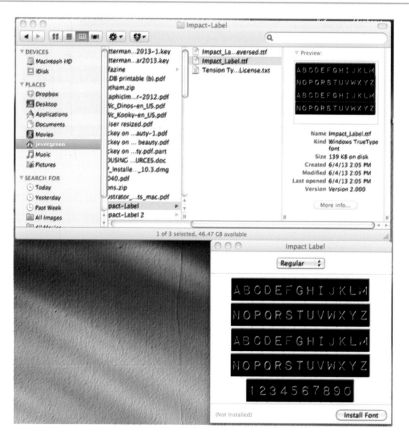

I double-clicked on the font's name in my *Downloads* folder and it opened a second window below. In there, I clicked *Install Font*.

Then my Mac's Font Book popped open, and there was my new font, ready to make my PowerPoint shine:

**Figure 3.12    Check your Font Book or open PowerPoint to see the new font**

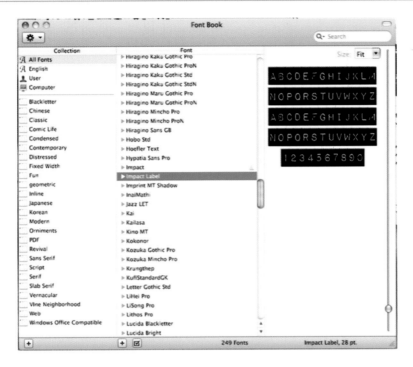

If you work in a place where you aren't allowed to add to your computer's *C* drive, you'll need to snag your IT person to help secure the right permissions. Either way, this process is as simple as downloading and opening an email attachment. So don't be intimidated! You are not restricted to the default fonts loaded onto your computer.

You may have tried using specialty fonts before, only to discover that when you passed your document along to someone (like a client) who didn't have the font, it didn't look right. Let's solve that problem right now.

## How Can I Protect Font Choices?

I used all of the procedures I've described above when I designed the report I detailed at the start of this chapter—and still, everything went awry. Let's break down what happened.

I set the report's narrative type in Gentium Book Basic, a typeface installed on my workplace PC. Gentium Book Basic is a decent font, holds up well on-screen, yet it is a serif that can be read at length. Sounds like a superstar, right? But when I shipped the report out to my boss, he opened it at home on his Macintosh, where that font was not in his Font Book. Oh, the trials and tribulations of PC–Mac compatibility!

His Mac did not recognize my text font (or the one I used on the headings), so it made a substitution, replacing Gentium Book Basic with another font so that my boss could read the document. Oftentimes, computers do not even let their owners know that a font substitution has been made. So when my boss opened the file, he presumed that what he saw was the product of an employee he knew cared a lot about font choices and assumed it was my preference for it to look that way.

It is painful to go to all the trouble of selecting the perfect font only to have it substituted when the report electronically leaves your hands. You might be tempted to think that this is why the PDF format was invented, right? Don't be fooled. PDF does not completely cure your font substitution ills, particularly when working with a PC–Mac translation. Nor does it make document cocreation any easier when you are producing data presentations as part of a team.

In those cases where the whole team is working in a PC environment, here is what I know now about document protection that I did not know then: Embed the fonts.

In Word 2016, you can automatically embed your fonts when you save.

**Figure 3.13**   Screenshot of a typical *Save* window—notice the arrow between the word *Tools* and the *Save* button

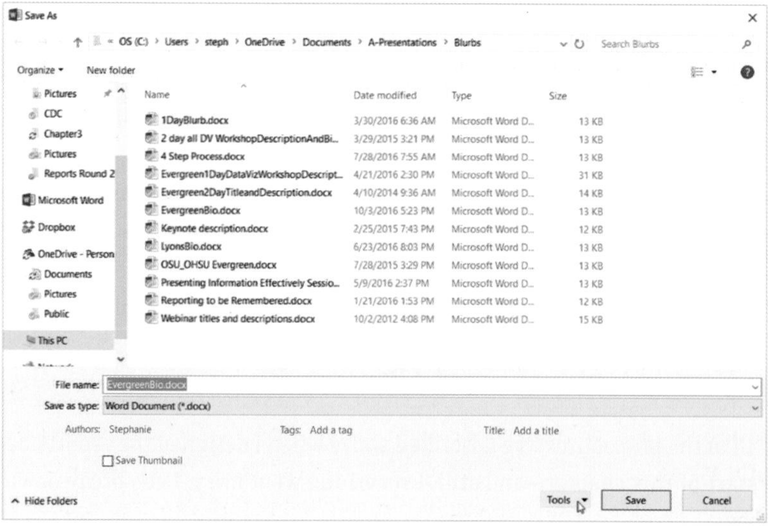

Before hitting that *Save* button, click the dropdown arrow next to *Tools* and choose the *Save Options* link. That opens up a pop-up box that looks like this:

Figure 3.14    **The bottom set of checkboxes shows where you can adjust the settings related to embedding your font**

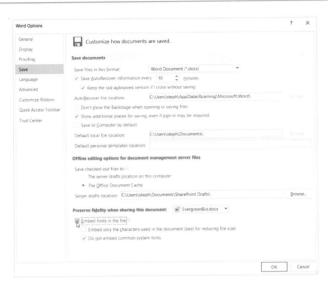

Then, make certain that the checkbox next to *Embed fonts in the file* is activated. Now, the font files travel with the document as it is disseminated. Your readers cannot download the font to their own computers, but they are able to see your materials the way you intended them to be seen. You can also ensure that the fonts are embedded in all new documents by choosing that option from the dropdown menu for *Preserve fidelity when sharing this document* (where, in this screenshot, the EvergreenBio file name appears). However, be careful—in my experience, embedding the fonts can raise file size by about 25%.

You can navigate the same path to embed fonts in any Office 2010 program on PCs. This way, you do not have to worry about your fonts getting substituted as you distribute your work or when you plug your flash drive into another computer.

PC–Mac compatibility is a little trickier, as Macs do not always recognize PC font embedding. In those cases, you can send the font to your colleague and have her download it to her Mac. If the recipient is a client or professor, and it might be awkward to ask her to download and install a font, then stick with fonts common to both computer types, such as Baskerville, Arial (PC)/Helvetica (Mac), or Segoe. As one final possibility, if you want to use uncommon fonts minimally (as discussed next), you can type those words into text boxes, then copy the text boxes and paste them right into the document as picture files. That is a pain, of course, so be selective about the use of nonstandard fonts.

As an extra precaution, you can also embed fonts into PDFs. Within Adobe PDF, look in the *Tools* tab for the *Print Production* area. Open this up and click the option for *Preflight Tools.*

**Figure 3.15    To be extra safe, embed your fonts in your PDF too**

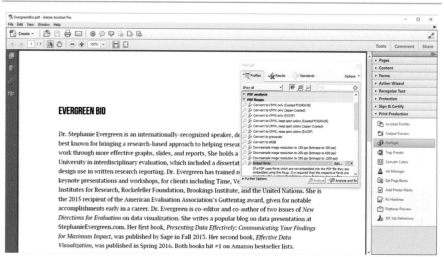

In *Preflight Tools,* open up the *PDF fixups* menu and click *Embed fonts.* It'll run through a check and take care of any font embed issues. From time to time, a font's author will restrict the font from being embedded, but otherwise, this should take care of it, honey.

## How Do Fonts Actually Communicate?

Psychologists debate the exact details, but we know that in reading, the eye–brain connection does not work by processing through each individual letter (Pelli, Farell, & Moore, 2003). Rather, curves of letters and the composition of ascenders (think of the tall stick on an *h*) and descenders (think of the stick that hangs down on a *y*) influence recognition of entire words. As such, fonts deserve our thoughtful attention because of their impact on our readers.

Beyond the words they compose, the individual characteristics that differentiate one font from the next also communicate subtle messages to the audience (Lewis & Walker, 1989). Sometimes this is obvious: Fonts that look like handwriting convey that the content is more informal or youthful, without the audience ever reading a single word.

Take, for example, these slides starting off a discussion on student enrollment within a history department.

The title slide in Figure 3.16 is from a PowerPoint template. The default font in the template, Century Gothic, is a sans serif—okay for screen reading, yes, but it can send a mixed message to the audience. The font may be too modern for a history department. Hang in there with me while I explain. Figure 3.17 is the same content in another PowerPoint template, this time set in Garamond, a serif font. Notice how Garamond feels more classic, more appropriate for the fine folks in history? It is more fitting for the subject, but serif is not great for screen reading. What a dilemma.

**Figures 3.16 and 3.17**    **Two template-based slides, one modern (on the left) with a sans serif font and one more classic (on the right) with a serif font**

**Figure 3.18**    **Selected words can be set in a decorative, mood-setting font, while the rest of the text supports readability**

A much friendlier option is to use the power of highly communicative fonts to set off a single word. Highlighting just one word or phrase still influences the flavor of the content and represents the subject well, as long as the surrounding fonts are somewhat neutral. In the revision in Figure 3.18, I used another standard PowerPoint template where the default font is Arial Black, but I offset one word using a more decorative font with an aged look, called Blackadder. Now, we've solved the issues of finding a representative font that communicates the subject and locating a font that reads well on-screen. The trick, however, is to restrict the use of the decorative font. Notice in the next example how the overuse completely obliterates the impact and even the legibility (that title actually says "KCC Enrollment Over Time").

**Figure 3.19**    **Overuse of the decorative font destroys good design and legibility**

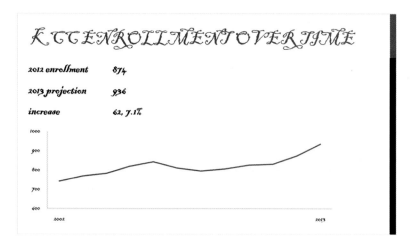

The best way to offset a single word or two is through the use of an extra text box. Definitely, you can keep "KCC History Department" in one text box and just change the font on "History," but that type of change throws off line spacing, especially if you increase the size of the highlighted word, as I did in the example in Figure 3.18. Insert text boxes as needed.

Let's look at one more example.

In these selections, same research, same poster layout, just two very different display fonts. The display font (used on the title, subtitle, and callout) for the poster in Figure 3.20 is Franklin Gothic Demi Condensed. By contrast, the display font used in the poster in Figure 3.21 is called Kids.

Now, we just discussed the need for appropriately matching font personalities to their subject matter, right? By that logic, at first glance it is easy to assume that Kids is the correct font to choose for the research presented on the poster. Yet the Kids

Figure 3.20    Research poster that communicates credibility

Figure 3.21    Same poster, just a different font—one that communicates immaturity

font does a disservice to the research—and, by proxy, the researcher. It communicates a personality of playfulness and immaturity, and it is these characteristics that are interpreted by the onlookers. In addition to impairing legibility, the font makes it difficult for a viewer to read through and digest the entire subtitle; it subtly undermines the credibility of the authors. (Let me say, as a former early childhood specialist and current parent, that kid-print typefaces also do not belong on newsletters, lunch calendars, report cards, or classroom walls. They neither model proper letter formation for children nor adequately represent the professionalism and respectability of the teaching field.) Do you think applying the Kids font on a single word in the title would be effective here? Maybe I have just been overexposed to kid-print fonts, but I would say fonts like these have no place in professional reporting situations.

The more serious display font in Figure 3.20 is not a serif, which traditionally tends to come off as more professional and classic than this sans serif, which is clear and crisp and condensed—everything we want on a research poster. This font is a better reflection of the competence of the research team, and it is this match between the font and the research that is more appropriate. The child-focused aspect of the study is effectively presented through the picture. The font here represents the integrity of the work.

## What Font Size Should I Use?

Did you know that you regularly read type set in point size 8, or even smaller? In printed materials, captions and less important information (think: photograph credits, newsletter headline subtext, magazine staff listings) are usually reduced to something between 7.5 and 9 points. We generally read that size type without much issue, such as the need for glasses. The reason we can comfortably read such small type is that the designers have chosen effective fonts that keep their clarity and legibility when shrunk.

Designers don't make the fonts that tiny to give you a headache. They do it to establish a font hierarchy. Our brains interpret the biggest size as the most important and the littlest as the least important. So we can create a hierarchy of font sizes to structure our work and communicate even more clearly. Let's see how this looks in a few examples.

Posters need to have large titles, often as large as 150 points, which is readable from about 25 feet away. In the poster in Figure 3.22, the green title is set in TheSans Extra Bold at 90 points.

Headings on a poster, such as "who are you?" in Figure 3.22, should be set in about 40-point size or larger (this poster uses 45-point type). Text at this size is legible from more than 5 feet. This means conference attendees can read your research poster title from down the aisle and come in closer to examine the details. It's a good idea to pick a sans serif font here, even though posters are on paper, because serif fonts tend to fall apart, with their thinner parts getting so thin that legibility can be diminished.

**Figure 3.22**    The different sizes of fonts within this poster help communicate what should be read first, second, and so on

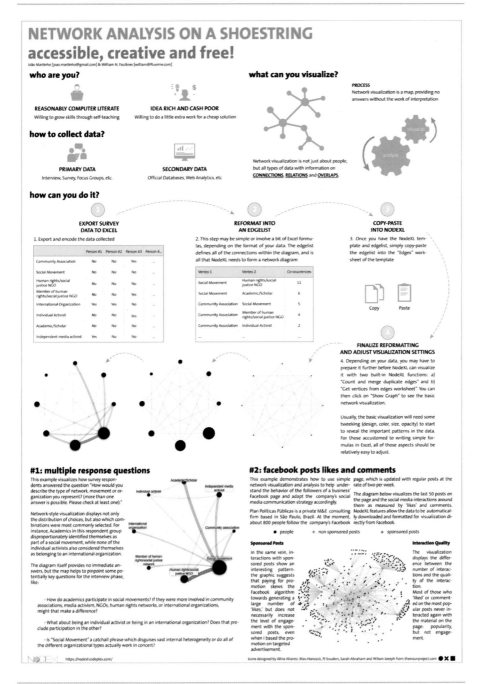

*Source:* © 2015. Reprinted with permission from João Martinho and William Faulkner.

This poster also has subheadings, like "Reasonably computer literate," which is set at 30 points.

The narrative text in this poster is set at 25 points. And either serif or sans serif would work here because it is pretty small. For the narrative portion of poster text, 18-point size, give or take, is common. At that size, it can be read comfortably from about 2.5 feet.

The tiniest print on this poster is used for the names and email addresses of the authors. These are tucked up right under the title, and should be something under 18 points.

Altogether, the sizes of the fonts sort the poster's various elements into a hierarchy of importance. This same method works in all of our reporting mechanisms, though they don't all have as much content on one page.

Slides will have very little text on them, which means that whatever text is there can be large and in charge. Go for headings set in 80-point type or larger. That can feel scary, but such size is important in a slideshow setting, particularly when you are presenting your research in a cavernous room. This means the folks sitting in the back row of your conference session or your classroom lecture hall will stay more engaged and less annoyed.

You can get a rough idea of whether your slideshow's type size is sufficiently large by using the slide sorter view. In PowerPoint, it looks like this:

Figure 3.23   **The slide sorter view provides a quick way of getting a sense of how your text looks to the audience members in the back row of a medium-size room**

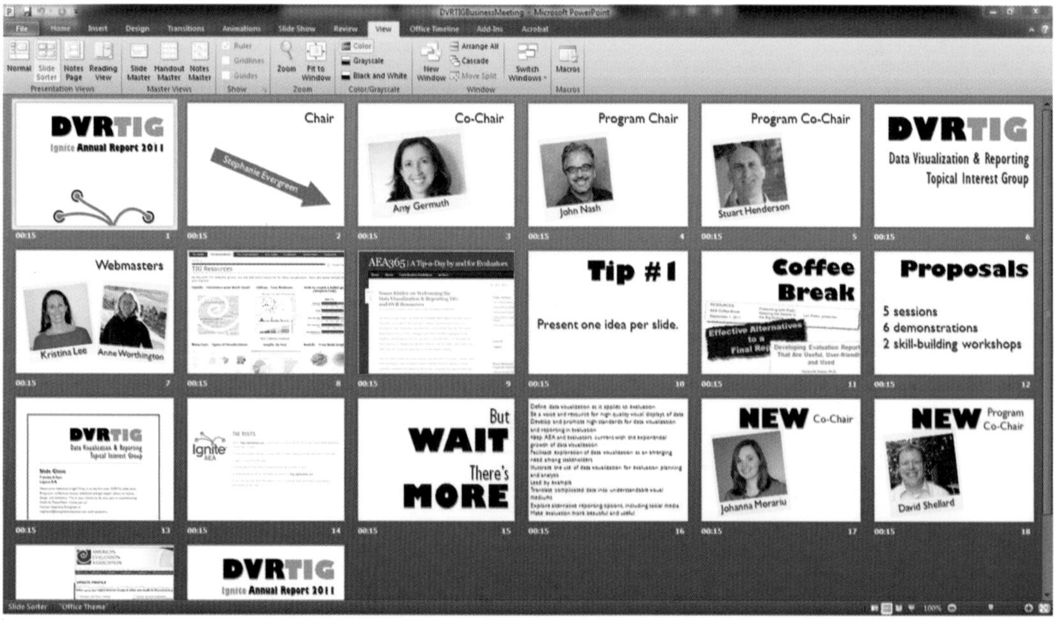

If you can read your words in the slide sorter mode, then chances are good that so can the audience in your presentation room.

To verify your size on a PC, click on the *View* tab and look to the left for *Slide Sorter* in the *Presentation View* group. In case you are wondering, the largest type displayed in the slides in Figure 3.23 is set in 115 point in Gill Sans Ultra Bold. The smaller text is from the same typeface family—Gill Sans MT, but in size 44. Slide 16 has lots of text crammed in at size 28, which may be too small. But, of course, the point of that slide was to create an overwhelming feeling.

If the text is too small, and enlarging it is impossible because there is too much text on the slide, guess what? It means there is too much text on the slide. Break those points apart so that each one has its own slide.

Report pages are more like posters than slides, in that there's a lot of content, but it's in a much more intimate format (who ever thought we'd used "intimate" to describe your report?).

**Figure 3.24** **Font sizes should vary within a page to mark sections**

*Source:* © 2015. Reprinted with permission from A. J. Drexel Autism Institute.

The report page shown in Figure 3.24 contains seven different font sizes. Generally speaking, headings should be 150% to 200% of the body text size. So, if the narrative text is set in 11 points, the headings should be set in something between 16 and 22 points. In Figure 3.24, the orange report headings are size 12 and bold, set in Arial, which tends to look big.

Important side note, while I have you looking at those orange headings: Check out how each heading is a whole statement. Sheer brilliance! It doesn't say something generic like "Social Participation" or, even worse, "Findings." It says the whole finding. Why does this matter? Because people are skimming your report. You know it, I know it. They are looking for the highlights and the things that jump out at them. They are going to look at the graphs and the headings. So make the headings the takeaway points! And then—total bonus—if you construct a table of contents, it will almost work as your executive summary. Take that one and run with it (for posters too!).

## Guiding Idea

Headings and callouts are emphasized

That long narrative prose in Figure 3.24 is about right in size 11. Studies show that 11-point text is easiest to read at length, but, as usual, it depends on the typeface. Some fonts, like Baskerville Old Face, are still too tiny at size 11. You can tell because the holes in the lowercase *e*'s are not yet visible (okay, fine, font nerds, the *bowl* in the lowercase *e!*). Some, like Verdana, look a bit too large at size 11, coming off as immature. If you love Verdana, just set it in 10 point. On the web, a larger font size is typically desired. Standard, reliable choices are Verdana, set in 12 points, and Arial/Helvetica, set in 13 points. Of course, when it comes to the font for your dissertation, use whatever is mandated.

## Guiding Idea

Long reading is in 9- to 11-point size

Graphs within a page need to fit into the hierarchy as well. The most important part of the graph, usually its title, should be the largest in size to draw a viewer's attention first. Notice again in Figure 3.24 that the graph titles are written like headlines, with key takeaway points. Since these titles fit within the hierarchy of this page, they have to be smaller than the orange headings. Graph titles here are set in Arial size 11, bolded.

A subtitle to a graph would be a point or two smaller than the title. In some cases, graph designers like to exchange a subtitle for an annotation, and they might plunk a callout box right next to a key point in a graph. These annotations should be treated the same as subtitles in terms of the font size hierarchy.

In the case of Figure 3.24, the graphs have no descriptive subtitles, so the data labels at the ends of the bars fill the second position in the importance hierarchy. They are still a larger size than the bar labels, which are larger than the axis labels.

The smallest text of a report is likely to be in the graphs, on source or note information, and it can get as small as size 9. Figure 3.24 uses sans serif fonts within the graphs, but your favorite narrative text serif font might be too tiny to read at 9-point size, and here is why. For the tiniest reading, look for a font that has what graphic designers call a taller x-height (named, cleverly, after the size of the lowercase *x*). For our purposes here, the point is simply the taller the letters, the more legible. Some fonts, such as Verdana, are also wider, which is helpful for those of us who get headaches from squinting too much. But what works at 9-point size does not always work at larger point sizes. Check out your nearest magazine. Chances are that the small-size captions are set in a typeface different from the larger text intended for narrative reading. Which means you might need three different fonts for a well-structured report. In the case of Figure 3.24, there are three fonts in seven different sizes.

Audiences interpret larger size as higher importance. In a hierarchy of information, largest is at the top. Varying type size communicates the organizational structure of the report and provides the reader with clues to the author's logic.

## How Should Lines Be Spaced?

Before we get too much further, let's chat for a moment about a closely related issue. Line spacing (i.e., the distance between lines within a paragraph) can affect legibility even when effective fonts are selected.

### Guiding Idea

Line spacing is 11 to 13 points

For lines within a paragraph, generally choose line spacing that is 1 to 2 points larger than the body text.

In Word, this can be done in two ways. Clicking on *Line Spacing Options* in the dropdown arrow in the *Paragraph* area of the *Home* tab opens up the box shown in Figure 3.25.

From the highlighted dropdown menu called *Line Spacing,* you can choose *Exactly* and type in something between 11 and 13. Alternatively, you can choose *Multiple* and type in something between 1.1 and 1.2, getting down with lots of decimal places available there.

Figure 3.25   **This window is where you can adjust the spacing between the lines of narrative text**

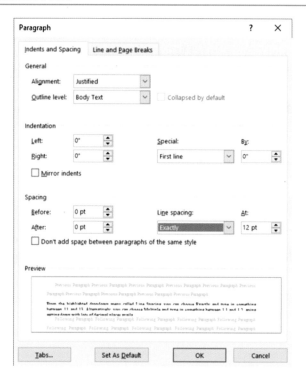

Figure 3.26   **Three line spacing possibilities, each influencing the readability of the text**

11 point text
11 point spacing
**Too narrow!**

Generally speaking, ideal reading conditions occur when the line spacing within a paragraph is set 1-2 points larger than the size of the text itself. If you know your type size, you can figure out proper line spacing.

11 point text
13 point spacing
**I can breathe!**

Generally speaking, ideal reading conditions occur when the line spacing within a paragraph is set 1-2 points larger than the size of the text itself. If you know your type size, you can figure out proper line spacing.

11 point text
22 point spacing
**I'm lost in space!!**

Generally speaking, ideal reading conditions occur when the line spacing within a paragraph is set 1-2 points larger than the size of the text itself. If you know your type size, you can figure out proper line spacing.

When the lines are too close together, the ascenders in one line bump into the descenders from the line above, making it difficult to discern the words and causing general feelings of claustrophobia. Line spacing that is too far apart, as in the last instance in the figure above, breaks up the fluidity of the paragraph.

## How Does Typeface Help Organize Data Presentation?

A change in font indicates a change in meaning and invites the audience to spend energy to interpret the meaning. This is why unnecessary font changes—whether in the font itself or in the size—cause audience frustration. So, be intentional about font changes and incorporate them only when you want to signal a shift in the narrative, such as the start of a new section or the title of a chart. Here are five places where a font change is warranted (I'll discuss a few others later on, in the context of data displays): headings, callouts, sidebars, quotes, and bullets.

### Guiding Idea

No more than three fonts are used

### Headings

Headings are a clue to the report's organization. They can be distinguished from body text by their placement above the narrative, and they can be further distinguished through the use of a font change. When moving between fonts, make them very different. If the sans serif heading looks too similar to the serif body type, it just comes off as a sloppy mistake. Be a little bold with the headings. Contrast with body text by using a different font category, size, style, and/or color. Looks that are too similar seem unintentional.

Subheadings should be set in the same font as the document's headings. In keeping with a hierarchical organization, the subheadings should be downplayed just a bit: smaller in size than the headings, or a more neutral color.

### Callouts

Callout boxes are those short bursts of text that highlight key points from the research. They are usually embedded within the narrative text; however, because they are used for emphasis, they must be visibly distinguished from the narrative text. In terms of content hierarchy, headings are more important than callouts, and callouts are more important than the narrative.

For example, in the research poster we dissected earlier in this chapter (Figure 3.20), the callout box in the lower right is set in 72-point size—the same size as the subtitle, and both are smaller than the main title.

**Figure 3.27**    **Callout boxes can be distinguished from the narrative text through adjustments in type settings, such as size and font**

In the report page shown here, the callout box is emphasized by its distinction from the narrative text. First, it is set in the same font as the heading—Segoe Black—so that it is visually different from the narrative, indicating to the reader that there is a change in meaning taking place. Second, the callout box has an ample margin separating it from the narrative text. It is also larger, set at 12 points rather than 11. The APA Guide (2010) recommends that figures and sidebars should be set in a sans serif font, at a size between 8 and 14 points. All of those settings then create a situation where the callout box is lifted out of the narrative to become higher in the hierarchy of importance on the page.

## Sidebars

Shifts in the narrative also occur with the introduction of sidebars. Sidebars are a way to showcase short, poignant stories or to describe details that are related but not a direct part of the narrative. The conceptual distinction needs to be physically presented in the report via sidebars.

**Figure 3.28    Sidebars are good places to introduce a third font**

Even though the program is focused on adolescent males, the functionality of each class session could improve with the exclusion of some age subgroups. However politically incorrect it may be, participants in both types of focus groups were very clear in their frustration over the ability of certain members to derail the course procedures and get the teacher off-topic. There are a few recommendations for managing such situations, which may attract and keep more participants.

**CONSIDER EXCLUDING MIDDLE SCHOOLERS.** Maturity and sophistication are hallmarks of this gentlemen's program. However, this academic cycle, the refinement didn't seem to occur for the youngest participants and their immaturity appeared to bring down the morale of the entire group. Eighth graders also scored considerably lower on the course assessments – indicating their lack of commitment to the group's main subject area.

**ESTABLISH GROUND RULES** and strategies for delivering consequences within the group to allow for peer leadership around group norms. Several participants were irritated by the tendency of others to arrive late, eat the snack, and leave – disrupting the flow on their way in and out. Some focus group participants suggested that establishing group norms on a large piece of paper – something that could be referred to throughout the program – might be an effective strategy for handling disruptive individuals. A thought-out, agreed-upon series of interventions might also help, so that there is a clear time when one's disruptions becomes so severe that the

**Mateo's story**

A ninth grader at City High School, Mateo Hernandez literally woke up one morning with the realization that he wanted to go to college. "It just dawned on me that I wanted do something and there are talents I want to work on."

But he had spent the bulk of his school years in detention or skipping out to the woods behind the school to hang out with his friends. His grades and extracurricular focus would need considerable attention if he was going to be able to advance on his new desire for higher education. That's when he found the MET group.

In the single academic year since Mateo has been with MET, he has become more satisfied with his grades and he has spent more time in the classroom than out. "I'm not there yet. There's a long journey for me to get my college applications looking good. But I'm headed there."

Mateo credits his focus to the MET schedule – it replaces his idle time with something fulfilling – and with his MET peers. He says knowing he has a group of friends with the same goals keeps him more accountable, even outside of program hours.

This example shows a sidebar that contains a small success case study. The content can stand on its own and serves as a complement to the narrative, making it suitable material for a sidebar. The sidebar is established with a gray background, and while color is commonly used to demarcate separate space, it is not totally necessary. As discussed in Chapter 4, on color, you need to be careful that the sidebar background color is light enough for good legibility.

What is more compulsory is that the sidebar content is set in a different font, so that it is not confused with the narrative text. In fact, sidebars are frequently set in a third font, not the one used for the text or the one used for the headings of the report.

Often, the third font is a sans serif that complements the other two. Identifying three complementary fonts can be tricky. Some font-matching resources are listed at the end of this chapter, but as a backup plan you can set your sidebars in the same font as your sans serif report headings and get the job done. Be attentive to the line length here—I used a condensed font for the sidebar in Figure 3.28 to get closer to the ideal of 8 to 12 words per line, which is discussed in Chapter 5, on arrangement.

## Quotes

Stylistic uniformity means that each narrative text section has normal text in sentence case. No bolded words. No all caps. Nothing underlined. In essence, if you blur your eyes just a bit, the narrative text should look like a gray blob with nothing in particular standing out or emphasized. Stylistic uniformity supports undistracted and speedier reading.

### Guiding Idea

Body text has stylistic uniformity

We talk about quantitative data displays at the end of each chapter, but we have not discussed how to display qualitative data very much. There are some cool ways (getting even cooler by the day) to visualize qualitative data, but for now, that is beyond the scope of this book (for more on this, see the entire chapter on qualitative data in *Effective Data Visualization*). The most basic way to show qualitative data is through the quotes of our research participants. *Do not put the quotes in italics.* That's funny. But, I am serious: Do not put the quotes in italics. Italicized text breaks uniformity. We think we are drawing attention and emphasizing text with italics, but they actually make text stand out even less. Italics also work against comprehension because italics are hard to read, especially at length. Quotation marks are sufficient to indicate a quote.

### When Should I Break the Uniformity Rule?

Of course, uniformity is the ideal, but there are some situations where there is no choice but to emphasize within the narrative text. For example, grant applications, journals, and dissertations are notoriously strict in their text settings, specifying the font and font size and restricting the use of other features like callout boxes. I even worked on a grant for one foundation where the application had to be cut and pasted into text boxes on a website. In these situations, bolding or all caps might be the only option for those critical pieces of text that must stand out to the reader. Because those emphasis methods can make it hard to read text, be judicious with your use.

I know it probably sounds like certain of my recommendations make data presentation pretty boring. And, given some of the restrictions I've outlined, it might seem like you are destined to make the most uninteresting typeface choices. This is actually what we want for our narrative text. We do not want people distracted by the shapes of our letters; we want them reading our letters to digest our data presentation. When the narrative text conveys information we want retained, it is okay to be boring. We have other methods of emphasizing and highlighting our key messages. Additionally, you save yourself the time and effort of styling the text. Uniformity is a win-win for you and your reader.

## Bullets

Personally, I think bullets kill—by that I mean that sometimes they create more problems than they solve. Too often, they are used whenever a sentence contains enough objects that it can become a list. Instead of a sentence with 10 commas, authors make a bulleted list; but bullets can be very distracting.

Notice in this example (Figure 3.29) how the darkness of the bullets is nearly the same as the bold heading text? Default bullets are dark. The black dots contrast with the white background more than the text on the page, and thus they pop out to the reader. The bullets are surrounded by white space, contributing to their emphasis as focal points. Our eyes are drawn to the bullets. That is a lot of power. Unfortunately, many authors tend to use bullets on anything that could be a list instead of reserving them for what really needs the reader's attention.

So, I will tell you how to use bullets, if you promise to wield them wisely. If you must use bullets, decrease their size to slightly less (70–80%) than the narrative font point size.

**Guiding Idea**

Bullets are slightly less thick than text

**Figure 3.29    Bullets are generally too dark and distracting to the eye**

**What changes, if any, should be made to the program for further success?**

**A few recommendations might improve achievement of program goals.**

Even though the program is focused on adolescent males, the functionality of each class session could improve with the exclusion of some age subgroups. However politically incorrect it may be, participants in both types of focus groups were very clear in their frustration over the ability of certain members to derail the course procedures and get the teacher off-topic. There are a few recommendations for managing such situations, which may attract and keep more participants.

- **Consider excluding middle schoolers.**
- **Establish ground rules.**
- **Let the students develop methods to obtain leadership roles inside the school.**
- **Adjust the standards.**

While performance standards were agreed upon at the start of the evaluation, some impact areas could have seen higher grades had we adjusted the standards set. For example, the self-esteem outcome is supposed to increase over the baseline by 95%. Such growth is realistically impossible. Given that we now have pre-post data for these outcomes from this year, we should rethink the anticipated growth levels and adjust the standards appropriately. The consequence could be that the evaluation grade masks some of the terrific work that was done.

Figure 3.30  **If you must use bullets, lighten them so they are less distracting**

**What changes, if any, should be made to the program for further success?**

**A few recommendations might improve achievement of program goals.**

Even though the program is focused on adolescent males, the functionality of each class session could improve with the exclusion of some age subgroups. However politically incorrect it may be, participants in both types of focus groups were very clear in their frustration over the ability of certain members to derail the course procedures and get the teacher off-topic. There are a few recommendations for managing such situations, which may attract and keep more participants.

- **Consider excluding middle schoolers.**
- **Establish ground rules.**
- **Let the students develop methods to obtain leadership roles inside the school.**
- **Adjust the standards.**

While performance standards were agreed upon at the start of the evaluation, some impact areas could have seen higher grades had we adjusted the standards set. For example, the self-esteem outcome is supposed to increase over the baseline by 95%. Such growth is realistically impossible. Given that we now have pre-post data for these outcomes from this year, we should rethink the anticipated growth levels and adjust the standards appropriately. The consequence could be that the evaluation grade masks some of the terrific work that was done.

It might be a subtle difference, but now the bullets are lighter than the heading and do not compete with the rest of the text for attention (Figure 3.30). Yet they still contrast enough to serve their purpose of pointing out a subset of important information to the reader.

My preference is to delete the bullets altogether (Figure 3.31). But I can bend on this preference, such as when the graphic designers at SAGE made the cute graphics for the page at the start of each chapter in this book.

A good, strong indentation can cue a reader to a subset of information, possibly as well as, if not better than, those dark dots.

Figure 3.31  **Adequate indentation can achieve the same effect as bullets**

**What changes, if any, should be made to the program for further success?**

**A few recommendations might improve achievement of program goals.**

Even though the program is focused on adolescent males, the functionality of each class session could improve with the exclusion of some age subgroups. However politically incorrect it may be, participants in both types of focus groups were very clear in their frustration over the ability of certain members to derail the course procedures and get the teacher off-topic. There are a few recommendations for managing such situations, which may attract and keep more participants.

   **Consider excluding middle schoolers.**

   **Establish ground rules.**

   **Let the students develop methods to obtain leadership roles inside the school.**

   **Adjust the standards.**

While performance standards were agreed upon at the start of the evaluation, some impact areas could have seen higher grades had we adjusted the standards set. For example, the self-esteem outcome is supposed to increase over the baseline by 95%. Such growth is realistically impossible. Given that we now have pre-post data for these outcomes from this year, we should rethink the anticipated growth levels and adjust the standards appropriately. The consequence could be that the evaluation grade masks some of the terrific work that was done.

## How Do I Apply These Ideas to Graphs?

Most of the time, our concerns about a graph's text are about removing the excess so that the graph is less cluttered. Data visualization is usually intended to replace a lot of text, so the little bits that do remain need to be awesome.

This section deals a lot more with the text itself and less with the font, so let me just clear this part up straightaway: I almost always use condensed fonts in my graphs. I mentioned these earlier when talking about sidebars: Condensed fonts are tall and skinny, usually sans serifs. This means you are more likely to fit a data label into the width of a bar in your bar graph, for example. Look for fonts that include "Narrow," "Condensed," or "Cond" in their names. Apply those condensed fonts to the text discussed in the rest of this chapter.

### 6- to 12-Word Descriptive Title Is Left Justified in Upper Left Corner

If you do nothing else to improve a weak visualization, you'll still seriously improve its interpretability by giving it an awesome title.

Often, we use weak titles that don't really tell the reader the point of the visualization.

Figure 3.32   **Weak titles don't tell us much**

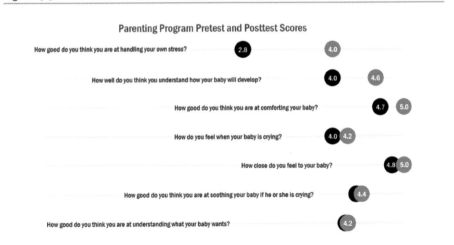

I think this is because we make our graphs in Excel, which pops in the two-word "Chart Title," and so we think we need to replace that with two equally generic words like "Graduation Rates." And this puts our audience in the really crappy position of having to figure out what we are trying to say about graduation rates, as if they are mind readers. They also must spend a lot of time decoding the visual display of the data to see if our point is discernible, when, chances are, the data could convey many points. And that's cool—data are rich and that's why we show them—but our point is lost with a weak title.

We can use that precious title space to frame our message such that when the visual is cut out of our report and spread all over Twitter, our point remains intact.

**Figure 3.33    A strong title frames the story**

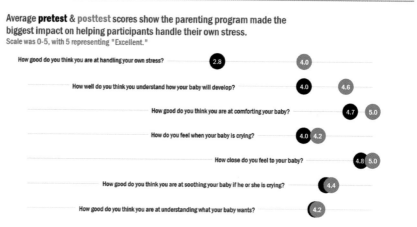

Coming up with a good title is deceptively tricky because it requires you to know your point—to have figured out what you are trying to say. And that can be half the work of solid data analysis and communication right there. But in the end, it's a very small change to the graph that will take you furthest. That's why a good title is the very first point on the Data Visualization Checklist. It's powerful.

But I sometimes see groups who completely reject the idea of a strong graph title. Usually these are academics or those with a heavy academic upbringing. They tend to think that moving from "Generic" to "Declarative" will somehow bias the audience, as if the audience wants to spend time figuring out your point. There is one audience that doesn't mind muddling through unclear data, and that's other academics. So if you are reporting for a journal article, sure, vague titles might be appropriate. But the rest of the time we are usually reporting to real people who have to make actual decisions and take actions based on our work, and they have paid you to cut to the chase. In other words, using strong titles makes us less annoying.

It doesn't have to be a strong-arm title like "Trump spoke more words at the debate, so he's obviously a blowhard." It can just be "Trump spoke more words at the debate." Which is still way better than "Number of Words Spoken at Debate." There's a middle ground here where the title describes what the visual shows so that the message is conveyed both visually and semantically, without jumping to conclusions beyond the data.

**Figure 3.34    Titles don't have to be too heavy-handed**

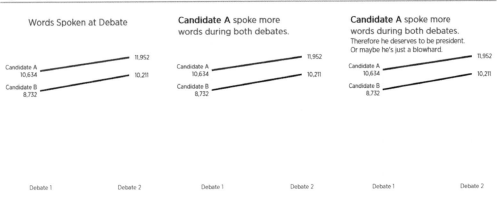

Recent research has also shown that awesome titles are a key element in making a visualization memorable. Borkin and team (2016) used eye-tracking methods to detect that viewers tended to look at the visual first and then at the title. Viewers spent more time on the title particularly when the visual wasn't something unique, like a social network diagram. But regardless of whether the visual itself was unique or standard, when asked to describe the visual later on, viewers were most accurate in describing those visuals that had strong titles. In fact, their descriptions were often very close paraphrases of the titles. Strong titles—the kind that are complete sentences with subject–verb agreement—hang in people's heads.

Shoot for a title that is a whole, complete thought, and put it at the top of the graph, in the upper left corner, left justified. It's a small change with big impacts.

## Can Text Sit on an Angle?

When the labels in a graph get long, many software programs will either wrap the text onto multiple lines (centered justification, at that) or tip it onto a 45-degree angle. Both of these options make the text harder to read. When you are in this situation, see it as your clue that you need to change up the graph type. Convert it from a column to a bar graph, for example, so that the labels stay horizontal.

The only time text on an angle is generally acceptable is when the *y*-axis label is rotated 90 degrees. However, as Jon Schwabish points out on his website, PolicyViz, for several reasons, the best place for the *y*-axis label could be under the graph's title, as a subtitle, especially if it is long or isn't otherwise obvious.

## Subtitles and/or Annotations Provide Additional Information

Subtitles and annotations are how we can answer the next set of questions viewers are likely to have when they are investigating the data display. Both are opportunities to extend the storytelling just a bit further.

In Figure 3.35, I have included an annotation inside the graph to further explain something happening in the data that the audience would want to know. It's as simple as inserting a text box, but annotations go a long way in explaining the data.

Subtitles are another option to convey just a little more information. Place the subtitle directly under the title, on a new line, slightly smaller, just as I've done in the rightmost graph in Figure 3.34 (though you need not be so heavy-handed). Sometimes I'll use the subtitle space to state important caveats, like the age of the data, or to articulate another aspect to the data story.

**Figure 3.35  Add a little extra text to support the story**

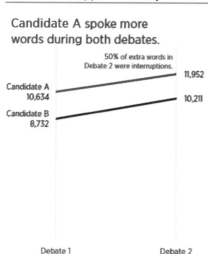

## Data Are Labeled Directly

In Chapter 2, we discussed how graphics and the related text need to be placed right next to each other, because flipping back and forth between pages hinders readers' working memory, impairing their ability to make sense of the associated words and images. Truly, the ideal situation for the brain is extremely close placement, and this also applies to the words and images inside data displays. Whenever readers have to seek and find to match up content, cognition is impaired. One way to get closer placement of words and images is to delete the legend. Yep, I just click on it and hit *Delete*.

In Figure 3.36, my client added labels with the identifying words from the legend to the rightmost point of each line, so it is totally obvious which line associates with which legend entry, thus eliminating the need for the legend. Cognition remains supported.

Sometimes it isn't possible to squeeze a lengthy label into a tiny part of a graph. But you can at least reduce confusion by placing the legend across the top of the chart (in the case of bars) so that the colors in the legend are laid out in the same order as the colors in the stacked bars, as in Figure 3.37.

In typical default chart production, the labels for the two bars shown in Figure 3.38, "Pretest" and "Posttest," are hanging off to the right, next to tiny squares filled with

Figure 3.36   **In lieu of a legend, the lines are directly labeled**

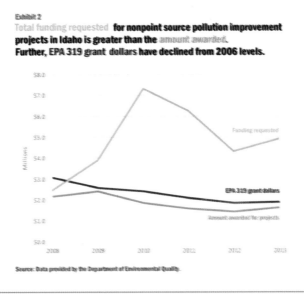

*Source:* © 2014. Reprinted with permission from Idaho State Office of Performance Evaluations.

Figure 3.37   **Reposition legends so they align with the order of the bars**

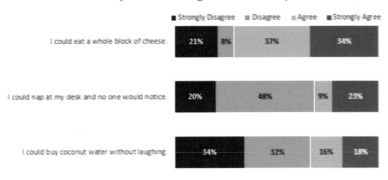

their associated colors. You can delete that legend and insert text boxes right over the bars that include the proper legend labels. In this example, it really only has to be done once, for seventh graders here, to establish the logic of the graph. A reader can immediately interpret the remaining bars without additional labeling or having to go back and forth between the bars and the legend.

**Figure 3.38**   Directly label the bars on their first appearance

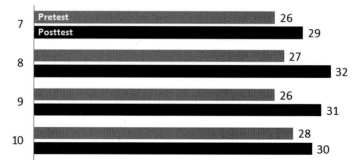

## Labels Are Used Sparingly

So far we've been talking about adding text to the graph so it can really stand on its own. This checkpoint, in contrast, is about removing the text that isn't necessary. No doubt, if you start looking for any unnecessary text in your graph, you'll find lot of places where you can hit that *Delete* key again. For example, if your axis is year, you don't need an axis label that says "Year," do you? If the years run from 2000 to 2016, you don't need to label every single one, because doing so clutters up the axis line and, after all, we all know what comes right after 2015.

Another place we often engage in overkill is with numeric labels. Do not add numeric labels *and* use an axis scale, since this is redundant.

**Figure 3.39**   **No need for both number labels and the *x*-axis scale**

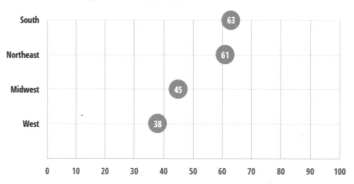

Figure 3.39 is a dot plot, and I have specifically made the dots so large that I can pop their labels right in the centers. If you want to know how many daily check-ins occurred in the South, the giant 63 makes it pretty clear. But I also left in the *x*-axis, marked off at every 10, with all those gridlines. I don't need both.

The general rule is that if the overall pattern is sufficient, use the axis and gridlines. If the precise values are important, use direct labels. *Not both.*

The only time I include both labels and an axis scale is when I have truncated the axis in some way.

Figure 3.40    **With a nonstandard *x*-axis, it can be helpful to note the start and end points**

**Patients in the South & Northeast had the most daily check-ins during the 80-day program.**

In my dot plot, the program lasted only 80 days, so there's no need to run the scale to 100. And the lowest score is in the 30s, so a start point of 30 makes more sense than a start point of 0 and puts my data more squarely in focus. However, I wouldn't want anyone to be misled by my truncated axis, so I keep the axis in the graph even though I have directly labeled the data. But I certainly don't need every 10 days marked off. In fact, I need only the start and end points. This takes out as much redundancy as possible while keeping in what the viewer needs to make the most sense of the graph.

## What Is the Bottom Line?

Choices in font category, size, and spacing affect legibility and influence the mood or environment of the reporting, as well as reflect the competence of the researcher. A hierarchy of importance, established through control and manipulation of the font, communicates to the reader the desired focus and order for attention. Thus, your font choices should be deliberate and consistent. Consistency in your presentations increases legibility and comprehension of the data. Apply your font choices to strong text in your headings and titles, changing a passive graph to one with an active voice that tells a story. Edit ruthlessly to get rid of any text that isn't necessary in your visuals and diagrams.

## Key Points to Remember

Typefaces communicate message and intent on their own, regardless of the actual words typed in the typeface.

- Legibility is impacted by the font. Generally, serif fonts are best for long narrative reading on paper. Fonts with an even thickness to their letter shapes—usually sans serifs—are better for on-screen reading.
- Check the details about the fonts installed on your own computer for a better understanding of their intended uses.
- Mood is also influenced by font choices. Serifs are perceived as more traditional and serious. More playful decorative fonts are useful to communicate a more obvious mood, but use them sparingly because they generally hurt legibility.
- Font size also sends a message. Importance is signaled by size so that the most important things are the largest, with the font decreasing in size as the significance of the displayed text decreases. Supportive text like captions can be set in something teeny, like 8 points. By contrast, titles of research posters can be set as large as 150 points, to accommodate reading from a distance.
- If bullets must be used, decrease their size so that they are less distracting.
- Lines of text that are too narrow or too far apart hinder readability, even if you have chosen a beautiful font. For narrative reading, adjust line spacing so it is 1 to 3 points larger than the size of the text.
- Using complete sentences in headlines and titles is one way to massively increase the interpretability of graphs.
- Embed legend labels directly inside the graph to make comprehension even easier.
- Add helpful annotations and take out any redundant text.

# How Can I Extend This?

## Check Out

What the Font? (**http://www.myfonts.com/WhatTheFont**): Have you ever seen a cool font and wondered what it is? Snap a picture or a screenshot and upload it to What the Font? This website looks for indicators and characteristics of certain fonts and churns out its best guess at the name of the font in question. (The site's main purpose is to then sell that font to the user, but you do not have to take it that far.)

Fontpark (**http://fontpark.net/en**): Graphic designers will not be happy that I am pointing out free font sites—they tend to think you should purchase entire type families from the typeface foundries and that fonts on free sites are a bit junky. Well, there may be some truth to that sentiment, but I still find Fontpark a great place to locate fonts, especially slightly funky ones to make certain words in my titles pop out. Be certain to watch the licensing here, since some fonts are okay for commercial use and some are listed as noncommercial.

Font Squirrel (**https://www.fontsquirrel.com**): All fonts on this site are free for commercial use. If you locate one you like, you can take some sample text for a test drive. But read the license agreement carefully—it may require that you use only PDFs when distributing documents with the font to third parties. Regardless, embed your font! Embed your font!

"'What Font Should I Use?': Five Principles for Choosing and Using Typefaces" (**http://www .smashingmagazine.com/2010/12/14/what-font-should-i-use-five-principles-for-choosing-and-using-typefaces**): This article by Dan Mayer for *Smashing Magazine* has a lot of great advice, but pay particular attention to Point 4, "A Little Can Go a Long Way," which depicts the practice of using decorative fonts selectively.

The Errol Morris Font Experiment (**http://opinionator.blogs.nytimes.com/2012/08/08/hear-all-ye-people-hearken-o-earth**): In a ruse that was published in his *New York Times* column, Morris randomly displayed some text in six varying fonts and provided evidence that text set in Baskerville was viewed as more trustworthy. See the experimental column and read his debriefing.

Jon Schwabish's blog post on where to place the *y*-axis label (**http://policyviz.com/where-to-position-the-y-axis-label**) provides multiple options and a solid argument on how to make the right choice. Read the post to get the nuance of this decision-making process.

*(Continued)*

(Continued)

## Try This

As in the history department example shown earlier, changing the font for a single word can have a big impact on the look and feel of a page or slide. Open up the report you are currently working on or the last one you finished, identify a keyword or two, and match it with a font that resonates with your subject matter. You may have to paste your emphasis words into their own text box to make this work.

Take a moment now to define your personal style. Pick your own heading and body font. Choose something that represents you well. Save the theme (see Chapter 6) and name it after yourself. Of course, there may be times when you'll need to downplay your personal branding choices in the service of blending in with someone else's branding, such as that of a client, a department, or a funder.

Send font pairs on a date at Type Connection (**http://www.typeconnection.com**). This site lets you test the font-pairing waters through a matchmaking game. If you are a nerd, you will enjoy the step that illustrates why certain fonts pair well together. Most fonts in the game are not native to PCs, but you can always look for the ones you like at the font-finding websites mentioned above.

## Where Can I Go for More Information?

American Psychological Association. (2010). *Publication manual of the American Psychological Association* (6th ed.). Washington, DC: Author.

Borkin, M. A., Bylinskii, Z., Kim, N. W., Bainbridge, C. M., Yeh, C. S., Borkin, D., Pfister, H., & Oliva, A. (2016). Beyond memorability: Visualization recognition and recall. *IEEE Transactions on Visualization and Computer Graphics, 22*(1), 519–528.

Chaparro, B. S., Shaikh, A. D., Chaparro, A., & Merkle, E. C. (2010). Comparing the legibility of six ClearType typefaces to Verdana and Times New Roman. *Information Design Journal, 18*(1), 36–49.

Lewis, C., & Walker, P. (1989). Typographic influences on reading. *British Journal of Psychology, 80,* 241–257.

Lupton, E. (2004). *Thinking with type: A critical guide for designers, writers, editors, and students.* New York: Princeton Architectural Press.

Modern Language Association of America. (2009). *MLA handbook for writers of research papers* (7th ed.). New York: Author.

Pelli, D. G., Farell, B., & Moore, D. C. (2003). The remarkable inefficiency of word recognition. *Nature, 423,* 752–756.

Song, H., & Schwartz, N. (2008). If it's hard to read, it's hard to do: Processing fluency affects effort prediction and motivation. *Psychological Science, 19*(10), 986–988.

Wheildon, C. (2005). *Type and layout: Are you communicating or just making pretty shapes?* Hastings, Victoria, Australia: Worsley Press.

# CHAPTER FOUR

# COLOR

## LEARNING OBJECTIVES

**After reading this chapter, you will be able to:**

- Identify the basic colors needed for optimal reading

- Pull colors out of an image

- Build a color scheme

- Replicate colors in standard software

- Distinguish among applications of color for decoration, navigation, and emphasis

- Check for legibility in different environments

- Apply color to data visualizations for stronger storytelling

O h, color! It's one of our strongest tools in telling stories with our data.

As before, we begin with another cathartic story about how I learned a big lesson, this time on the use of color.

I made Figure 4.1 (it was not my finest hour) as part of a report I submitted several years ago. As you readily recognize, it uses the default rainbow color scheme of Excel. As was my typical process, I created the report in color, and I then translated it into a PDF file and sent it to the main contact person at my client's office. Some of you are probably using a similar process to submit papers to your professor, or status updates to your supervisor. And as was her typical process, my contact printed the file on her office printer (in this case, a black-and-white printer—she worked for local government) and then made copies of that printout for the other panelists to review.

## Guiding Ideas

Narrative text is dark gray or black

Background has white or subdued color

One or two emphasis colors are used

Color reprints legibly in black and white

Color changes denote meaning changes

**Figure 4.1    Line graph made with Excel's default colors**

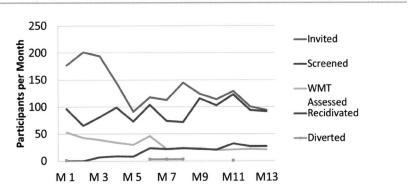

When I arrived a few weeks later to discuss the findings in person, I circulated around the room before the presentation began to introduce myself to the panelists. One of them said to me that he was looking forward to the presentation because he did not actually read the report. Inside my head, I thought of all kinds of snappy responses, but out of my mouth I joked about how he must be busy, and then he said that was not the issue. He opened his copy of the report to the page where this graph appeared in the executive summary. Here is what it looked like to him:

**Figure 4.2** **Same line graph as it appeared to a reader, having been copied and faxed**

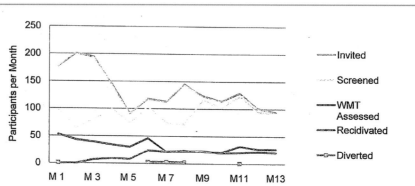

You can immediately notice that the color of the top two lines had degraded significantly, which is often the case when we distribute our work electronically and our professors or clients or supervisors print it, fax it, and then copy it for dissemination.

I learned the hard way: He was only going to look at the graphs, not read. If the visual did not pull him in, he would not proceed. All of the information in the graph was summarized in the text around it, but he was not going to bother with it. Our graphics carry the weight in our reporting. Consequently, I now always check how my color choices look when printed in black and white. Sometimes that means I work only in grayscale or color schemes that will translate well in black and white. Other times, I take greater control over the distribution of my work, creating and shipping physical color copies.

Either way, I learned to be more mindful of my color choices. In this chapter, I help you to become more mindful as well.

## Why Is Color Important to Memory?

Color is among the first elements that grab our earliest attention, and this fact is not just true of humans. Animals also know that color communicates; the more colorful the frog, the more poisonous. Contemporary graphic designers use color in a similar way—to draw attention to selective elements of interest (Samara, 2007). Color is one of the primary attributes of objects readily recognized by the eye–brain system. Effective data presentation uses color to draw the reader's attention quickly.

Color is not just for looking flashy, however. Viewers actually need text color to be pretty toned down to be able to read it. Legibility, of course, is critical for information to be read and remembered. A muted setting aids legibility, but it also lets chosen elements pop out appropriately when selected emphasis colors are applied. For color to stand out, the surrounding text or data points must be in a neutral color, like a shade of gray. Then color can be applied, such as through color-coding systems, where colored icons correspond to colored report headings, to significantly speed navigation (Campbell & Maglio, 1999).

Even more than improving legibility and efficient engagement with our data presentation, though, the smart use of color connects to the emotions of the viewer. Studies indicate that color is closely related to invoking and building new memories and associations that are often steeped in culture, stereotypes, and personal experience (Clarke & Costall, 2008). Thus, color choices should always be intentional—never fall back on the software default color scheme.

## What Colors Should I Choose?

Like most things in life, the answer to this question is the dreaded "It depends." But the fork in the decision road is actually pretty clear. It depends on the data presentation purpose. If the presentation piece at hand is intended for study and requires extensive reading of narrative prose, the color combinations should be fairly bland and nondescript. If parts of the data presentation—like callout boxes or key data points—need to leap out at a reader, a more colorful scheme is warranted. Let's discuss each of these in turn.

### The Best Color Combinations for Reading

On the next page is a bad slide I created a long time ago for a real client. I am showing you this to hurt your eyes so much that you will never forget how bad design looks.

The research on color contrast says that color text on a color background hinders reading (Ware, 2013). This slide contained dark blue text on a bright blue background—a kind of combination that makes any content difficult for people to read, especially outside of a slideshow context, such as in the long passages of a report.

In a famous readability test conducted by Wheildon (2005), 53% of the study subjects did not even attempt to read the study materials when the page background color was as dark as the background in Figure 4.3. For those persevering people

### Guiding Idea

Narrative text is dark gray or black

Figure 4.3  **Generalized version of a slide with ineffective color combinations that I actually delivered to a client**

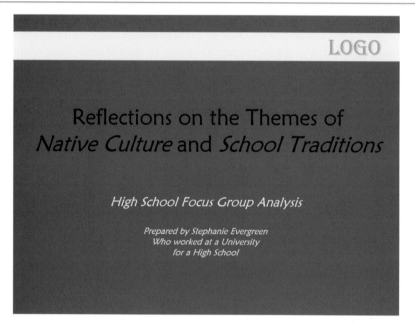

who did continue to read, less than 50% were able to correctly answer questions on a comprehension test about the content they had just read. When color text is on color background, both legibility and comprehension are impaired. Black text has the highest comprehension level when positioned on a white background, followed closely by dark gray text. We will discuss other color options below, but keep in mind that all of them come in a distant third place.

### Guiding Idea

Background has white or subdued color

The issue is not so much about color combination as it is about contrast. The two colors must contrast sufficiently for a reader to be able to distinguish the letters from the background. Since black and white have the strongest possible contrast, some folks also like to use white (or light) on black (or very dark) backgrounds, as I did at the bottom of the worst slide I ever created in Figure 4.3. Graphic designers refer to this color combination as "reversed out." The contrast is there, but it still produces weaker comprehension scores than black on white. Thus, such combinations should be restricted to short bursts of text in sans serif fonts that are fairly large in size, so that legibility is stable.

Studies show that you can stretch the contrast without hurting legibility if the background is no more than a 10% tint (Wheildon, 2005). It is probably fair to say that the concept of "tint" is not really one that most of us in report writing and graph making are familiar with (though professional printing services know how to handle it). Neither is it a language or concept that Microsoft speaks very well. But, for a good rule of thumb, refer to the second row of color options in Microsoft's default Office color menu.

**Figure 4.4** **The page color option highlighted in this screenshot is about as dark as you can go before hindering legibility**     **Figure 4.5** **Screenshot of a completely white background, for comparison to the "dark" background in Figure 4.4**

The only option shown in this example that is suitable is the choice on the left. Notice how, on hovering, it tells us that this is "Darker 5%," which means a 5% tint.

Compare it to the regular white background, shown in Figure 4.5.

As you can see, the difference between the two backgrounds is incredibly subtle, but the slightly darker version may add some warmth to your data presentation.

The slightly darker gray option just below it is a 15% tint, which is too much. The other colors in the second row, extending to the right of the ideal color, are also too dark, usually at 20% tint. If you really want to work with one of those colors, select the 20% tint option, then click on *More Colors,* and scale back the slider in the *Custom Color* tab to lighten it up a bit.

That said, the ad on the next page from the Ad Council and Feeding America breaks those rules and gets away with it. Here we have green color text on an orange color background (Figure 4.6). The reason it works is that the text is a very large sans serif, the colors are still far from each other in terms of contrast, and there is very little text to begin with. Sometimes we make choices like this for aesthetic reasons, to fit in with our university's color scheme, for example. Generally, though, in that case the best option is to use black, white, and one of the university's colors for emphasis.

## The Best Colors for Emphasis

Although we have clearly justified the predominant use of black and white, we still want some additional color because we need some method of emphasis, something that grabs early attention and lands our content in long-term memory—something effective.

### Guiding Idea

One or two emphasis colors are used

Emphasis colors can be applied to headings (muted for subheadings), used for backgrounds in callout boxes where the text is short, or used to call attention to key data points in graphs.

As noted, often the emphasis colors are an easy choice, based on company or school color schemes. In my experience, organization and university color palettes sometimes do not include enough variation—that is, there may be several shades of just one color. On many occasions, you will need to construct your own color scheme completely from scratch.

**Figure 4.6** **Advertisement uses dark text on a colored background yet maintains legibility**

*Source:* Feeding America and Ad Council. © 2012. Reprinted with permission from Feeding America.

### Using a Color-Picking Tool

Here is a procedure I use all the time to help me select color combinations for my data presentations. It makes use of an online program that incorporates all the scientific color theory stuff and then translates it for those of us without a master of fine arts degree.

If I do not already have a departmental template or style sheet to work with, I first head to the organization's or client's website and take a screenshot that includes the main color scheme.

Then I use this cool, free color-picking website, Adobe Color (https://color.adobe.com). I upload my selected image (in this case, the SAGE screenshot), and the program picks out the colors from the image.

Figure 4.7    First, grab a screenshot from the organizational website

Once I like where the program is pulling colors from in the image (Figure 4.8), I can click a little color wheel icon in the upper right to reveal the recipes for re-creating those colors. That gives me the RGB (red/green/blue) color codes (Figure 4.9). With those color code numbers, I can customize the palette of my word-processing and presentation and graphing software programs to match the colors to those in the source image screenshot file. Nice, right?

Figure 4.8    Then upload the screenshot to Adobe Color

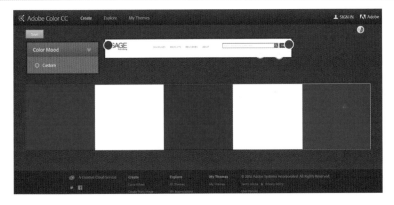

Figure 4.9    The program provides the color codes you need, in many forms, to customize the palette in your reporting and graphing software

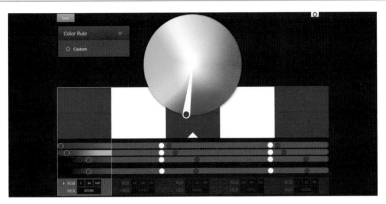

# Shouldn't Screen and Print Colors Match?

Chances are, if you go through this process of pulling out colors from a screenshot and adjusting your color palette in your report, when you print your report you will feel a ping of disappointment. Color rarely looks the same on paper as it does on the screen, even when you're working with color codes (and goodness knows it even looks different on different screens). Screen monitor colors, printing ink levels, and other factors influence how well the colors match from screen to paper. But, as Ware (2013) notes, precision is less important than perception. Aim to get as close as possible, without worrying about an exact match. RGB is most appropriate for things viewed on a screen. Printed materials look best with colors selected using another color code, called CMYK (cyan, magenta, yellow, and black—yes, K stands for black). Both sets of color code numbers are available through most color-picking tools. If you plan to print, then follow the same instructions listed here, just pop the CMYK colors into Word. However, just know that slight differences in color are such a rampant problem that they are accepted as normal.

**Figure 4.10**    **Screenshot showing how to navigate to the window where you can type in color codes**

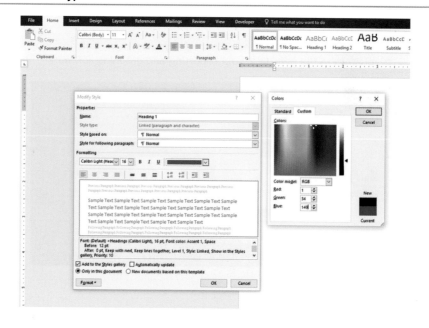

I then write down those RGB color codes and head over to Word. This screenshot shows where I transferred the RGB codes from Adobe Color into the *Custom Colors* option (right-click on, say, Heading 1 in the *Styles* menu and select *Modify,* then click on the arrow by the color menu, go down to *More Colors,* and click on the *Custom* tab).

Once you have set up your page layout to your preference, go to the *Themes* button and select *Save Current Theme* (see Chapter 6 for detailed instructions and screen-shots). This process makes your color scheme available in Excel, PowerPoint, and any of the other Microsoft programs running on the same machine.

Sometimes, as I mentioned, the color scheme of the client organization is not extensive enough for your purposes. In the example shown here, we pretty much have only SAGE blue and a light gray.

No problem. In the Adobe Color program, you can choose one of the colors as a "base" and then click on the optional color combination rules to generate schemes that align with color theory and play nicely with your original color.

Now you have some lighter and darker options that can serve as report accents, suitable text shades, and additions to a color-coding system.

Why go to all that trouble? Because now you have created an intentional tone that communicates consistency and belonging with the branding of your department or client.

Figure 4.11    **Adobe Color also generates alternate palettes from your selected base color**

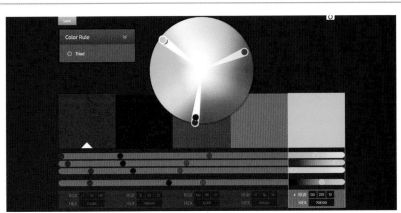

## Other Color Combination Sites

If you must come up with totally original schemes because no source color is available, all is not lost. At this very moment, there are legions of folks just like us adding color scheme possibilities to crowd-sourced websites. Adobe Color has a "Community" section where you can peruse the contributions of others. Design Seeds (www.design-seeds.com) and COLOURlovers (www.colourlovers.com) are two other resources for submitted color palettes where you can locate lovely options.

Figure 4.12   **COLOURlovers has user-generated color palettes to browse—just be mindful, not all are designed for presenting data effectively**

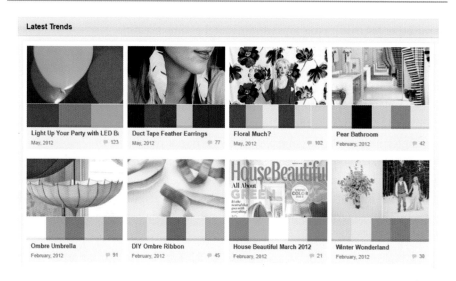

Choosing a color palette from scratch gives you the opportunity to explore how color can shape a feeling of relevance or create a mood (Carruthers, Morris, Tarrier, & Whorwell, 2010). For example, check out the DIY Ombre Ribbon color scheme in Figure 4.12. It may be difficult for some people to connect to a document using those colors because of connotations related to childishness or, even more stereotypically, severe femininity. Yet this scheme might work well in certain contexts. The color scheme called House Beautiful March 2012 consists of shades of greens and blues. While some might associate that with hospitals, others might see it as the color scheme of corporate America (for better or for worse); still others might associate the colors with a rival university's football team and begin to feel some hostility. Colors definitely influence pleasure and displeasure, so it is worth running your ideas past a few classmates or colleagues to get a sense of how any color scheme you select is perceived in your localized culture.

Just keep in mind that you want a palette that includes a very dark, a very light, and at least one emphasis color. As you can see, the Ombre Umbrella palette in Figure 4.12 does not have enough contrast to suffice for data presentation purposes. There are also other considerations to be mindful of when making color choices.

## What Should I Watch Out For?

Working with color can be exciting for you and your readers. Here are three common mistakes to avoid so that your color choices complement rather than compete with your data presentation efforts. Be alert to the overuse of color, color-blind readers, and reprinting in black and white.

### Too Much Color

The use of color for emphasis impedes comprehension if too many colors are used indiscriminately; readers expect that a change in color indicates a change in meaning, and they spend valuable time and effort trying to understand the meaning shift (Jamet, Garota, & Quaireau, 2008; Tourangeau, Couper, & Conrad, 2007).

Observe the two logic models in Figures 4.13 and 4.14, identical save for the application of color. The colorless logic model may look plain, but there is conceptually a lot going on, with arrows crossing arrows and multiple boxes in one column leading to single boxes in the next. The organizational program represented by this logic model is complicated in and of itself. The addition of color in the model in Figure 4.14 does not add clarity.

Figure 4.13    **Basic logic model without color**

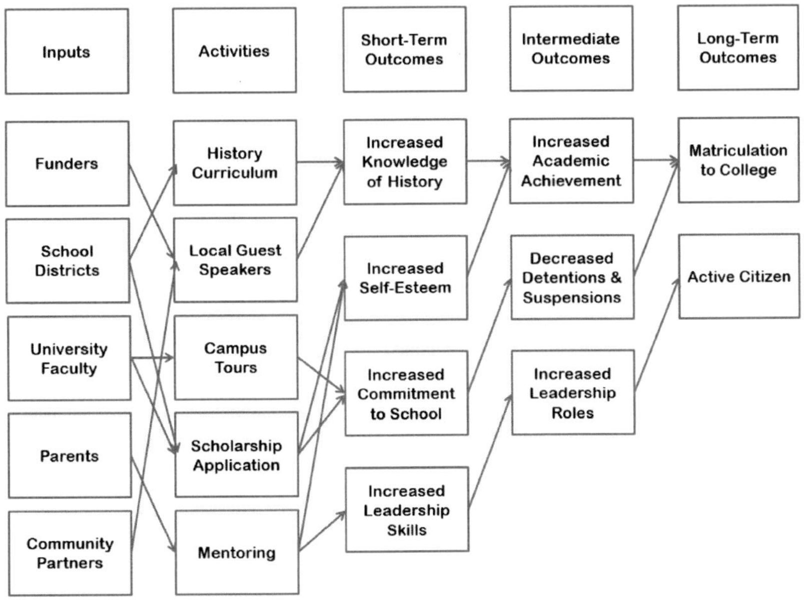

Figure 4.14    **Same logic model, but with color**

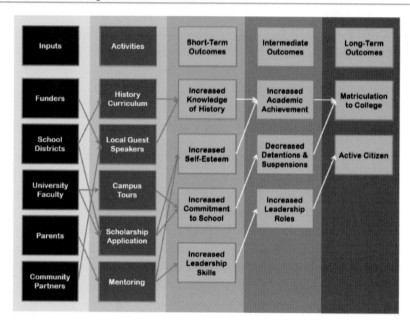

In fact, I believe that the color in the logic model in Figure 4.14 adds clutter. The color blocking behind each column in the model is probably unnecessary, as the columns are already spaced far enough apart to distinguish them from one another. Because of this change, readers spend time and mental capacity trying to understand if the change is meaningful. Aside from the headings naming each column, what does the background color add? The color change is conceptually meaningless. Yet the outcomes are all assigned the same shade of blue in order to set them apart from inputs and activities—so in that area of the logic model, color is meaningful. This example quickly gets confusing; too much color gets in the way of comprehension.

Another reason to be wary of too many colors is that colors are expensive to print. The computer lab's color copies are always more expensive than the black-and-white machine for a reason. Professional printing shops charge significantly more to run a full-color, or what they call "four-color," copy job (the four colors are cyan, magenta, yellow, and K—or black—this is the CMYK term discussed in the sidebar earlier). It is much less expensive to print and work with a black-and-white setting. In that case, shades of gray can accomplish a lot. Two-color printing is slightly more expensive, but not as bad as four-color. Two-color printing is usually black plus an emphasis color. Again, shades or gradations of both can actually provide a pretty wide variety of options to work with. Most journals still opt for a black-and-white or two-color scheme.

That said, don't fall into the trap of using too many shades of your emphasis color, either. Readers have a hard time distinguishing among more than four shades of a single color (Ware, 2013). So when the guiding idea states that we should have two emphasis colors (at most), include shades of one color in your count if that's all you have.

## Color-Blind Readers

Another issue to keep in mind when choosing color is color blindness. Color blindness on the red/green spectrum affects roughly 10% of the population in the United States. It is more common in white men than in other segments of the population. There are also people affected by color blindness on the blue/yellow spectrum, though that is not as common. Federal regulations specified in the Section 508 amendment to the Rehabilitation Act require designers of information technology to create designs that are color-blind-friendly (adherence to these regulations is known as 508 compliance).

Dealing with potential audience color blindness is not as mysterious as it seems. (When taking color blindness into account, an added bonus is that you also fortify your data presentation against the dim bulb in the projector or the color settings on the conference room laptop that skew your established color scheme, and you usually handle the black-and-white issue too.)

Several programs are available online or downloadable to your computer that can help you assess whether your work is accessible to those with color blindness. Some are listed at the end of this chapter. The simulators render your files into how they appear to people with various types of color blindness.

With the following example (be prepared to cringe), I used a program called Vischeck (www.vischeck.com) on a slide I developed to look like others I have seen. My slide is on the left—green text with a red background. The slide on the right shows what it looks likes if you are affected by red-green color blindness (the condition known as deuteranopia).

**Figure 4.15**  **Vischeck shows how images appear under certain variations of color blindness**

True, the image is terrible, but the original image on the left is pretty bad in the first place! So, the problem is not really about the red-green color combination—it is about the contrast of the two colors. Below, I still used red and green to make my original slide, but note the improved readability, both before and after Vischeck:

**Figure 4.16**  **A stronger contrast between colors used on text and background boosts legibility, even under color blindness or black-and-white printing**

The message is to not be afraid of color combinations—but do focus on making certain that you have a light-dark color pairing that is maintained regardless of the projector quality, presentation laptop color settings, or audience impairment.

For RGB color schemes that are appropriate for those with color blindness, check out ColorBrewer 2.0 (http://colorbrewer2.com). This is a free web program that lets you select the number of colors you need and the nature of your data (sequential or diverging, for example) and then produces color palettes that are color-blind-safe. Originally intended for cartography, ColorBrewer is useful for obtaining effective color codes that are applicable to any sort of data presentation.

## Does Color Apply Universally?

When choosing an emphasis color, always keep in mind the possible cultural connotations your choice may carry and how those connotations vary globally. The field of color psychology investigates the associations that different cultures bring to particular colors. Blue, for example, is commonly associated with liberal politics in the United States. In the United Kingdom, it represents conservatives. Baby blue

*(Continued)*

(Continued)

is often associated with boys in the United States, while in China some presume that blue is a feminine color. It also can represent authority; conversely, it can mean depression. Blue is often believed to be one of the safest colors to use worldwide; nevertheless, it still communicates different cultural messages based on the shade and the context. Other colors are even less universal in their associations; therefore, the context of your dissemination should influence your color choices.

## Reprinting in Black and White

As demonstrated by the way the lines in my graph deteriorated under the normal wear and tear of research dissemination, you should always check that your intentional color choices and emphasis are stable after normal transmission methods. And yes, printing in black and white is still a normal transmission method in many parts of the world.

### Guiding Idea

Color reprints legibly in black and white

In this sample report page, the original in Figure 4.17 uses only black and purple. There are a few leader words at the start of the main paragraphs that are in a light

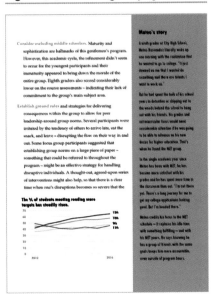

Figure 4.17    The original page

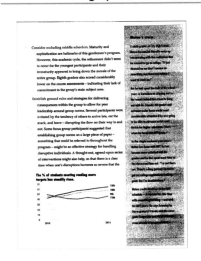

Figure 4.18    The result, after normal wear and tear, shows some degradation to the intentional use of color in the graph

gray. In the graph, shades of purple distinguish each line. I copied that page, faxed it, and copied it again to replicate a normal dissemination route. The result is Figure 4.18.

While the content generally held up all right, we can see that the leader text disintegrated somewhat, making it harder to read. The colors in the graph became meaningless and hard to see. And the background of the sidebar is distractingly grainy, impacting legibility.

To check legibility, print using your printer's grayscale settings, then make a black-and-white copy of that printout (and then maybe a copy of that copy) and scan it. In this case, rather than changing the leader text to gray, I could have kept it black and bolded it. I also could have started the lightest color in the line graph a bit darker and darkened even more from there.

## Using Red/Yellow/Green

We must stop using the red/yellow/green stoplight color system.

In addition to being uninterpretable for people with color blindness (Figure 4.19) and not reprinting legibly in black and white, the stoplight should be avoided for another reason: It puts a color on everything, and when everything has a color, nothing stands out. And the whole point of using icons and color-coding is to alert the viewer to problems (or successes).

It's way more efficient to pick a side. Either highlight your successes with green (with the understanding that everything that isn't green is not up to par) or highlight the places that need work with red (and be clear that the things without a red icon are fine). Selective color-coding actually serves the original intention, which is to point attention to areas of interest.

I know some organizations are really wedded to the stoplight color scheme, and I will have to pry it from some people's cold, dead hands. If you are at all interested in becoming more 508 compliant, efficient, and streamlined, stop with the stoplight. Focus decision makers' attention on the areas that need it and—BAM!—you shine, you're the rock star, you get the promotion. You're welcome.

**Figure 4.19    A red/yellow/green color scheme doesn't communicate to people with red-green color blindness**

## Try Vischeck on Your Image Files

Your Results:

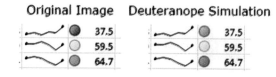

## How Do I Apply Emphasis Colors?

Now that we have taken the care to develop an intentional color scheme, let's look at effective ways to use those colors in our data presentations. Usually, color serves one of three purposes: decorating, navigating, or spotlighting.

## Decorating

It may sound as if this reason to use color is superfluous, not for those interested in seriously effective data presentation. However, applying colors for decoration adds balance and professionalism to reports, contributing to perceptions of credibility and quality.

**Figure 4.20**    **Report cover where text color and text background color have been pulled from main image**

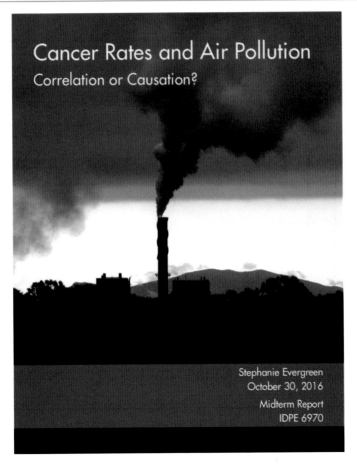

In this midterm report cover (Figure 4.20), a large photograph of a factory smoke-stack consumes the page. The photograph is cast in shades of blue and gray. The author's information is listed at the bottom of the report cover, placed against a blue strip of color—the same blue that appears in the photograph. Even the light gray-blue used for the title text comes directly from the photograph. The repetition of color adds a cohesiveness that communicates forethought and planning—just what we want to express. You can readily replicate this look by using any of the color-picking tools described in this chapter to pull out the exact color from the photograph and then customize the fill color of a text box in Word.

**Figure 4.21**   **Slide uses a limited color palette to convey the key message of influence**

This slide (Figure 4.21) shows another use of color as a decorative tool. The background on the left is a dark blue, and the text shifts from dark gray to very light gray as it progresses down the slide. We know this sort of situation can impact legibility. The gray on the word "Design" is too dark, and the blue background is technically unnecessary. However, the use of color here suggests a change. The progression of grayscale is used to reflect the way good design can change a reader's mind. There is a purpose to the decoration, an intentional color selection. The background on the right, behind the image, even matches the very light gray on the word "Persuasion." So although the color choices may not be entirely ideal by legibility standards, they work well to express a concept, and they fit together as a united package. Furthermore, this example illustrates the effective decorative use of color even when full-color printing is not an option.

## Navigating

The second way to use color is as a tool to help readers navigate through your work. Color-coding long reports is an easy way to decrease the labor required to get to specific passages quickly, especially now that most of us are in a digital reading environment, where printing costs are not a factor.

**Figure 4.22    This award-winning report from Drexel University uses color to help readers navigate to sections most relevant to them**

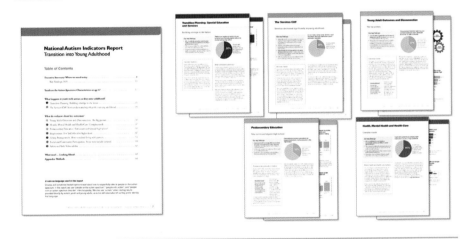

*Source:* © 2015. Reprinted with permission from A. J. Drexel Autism Institute.

On a regular basis, Drexel University issues reports on autism indicators. The reports are lengthy because they have to cover many different aspects of life. We made the reports easier to navigate by leveraging color as an organizing principle.

We introduced this idea by modifying the typical table of contents. We inserted a tiny colored dot next to the title of each major chapter of the report, covering each aspect of life with autism to be discussed. This essentially color-codes the contents and tells the reader what to expect later on. Then, within the body of the report, we used the corresponding colors throughout the respective chapters. One dominant color appears in each chapter, in the data visualizations, the backgrounds of the call-out boxes, and the bands that stretch across the tops of the pages.

Using color as the organizing principle makes it easy for readers to make their way. For example, if I'm looking at the table of contents and I decide I'm mainly interested in postsecondary education, I can see the green circle and then just hit my scroll wheel until I see green again. And then readers love us because we've made their lives easier. And they've learned something. And they can handily pass this info and love on to others.

## Spotlighting

The third important way to use color (and the one we spend the most time on throughout this chapter) is in applying emphasis to bring attention to your data.

**Figure 4.23**   **Repeating the background color of the title text box in the callout text box helps to spotlight the key takeaway message**

While we know light text on a dark background is less than perfect, it is still effective in drawing attention to short bits of text. The callout box on this poster (Figure 4.23) does just that. The fill color of the callout box is a gold to draw the eye, emphasizing the study's main finding. Then, I changed the text box fill color behind the title to match, in order to add balance to the poster. If I had applied the heaviness of the dark text box only to the callout on the right, the poster would look a bit odd or lopsided. Although I elected to use gold here to achieve this look, other appropriately dark emphasis color choices would also work.

Further, I added bolding to one sentence in the middle of the narrative text. In essence, this made that sentence blacker. As a general rule of thumb, it is best to keep the narrative text uniform, but note that sometimes a color change (even bolding) can call a reader's attention as well. As usual, we would not want to overuse this color emphasis technique.

### Guiding Idea

Color changes denote meaning changes

**Figure 4.24**  **A callout box or a slide can use color on the important statistic to help it draw reader attention and memory**

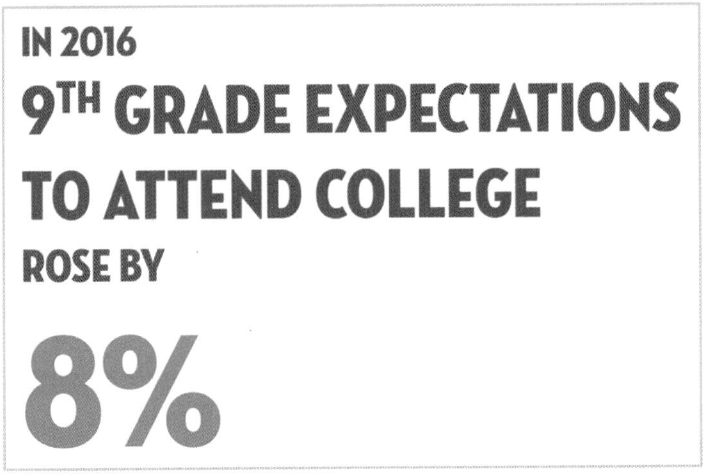

IN 2016
## 9TH GRADE EXPECTATIONS TO ATTEND COLLEGE
ROSE BY

# 8%

You can also use color to call attention to an important sidebar or statistic. Here, Figure 4.24 illustrates the very selective use of color to make the "8%" pop out. Note how the rest of the text must be in dark gray rather than black. Black and white provide the strongest contrast, so anytime we use color to emphasize text, we actually weaken the contrast and make the important text stand out less. Ironic, right? This problem is not always noticeable—it depends a great deal on the emphasis color in question. The lighter the emphasis color, the less it actually stands out when applied. However, by using dark gray for the rest of the narrative, we make the color text pop out even more.

To transition us into talking about color in graphs, here's one more example of how color can be used to spotlight information inside a dashboard (Figure 4.25). After feeling some frustration that their spreadsheet wasn't getting a lot of play from the board of directors, one of my clients asked me to add some simple data visualization so that the numbers would be easier to interpret.

Figure 4.25 **Big red dots spotlight trouble areas for quick action**

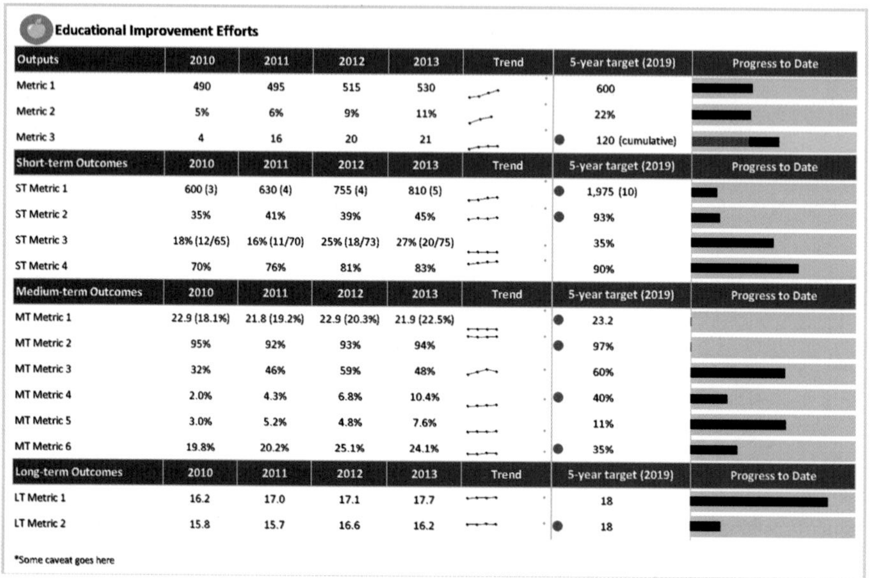

**Educational Improvement Efforts**

| Outputs | 2010 | 2011 | 2012 | 2013 | Trend | 5-year target (2019) | Progress to Date |
|---|---|---|---|---|---|---|---|
| Metric 1 | 490 | 495 | 515 | 530 | | 600 | |
| Metric 2 | 5% | 6% | 9% | 11% | | 22% | |
| Metric 3 | 4 | 16 | 20 | 21 | | ● 120 (cumulative) | |
| **Short-term Outcomes** | **2010** | **2011** | **2012** | **2013** | **Trend** | **5-year target (2019)** | **Progress to Date** |
| ST Metric 1 | 600 (3) | 630 (4) | 755 (4) | 810 (5) | | ● 1,975 (10) | |
| ST Metric 2 | 35% | 41% | 39% | 45% | | ● 93% | |
| ST Metric 3 | 18% (12/65) | 16% (11/70) | 25% (18/73) | 27% (20/75) | | 35% | |
| ST Metric 4 | 70% | 76% | 81% | 83% | | 90% | |
| **Medium-term Outcomes** | **2010** | **2011** | **2012** | **2013** | **Trend** | **5-year target (2019)** | **Progress to Date** |
| MT Metric 1 | 22.9 (18.1%) | 21.8 (19.2%) | 22.9 (20.3%) | 21.9 (22.5%) | | ● 23.2 | |
| MT Metric 2 | 95% | 92% | 93% | 94% | | ● 97% | |
| MT Metric 3 | 32% | 46% | 59% | 48% | | 60% | |
| MT Metric 4 | 2.0% | 4.3% | 6.8% | 10.4% | | ● 40% | |
| MT Metric 5 | 3.0% | 5.2% | 4.8% | 7.6% | | 11% | |
| MT Metric 6 | 19.8% | 20.2% | 25.1% | 24.1% | | ● 35% | |
| **Long-term Outcomes** | **2010** | **2011** | **2012** | **2013** | **Trend** | **5-year target (2019)** | **Progress to Date** |
| LT Metric 1 | 16.2 | 17.0 | 17.1 | 17.7 | | 18 | |
| LT Metric 2 | 15.8 | 15.7 | 16.6 | 16.2 | | ● 18 | |

*Some caveat goes here

*Source:* © 2013. Reprinted with permission from the Walton Family Foundation.

I added tiny sparklines to visualize the trend over time, and I modified bullet graphs to show progress against the long-term target. But perhaps the most useful visualization on this dashboard is the bright red dot. The dot's purpose is to show when, based on the existing trend, there's no way the organization will meet its target on time without some intervention. The board of directors pretty much gave high fives back and forth forever, because now they had a dashboard that was useful for their decision making. Rather than fuddling through a spreadsheet of numbers, taxing working memory, or picking the red dots out of a red/yellow/green color scheme, they could take decisive action based on the bright red dots spotlighting trouble areas.

## How Do I Apply These Ideas to Graphs?

We are going to start by talking about how Excel, as great as it is, has color default settings that for several reasons are not preferable. Let's talk about how color can help us tell our stories. To begin, let's cover the basics.

## Text Sufficiently Contrasts With Background

Backgrounds should be white. Some default chart templates in Excel and other programs apply a gray color to the background that makes it even harder for the colors of the data points to contrast and maintain legibility. The APA Guide (2010, p. 161) advises that shading should be limited and distinct; therefore, it is best to reserve the use of color for the data, not the background.

The text itself should contrast with that background, which means it should be dark enough for people to read against the white. I usually use black or dark gray for titles. Axis labels and subtitles can become a medium gray, dark enough to still read, but not so dark that they distract from the data.

## Color Scheme Is Intentional

Working with that default color scheme may be appropriate when you are analyzing the data. When you are in your office looking for patterns or abnormalities, it can be helpful to distinguish lines or data points by marking each with a different color. But when reporting and presenting the data, it's a bad idea to use the default colors.

First of all, everyone can recognize those colors as the defaults. Anyone with even a slight awareness about the issues covered in this book will look at those default colors and judge you. They'll think you're not even trying. That you didn't even bother to go beyond the bare minimum. That you, friend, are default. And I'm guessing that's not the image you are trying to project.

Beyond avoiding that judgment, research shows that the typical way of assigning random colors to different parts of graphs causes confusion. Color changes signal changes in the hierarchy of the information; however, in spite of this, designers often do not have any kind of hierarchy in mind—the colors are chosen just to be pretty, or, worse, color isn't even a consideration. Numerous scholars suggest that the use of random rainbow colors impedes comprehension of the data (Few, 2006; So & Smith, 2002; Tufte, 2001). Now that we have those basics covered, what should we do with color to help us tell our story?

Let's imagine that I want to report the responses to some survey questions, and the response options are on a standard Likert-type scale. In this scenario, I like my readers to generally group the positive responses into one mental chunk and the negative responses into another—in other words, the "Strongly Agree" and "Agree" responses conceptually group together, as do the "Strongly Disagree" and "Disagree" responses. But I also want to show the responses for each category, because of the need to pay attention to those who marked "Agree" and

"Disagree" in order to focus on tipping them one way or the other. It's important that these responses are distinct.

Figure 4.26    **Diverging color schemes can visually group similar survey responses**

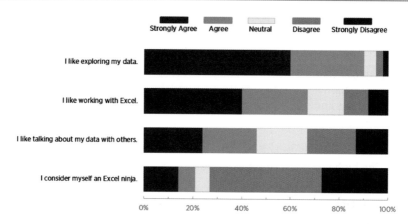

This is the type of research condition where a diverging color scheme comes in very handy. The positive responses here are in shades of blue, with the stronger response in the darker shade. The negative responses are in shades of gray. Shading within one color identifies those data points as a group but also lets them maintain some distinguishability from one another. Then, throughout my narrative, I use blue and gray to reinforce the color-coding and increase engagement with the data presentation. With separate graphs focused solely on the negative responses, the data points are in a gray palette. If I have a callout box in my narrative that captures a positive comment, the background of the box is blue. Clarity is achieved through the color choices.

## How Can I Handle Light on White?

In Figure 4.26, the neutral category is set in a very light blue-gray. Generally speaking, light colors on a white background are the worst color combinations for legibility. The light colors do not contrast well with white. Yet, in this diverging color scheme, it is important to have a neutral shade in between the blue and gray poles. Instead of adjusting the light color, I added a thin, slightly darker border around the neutral-colored data point in the stacked bar to help set that color off from the white background.

Alternatively, if the data display is being shown to an audience with the explicit hope that they compare data points, assigning scales within one color can speed interpretation and increase its accuracy (Breslow, Ratwani, & Trafton, 2009). This idea of using gradations of one color also helps with the interpretation of line graphs when the lines cross one another substantially, or of scatterplots where the chart area holds different categories of data.

In Figure 4.27, a gradated color scheme makes sense as applied to an ordinal scale of high school grades. The higher the grade, the darker the color. I could have even reinforced the color scheme by making the data labels at the end of each line the matching color but chose not to here because the lightest purple might not work well for reading on a white background.

Eventually, we refine the color use so that a graph displaying more complex data, such as in this scatterplot (Figure 4.28), does not even need a legend cluttering it up in order for the reader to understand what each color signifies.

Consistent use of the color-coding system results in faster interpretation and easier engagement. Keep in mind, however, that it is difficult for readers to detect differences when more than four shades of a given color are used.

Once a color code is assigned to each category, it should not change. The color assignment should be listed in the project's design plan or style sheet (see Chapter 6) and unwaveringly followed. When the color scheme shifts, the audience gets confused and exerts precious mental energy and attention trying to decipher the meaning behind the shift.

In Figures 4.29 and 4.30, the direction of the color progression reverses between graphs. Even more, the lightest blues in the two graphs ("Strongly Disagree" for Classroom A and "Strongly Agree" for Classroom B) are actually two different shades, which could spur a careful reader to wonder what the difference between the two light blues represents. This kind of confusion persists even when the graphs are separated

**Figure 4.27**    **Color gradations applied to ordinal categories can also visually organize data**

**Figure 4.28**    **Introducing a consistent color-coding system can bring understanding to a graph without the use of a legend or labels**

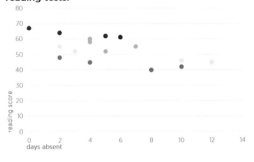

by pages of narrative or explanatory slides. So, decide on a color-coding system and stick with it. Once established, the color-coding system works to assist your presentation in powerful ways.

Figure 4.29    **This chart may appear in one part of a report . . .**

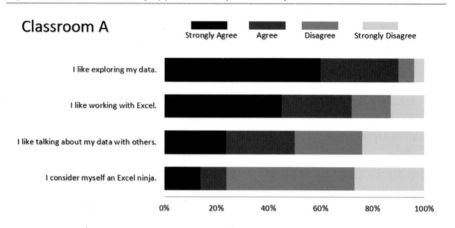

Figure 4.30    **. . . while this chart appears in another; inconsistent color-coding within a single report leads to confusion**

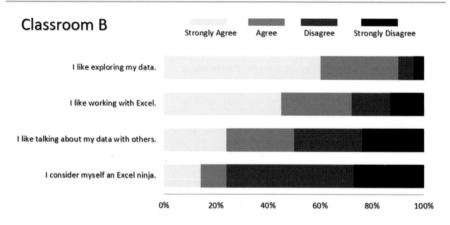

Diverging and sequential color schemes support our work because they communicate on our behalf in ways that sync up with how our readers think. A sequential data set gets sequential colors, and readers have an easier time keeping track of the sequence. Readers associate reds with negativity, so using red on data showing need for improvement cooperates with how people already interpret the world. When we use color intentionally, it carries some of the communication task for us.

## Color Is Used to Highlight Key Patterns

Diverging and sequential color schemes definitely help organize our work, but even with those, readers have to devote some mental energy to figuring out our color-coding system. It shouldn't be difficult for them to commit the system to memory, because we make intentional color choices that cooperate with how people think in the first place. But for even quicker communication, consider using gray and an action color to spotlight key data.

In Figure 4.31, I de-emphasized the less important data by switching the colors of those lines to shades of gray, and I used my highlight color to support the communication of my message, which is then reiterated in the chart title.

Figure 4.31   **Highlighting important information with a single emphasis color makes the graph's takeaway message more obvious**

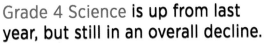

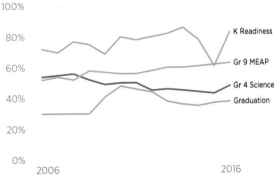

When using a palette of grayscale plus emphasis color, keep in mind that the gray should still be fairly dark. As the APA Guide (2010) notes, data should be darker than the gridlines, just as shown in Figure 4.31.

In Figure 4.32 you see the smart use of color in a bar graph. No question about what I want you to notice, is there? My main category of interest is the Michigan bar, so I applied my project's chosen blue color to bring attention to it. In this particular example, I also added a red vertical line, to indicate a predetermined score cut point or goal. I don't even have a title on this graph, but you can easily see what I want you to pay attention to. I'm using color to guide your big eyeball brain where I want it to go.

Figure 4.32    **Using an emphasis color on the bar for Michigan highlights that part of the data for the reader**

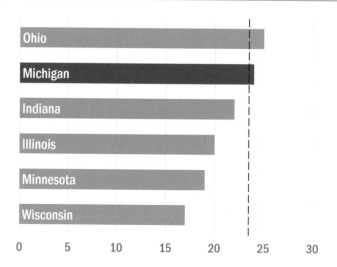

Figure 4.33    **This dashboard relies on a color-coding system introduced in the top row, which keeps the bottom row uncluttered**

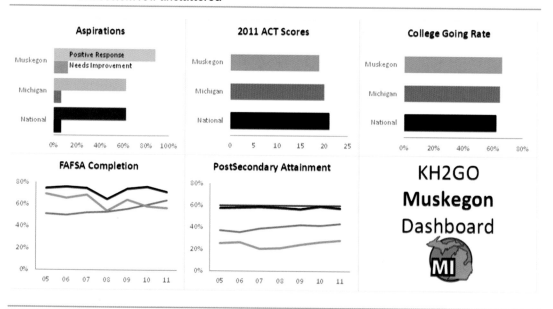

Source: © 2011. Reprinted with permission from the American Council on Education. KnowHow2GO is a registered trademark used with permission from the American Council on Education.

Color-coding might operate at peak efficiency levels when used on data dashboards. This sample dashboard (Figure 4.33) works with a fairly restricted project color scheme I developed—just orange, red, gray, black, and a tiny hint of blue (in the background of the circle behind the shape of Michigan). Notice how we built a color system where, in most of the graphs, the city is in the emphasis orange color, Michigan is gray, and the National scores are black. Then, when we get down to the line graphs in the second row, I can even get away with having no labels at all, because the interpretive system is now established. The only place this system requires extra elaboration is in the very first graph in the upper left, where each location had some subcategories that needed labeling. In these areas, I used lighter shades of each assigned color.

The color-coding system supports the primary purpose of dashboards—to provide rapid and easy engagement and interpretation for the audience so that they can quickly move into informed discussion and decision making.

## What Is the Bottom Line?

Selective use of color is one way the designer (you) can "prechunk" information, easing some of the thinking and cogitating that readers normally have to do, thus increasing both their mental capacity and their depth of thinking. The effective application of emphasis colors absolutely hinges on two things. First, you must identify the key message you are trying to communicate in your diagram, graph, or slide in order to emphasize that message with color. Second, once you have set up a palette of colors, you must use those color choices intentionally to create a predictable system for your readers that speeds up their ability to understand and remember your effective data presentations.

## Key Points to Remember

- RGB color codes are best suited for things that appear on-screen. CMYK color codes are intended for things you want to print. You can translate between the two closely, but if they do not match precisely, don't stress out.
- Dark gray or black should always be applied to text intended for long, narrative reading. Shorter bursts of text and those less essential to comprehension can be set in different colors or can appear on a colored background.

(Continued)

(Continued)

- It is almost never a good idea to use Excel's default color scheme. Apply color intentionally to specific areas of a graph to communicate a point or to highlight information for greater focus.

- Color choices degrade in black-and-white print settings and regular dissemination routes. Replicate a typical distribution of your report by copying a copy of a key page to determine whether your color scheme holds up well.

## How Can I Extend This?

### Check Out

Adobe Color (**http://color.adobe.com**): This is the color-picking site described earlier in this chapter. Upload your own photos here to pull out colors, type in one color code you have on hand to generate a full palette, or browse the color schemes invented by others.

MulticolorEngine (**http://labs.tineye.com/multicolr**): Produced by the folks at TinEye Labs, this search engine lets the user locate images from Flickr based on their color. Type in the color codes you have (it only works with web codes), and the search engine produces an amazing generation of graphics containing those colors. On other stock photo websites, add the color name to your search parameters to retrieve photos with that color in them.

Color Code Converter (**http://easycalculation.com/colorconverter/colorconverter .php**): If you have RGB codes and need to know how to translate them to CMYK or web codes, this is your spot. Type in what you have, click, and generate what you need.

ColorBrewer 2.0 (**http://colorbrewer2.com**): This site is designed to provide color advice for maps, but you can use the settings to produce color codes for palettes that are both color-blind-safe and printer-friendly.

Rob Simmon's "Subtleties of Color" (**http://earthobservatory.nasa.gov/blogs/ elegantfigures/2013/08/05**): My friend Rob used to work for NASA, where he did cool stuff like tweak colors in that famous blue marble photo of Earth. He's my go-to color resource, and he wrote this six-part series on color in data visualization that you can scan for free to dig deeper into color theory.

## Try This

Download Colorblind Assistant (**http://www.littlesky.org**), a free, lightweight tool that allows you to hover on colors to reveal their color codes. Then go snag your school or organization's RGB colors.

Download Color Oracle (**http://colororacle.org/index.html**) right to your computer—it runs through your selected documents and shows you what they look like under the various types of color blindness.

Test out some color palette ideas by scribbling with Crayola crayons, keeping in mind the need for a light, a dark, and an emphasis color (or two). Then look up the web and RGB codes on Wikipedia (**http://en.wikipedia.org/wiki/List_of_Crayola_crayon_colors**) to replicate that color scheme in your data presentations.

Grab Adobe Capture's app from your phone's app store. With this app, you can snap a photo of your favorite place, or the school you are studying, or the subject you are interviewing, and the app pulls out the colors and provides you with the color codes. It'll even give you alternative color schemes that work with one color from the photo. With both the picture and the color palette, you are on your way to a cohesive design for your data presentation.

## Where Can I Go for More Information?

American Psychological Association. (2010). *Publication manual of the American Psychological Association* (6th ed.). Washington DC: Author.

Breslow, L. A., Ratwani, R. M., & Trafton, J. G. (2009). Cognitive models of the influence of color scale on data visualization tasks. *Human Factors, 51*(3), 321–338.

Campbell, C. S., & Maglio, P. P. (1999). Facilitating navigation in information spaces: Road-signs on the World Wide Web. *International Journal of Human-Computer Studies, 50*(4), 309–327.

Carruthers, H. R., Morris, J., Tarrier, N., & Whorwell, P. J. (2010). The Manchester Color Wheel: Development of a novel way of identifying color choice and its validation in healthy, anxious and depressed individuals. *BMC Medical Research Methodology, 10*(12). Retrieved from **http://www.biomedcentral.com/content/pdf/1471-2288-10-12.pdf**

Clarke, T., & Costall, A. (2008). The emotional connotations of color: A qualitative investigation. *Color Research and Application, 33*(5), 406–410.

*(Continued)*

(Continued)

Few, S. (2006). *Information dashboard design*. Sebastopol, CA: O'Reilly.

Jamet, E., Garota, M., & Quaireau, C. (2008). Attention guiding in multimedia learning. *Learning and Instruction, 18*, 135–145.

Johnson, J. (2014). *Designing with the mind in mind: Simple guide to understanding user interface design guidelines* (2nd ed.). Waltham, MA: Morgan Kaufmann.

Samara, T. (2007). *Design elements: A graphic style manual*. Beverly, MA: Rockport Press.

So, S., & Smith, M. (2002). Colour graphics and task complexity in multivariate decision making. *Accounting, Auditing & Accountability Journal, 15*(4), 565–593.

Tourangeau, R., Couper, M. P., & Conrad, F. (2007). Color, labels, and interpretive heuristics for response scales. *Public Opinion Quarterly, 71*(1), 91–112.

Tufte, E. R. (2001). *The visual display of quantitative information* (2nd ed.). Cheshire, CT: Graphics Press.

Ware, C. (2013). *Information visualization: Perception for design* (3rd ed.). Waltham, MA: Morgan Kaufmann.

Wheildon, C. (2005). *Type and layout: Are you communicating or just making pretty shapes?* Hastings, Victoria, Australia: Worsley Press.

# CHAPTER FIVE

# ARRANGEMENT

## LEARNING OBJECTIVES

**After reading this chapter, you will be able to:**

- Choose the proper text justification settings so that your research is easier to read

- Arrange text, graphics, and callout points to maximize impact

- Position graphics consistently

- Ease cognitive overload by grouping data with text

- Modify your reporting for quicker navigation

- Revise your work so it fits modern reading expectations

- Report to multiple audiences at the same time

- Produce clearer data displays

- Revise a data display so that it represents data accurately

When someone asks me how effective data presentation actually contributes to a better bottom line, I tell them this story. Some time ago, I sat in a meeting with 10 other people. We were reviewing research findings, presented via graphs that were created by another researcher who was not present. You know this scene. You have been there a hundred times. The group spent 20 minutes just trying to decode and interpret a single graph. It was not the data that baffled us. It was not the graph type, either. Rather, it was the little things, like the placement of the labels, that confused the 11 of us (an educated group, I should point out) and led to a lengthy graph deconstruction discussion. So, what did that weak design cost?

Six people at that meeting were paid $800/day (or $100/hour), which means we spent $200 on their confusion. Add to that:

1 person at $600/day = $25

1 person at $400/day = $17

1 person at $300/day = $13

2 people at $1,500/day = $125

# Guiding Ideas

Important elements are prominent

Lines of narrative text are 8 to 12 words in length

Narrative text is left or full justified

Alignment is consistent

Grouped items logically belong together

Empty area is allocated on each page

That one poor graph design cost our group $380, which was actually more than the daily rate (salary and benefits) for one of the meeting attendees. If the cost of living is higher in your town, or you work in a more profitable sector, then raise this amount accordingly.

Ouch. Additionally, this does not include the time it took for the report author to develop the weak graph in the first place, or the subsequent time to make the graph clearer. As common as this situation seems, it is even more costly when weak graphs are published in textbooks, magazines, or newspapers, and the costs of printing and reprinting and confusion are incurred on a larger scale. Bad design is expensive. An up-front time investment in learning about good design principles and applying them to data displays and presentations literally pays off in the end. The arrangement of the data tends to be the least obvious aspect of effective data presentation, but it's what makes the difference between sloppy and professional work. So let's turn now to discuss what to do with all those bits and pieces of information.

## Where Do the Bits and Pieces Go?

The bits and pieces referenced here are the graphs, images, and blocks of text that make up your presentation documents. Thus far, we have talked about what we know we need to have—compelling images, intelligent colors, and intentional typefaces. In this chapter, we focus on how to arrange those elements on pages, slides, posters, and data displays so that they support reader cognition.

Basically, we want the most important information on a page or slide to go where it dominates attention. It naturally follows, then, that in order to arrange the pieces in a document, we must make decisions about what aspects of the data presentation are most important, second in importance, and so on. Just as discussed in Chapter 3, we are essentially creating a hierarchy for the prominence of the data.

In general, it is easiest to create a hierarchy of information when the reporting format is limited to just one idea or image per page or slide, thus avoiding competition between report pieces. Once the hierarchy is established conceptually, the information is ready for arrangement in the actual software. Effective arrangement organizes presentations to support comprehension and readability. This may be one of the most advanced steps you can take as a research information designer, so hang on.

**Guiding Idea**

Important elements are prominent

## Two Models for Layout

I am about to introduce two options for arranging report pieces, but first we must lay a foundation for that work with a quick discussion of grids. When I suggested the idea of writing about grids to the graphic designers on my dissertation panel, half of them advised that I avoid doing so, explaining that grids are complicated concepts that are troublesome even for some professional graphic designers. I rejected their advice (usually not a good idea if you want to graduate) because we are, after all, researchers—we love systematic organization, and that's what grids do. You will be good at this, if you follow my lead.

Essentially, grids divide pages into columns and rows so that designers can achieve consistent and predictable placement for each reporting element (Müller-Brockmann, 1981/2009). Let's review the Greenpeace report I introduced in Chapter 2, because that report's creators did such a nice job of organizing their information. You can download the entire report at www.greenpeace.org/international/Global/international/publications/climate/2010/fullreport.pdf.

**Figure 5.1    Black lines mark the grid—the rows and columns used by the designer to arrange the report pieces**

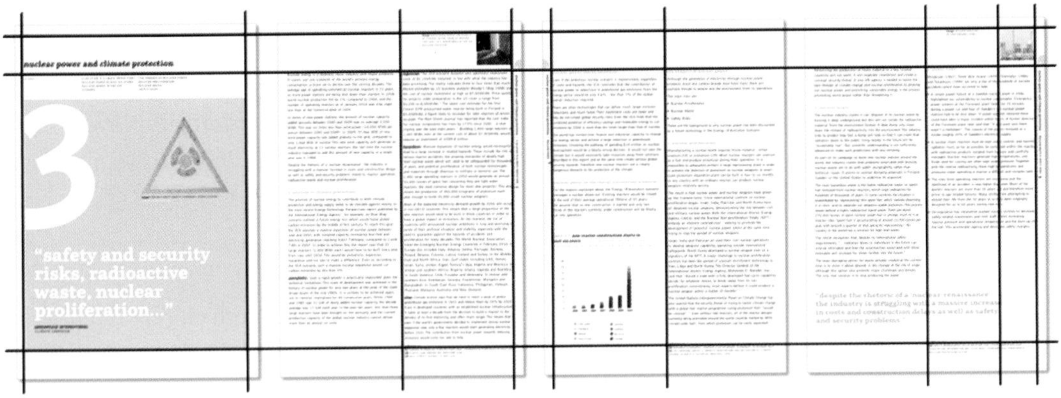

*Source:* © 2010. Reprinted with permission from One Hemisphere/Greenpeace.

In Figure 5.1, it appears that the report's designer chose a grid that divides the pages into several rows and columns. I drew in the black lines to give you a sense of the grid structure. One line marks the placement of the supplementary text on page 1 and where the narrative text begins on other pages. Another line across the bottom marks a row where the graphic ends on page 1, and some tiny print is placed on the rest of the pages. The columns that mark the margins on the first page are also the guides used to place the tiny pictures on pages 2 and 4, as well as the vertical text off to the right.

You can probably see other gridlines, both horizontal and vertical, that I did not draw but that signal the organization of the report.

For the research report designer, using a grid structure means rarely having to spend time on decisions about where to place a picture on a page, because the arrangement is dictated by the grid. And for the reader, it is easy to see that whenever a photo takes up three-fourths of the rows, it marks the start of a new section of the report. That sort of organization speeds navigation and increases information retention in an audience. Grid systems take out the guesswork and produce a more organized report.

To establish a grid structure, choose the numbers of rows and columns you would like and space them evenly on a page. Use the ruler along the top and side of the page in your software program and make note of where the gridlines fall. On an 8½-by-11-inch page, if I want four rows, I need to divide 11 by 4. But wait a minute. The rows would look more even if I took the margins into consideration. So subtracting the

1-inch margins from the top and bottom leaves me with 9 inches of working room. I divide 9 by 4 and see that my rows will each be 2¼ inches tall. Later, this will help me position the bits and pieces because I can just nestle my pictures and text boxes right up against the gridlines.

Position within the grid is important to attraction and comprehension. Viewers pay more attention to elements that compose key positions. Information lower in the hierarchy is toned down and placed in subordinate positions. Here are two models for placing elements within a grid.

## Gutenberg Diagram Arrangement Model

The Gutenberg Diagram is based on research specific to Western cultures identifying the way eyes travel around a page when people engage with a document. Some studies show that deviation from this diagram throws off comprehension of the material (Wheildon, 2005).

**Figure 5.2    The Gutenberg Diagram signals where to place (and not place) key report pieces**

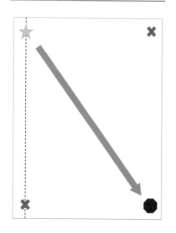

Imagine you have all of the content you need to create a research poster about your dissertation. You sit down at your computer, open your poster software, and stare at a blank screen. According to the Gutenberg Diagram, you want to place your elements according to what people naturally look at first.

The first area on a page where a person's eyes tend to go is represented here by the star. This is known as the *primary optical area,* the most ideal spot to grab attention. In Western culture, the top left area is a key position.

The arrow represents the direction eyes flow through the material. People in Western cultures are most comfortable reading according to this *reading gravity*—left to right and top to bottom. Layouts that go against this reading gravity tend to make a reader feel subtly uncomfortable, which sometimes can work to the designer's advantage.

The dotted line marks the *axis of orientation,* where eyes want to return after reading each line. Readers want a strong and predictable axis of orientation, probably at one of your gridlines. A bit further into this chapter we talk about alignment and justification of text in more detail, but the basic idea is that the narrative text should align.

The stop sign signals the *terminal area.* It is the last place eyes tend to go before leaving a page, even if the reader is just skimming.

The *fallow areas* are represented by the location of the *x*'s. Usually, these corners are left blank, or fallow. Placing stand-alone elements in those areas puts demands on the eyes to work against reading gravity. Sometimes, continuous narrative text can run through the fallow corners, and sometimes those corners can be activated with eye-catching graphics.

The Gutenberg Diagram applies more to text-heavy materials, such as posters and reports.

How well does the Gutenberg Diagram hold up? Pretty well.

Figure 5.3 is an advertisement from one of my clients, the Ad Council. I saw a version of this on a billboard near my house and loved it because of how well it catches the eye with its novelty. Now, you are not in the business of designing billboards, but think how revolutionary it would be if our research report covers and posters looked like this.

The ad follows the Gutenberg Diagram nicely. The paint can is located in the primary optical area. The arrow shows that the whole ad generally moves according to reading gravity. The axis of orientation is roughly in the middle of the page but still clearly evident. Organizational logos are placed in the terminal area, the last place our eyes will go, so as to leave a lasting impression. And the fallow corners are generally left blank, except perhaps for the intriguing cereal bowl.

**Figure 5.3** **The arrangement of this advertisement aligns with the Gutenberg Diagram**

*Source:* Ad Council and the Coalition to End Childhood Lead Poisoning. © 2012. Used with permission..

Let's look at the interior page of a report in Figure 5.4. The primary optical area is somewhat weakened on interior pages, but in this case the heading there is stuck way out to the left. This arrangement is effective for a report. It makes locating information a faster process for the reader, particularly when a grid structure is used to ensure that the placement falls in the same location on each page. The axis of orientation aligns the heading, subheading, and paragraph starter sentences. A second axis of orientation could be inserted to mark how the remaining narrative text aligns. The narrative text follows reading gravity. The terminal area is also less strong on an interior page, because the intent is that there is more reading continued on the next page, but tucked behind that stop sign is the page number. The fallow areas are often filled with text, though they are empty here.

## Rule of Thirds Arrangement Model

While the Gutenberg Diagram is a good option for text-heavy documents like reports, the Rule of Thirds, which stems from photography, is better suited for slideshows.

**Figure 5.4    Interior, text-heavy narrative pages fit the Gutenberg Diagram less well but can be modified to the extent possible**

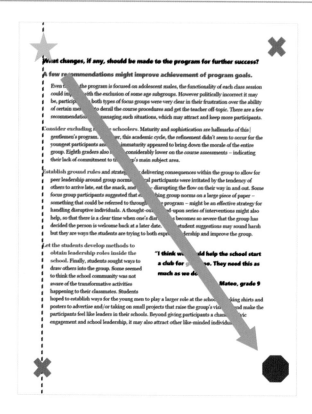

Watch a short tutorial on it here: vimeo.com/14315821.

Okay, you have your content and your slide software open to a blank canvas. Here is how to envision the Rule of Thirds.

In this layout method, the blank canvas is mentally divided into a grid structure of thirds both horizontally and vertically, creating four points of intersection (Figure 5.5). Designers use either the *fill a third* strategy—where an image fills one, two, or all three thirds—or the *intersection point* strategy—where important imagery is placed at one of the stars.

Because the Rule of Thirds comes from the world of photography, a lot of stock photos are already designed to fill a third. In Figure 5.6, the girl consumes the right third of the slide, while the rest of the picture is blurred in the background. I knew where to place my text box with title information because I knew it needed to align with the grid created by the thirds in the upper right.

**Figure 5.5** Gray lines divide the page into thirds in both directions, while orange stars show where to place critical pieces

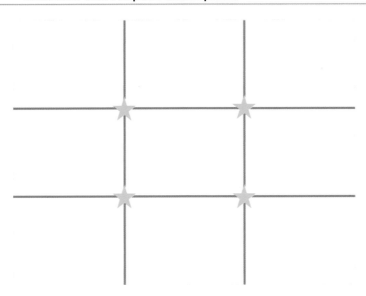

**Figure 5.6** The girl fills the right third of the slide

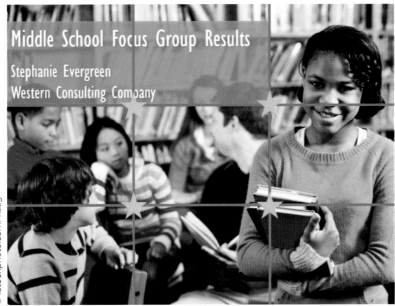

© iStockphoto.com/kalig

## What Is White Space and How Do I Use It?

You have probably noticed that most of the examples in this book leave open swaths of empty space on one side of a page. You might be thinking, "What a waste of paper." Those of us who are efficiency-minded tend to want to cram as much information as possible onto as few pages as possible, and maybe in doing so we would actually decrease the number of pages in the report, save a couple of trees, and fall within our semester printing limit at the campus computing lab. This might be true—but it does not assist reader cognition.

### Guiding Idea

Lines of narrative text are 8 to 12 words in length

When thinking about grids and line length and functionality, we need to keep in mind how the design hinders or enhances readability for the audience. This is where we can create and use white space to knock out several readability-enhancing checkpoints.

### Line Length

Comprehension studies show that readers can best track a narrative when lines are 8 to 12 words in length (Wheildon, 2005). (The number depends on the choice of typeface, type size, and number of columns.) For those of us who like long words, let me translate: For optimal reading conditions, this means about 50 to 80 characters per line. Longer lines make it difficult for readers to track even when there is a strong axis of orientation, which means that they falter a bit when trying to finish one line of narrative text and start another. Shorter lines tend to create too many hyphenated words, distracting the reader and breaking up the reading flow. So, that is why a large margin on one side of the page, despite potential ecological impacts, literally makes more sense.

These suggestions align with APA (2010) guidelines, which specify that the line length should be a maximum of 6.5 inches (the default setting of one column with 1-inch margins on all sides, using default font settings), thus restricting line lengths to shorter than that maximum is acceptable. The MLA (2009) style guide proposes 1-inch margins all around, so keep that restriction in mind when aiming for publication in an MLA journal. Of course, follow whatever directions you are given for your dissertation or journal article (probably 1-inch margins), but consider more reader-friendly margins when publishing elsewhere.

In the example in Figure 5.7, the left margin is set at nearly 2 inches, with regular 1-inch margins on the rest of the page. Using multiple columns also works, depending

Figure 5.7    A wide margin reduces line length to a comfortable size

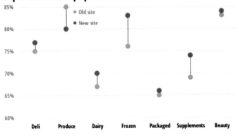

**Customers were generally satisfied with prices after the move.**

Everything in the paragraph and the next is talking about the graph below, customer satisfaction with the prices in different parts of the market, as compared to the market at its old site and its new site. Notice how satisfaction has generally been quite high, except in the areas of packaged goods, where satisfaction remained somewhat low even after the move to a new site. Notice how satisfaction with the produce prices actually decreased after the move, even though the produce section itself expanded greatly in size.

In general, price satisfaction rose for the deli, diary, frozen, supplement, and beauty sections, though only the gains in frozen and supplements were statistically significant. The decrease in satisfaction with the produce section was also statistically significant. Everything in the paragraph and the next is talking about graph below, customer satisfaction with the prices in different parts of the market, as compared to the market at its old site and its new site. Notice how satisfaction has generally been quite high, except in the areas of packaged goods, where satisfaction remained somewhat low even after the move to a new site. Notice how satisfaction with the produce prices actually decreased after the move, even though the produce section itself expanded greatly in size.

**Market price satisfaction increased for all departments except produce.**

on the size of the text. To meet this guiding idea using columns, I had to adjust the default settings in Word. For a two-column setting, I had to decrease the font size to 10 points, decrease the margins from 1 inch to 0.75 inch on the left and right, and increase the width of each column to 3.4 inches. Whichever way you arrange it, the white space, meaning the parts of the page with no words, will increase.

On wider layouts, such as for a research poster, effective data presentation should still include white space. In one method, the poster's grid structure makes use of columns. In Figure 5.8, the grid structure includes three columns, with the image taking up one of those three. White space still counts, even if it is filled with an image.

Figure 5.8  **A wide margin on a poster creates adequate line length and leaves space for a picture**

© iStockphoto.com/SteveLuker

# Rule of the Dollar Bill

Some graphic designers refer to the "Rule of the Dollar Bill." This rule says that if a block of text is larger than a dollar bill, it is too big. At that size, it appears intimidating to the reader, who presumes that it will take a lot of cognitive work to read and digest the information (unless the reader has a vested interest, such as when she is paid to understand what you wrote). Graphic designers suggest using wider margins, creating more paragraphs, adding some graphic elements, or simplifying language to remedy the situation. The Rule of the Dollar Bill might not be backed up by research, but it is a good barometer for you to use in determining whether text should be broken up when you are working with 8½-by-11-inch documents. Convey the same intention of supporting the reader when working with larger documents, such as research posters.

## Sidebars

Readable line lengths give us white space and the opportunity to use that space for happy things like sidebars. Sidebars are places to offload tangential content—the stuff that would interrupt your main narrative. Mission statements, acknowledgments, contact information, and definitions perform their supporting roles better when they appear in sidebars.

**Figure 5.9    Sidebars hold tangential content**

*Source:* © 2014. Reprinted with permission from the Idaho State Office of Performance Evaluations.

In this report from clients, sidebars are inserted on several pages to contain somewhat irrelevant information. On this particular page in Figure 5.9, the sidebar is where the icon for that section is located. Gorgeous! But perhaps more important, this is also where the team defines acronyms that appear in that section. That's one way to make reading long reports even easier. Usually what I see is a page in the front of the report listing the definitions of all acronyms. But this isn't a great idea.

Why? Well, because people read reports online these days. Back when we always read reports on paper, sure, it might have been handy to dog-ear the acronyms page so you could quickly return to it when you forgot what a certain acronym meant. But people don't dog-ear PDFs. In PDF land, people scroll right past all those boring pages up front and then have to scroll back and forth, getting more annoyed with you at each scroll, to remember those acronyms. A smarter idea is to define each acronym close to where it is actually used in the report via sidebars. So we have made it easier to understand our writing with better acronym placement, provided an appropriate line length for reading, and added in some white space? Yes, please!

Sidebars also rock at helping you report to multiple audiences within the same report.

**Figure 5.10    Sidebars provide background information for broader audiences**

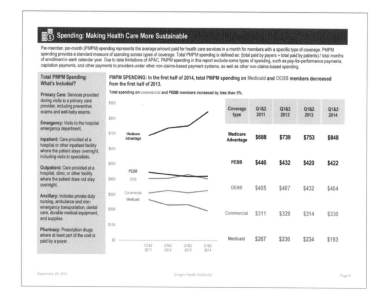

***Source:*** © 2015. Reprinted with permission from the Oregon Health Authority.

What an amazingly clever use of sidebars in another client report (Figure 5.10). The topic here is PMPM spending. Um, what? I have no idea. But then again, I am not the main audience the Oregon Health Authority is trying to speak to here. The primary audience is composed of people in health care, who are 100% clear on what PMPM spending means. They just want to get to the good stuff. But the Oregon Health

Authority knows that the report will be posted online, where anyone with an Internet connection can access it, and most of those people are like me—clueless about this PMPM stuff. So the report authors need to define what PMPM spending is. If they took up the main narrative space to do so, as we commonly see, their main audience of health care folks would read it and think, "Oh, this is kindergarten stuff not meant for me," which would be a mistake! So the authors put the definition of PMPM spending off in a sidebar. It's gray text on a gray background, specifically to de-emphasize it so it isn't viewed as critical to the main audience. But it provides the support needed for the rest of us. Sidebars are amazing in that they serve lots of roles for our reporting.

## The Wrong Kind of White Space

Long-form reports suitable for a digital reading age require other adjustments as well. Printed reports, like books (including this one), often have extra blank pages at the front and back. This probably gives printed materials a sense of refinement, or maybe it's used to build anticipation. But in PDFs, this doesn't work out well. What happens when you open a PDF, start scrolling, and encounter blank pages? You probably think, "Oh, this thing is still loading." So you go check email. And you never come back! Those folks who choose to print PDFs also get annoyed by having to waste paper on blank pages. That's some seriously unnecessary white space.

**Figure 5.11    This 30-page report wastes a lot of space in its front matter**

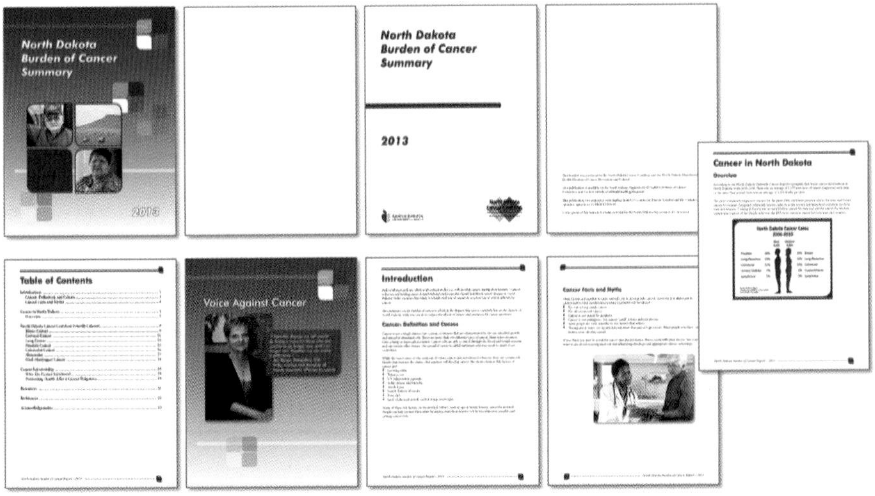

*Source:* © 2013. North Dakota Comprehensive Cancer Control (ND CC). Used with permission.

My clients in North Dakota had been adding way too much white space to the front of their report (emphasis on "had"—their latest work is right on point). In their old work, first there's a cover page. Okay. Then a blank page. No. Then another cover page. No. Then some copyright information that could be a sidebar or part of the following page, which is the table of contents. (Sure.) Then there's a page of decoration. No. This could be a cool sidebar elsewhere in the report. Then a two-page introduction that could be condensed to one page. The real content doesn't start until page 9, out of a 30-page report. No one wants to scroll past all of that dead weight to get to the good stuff.

Figure 5.12   **The end matter is also nearly useless**

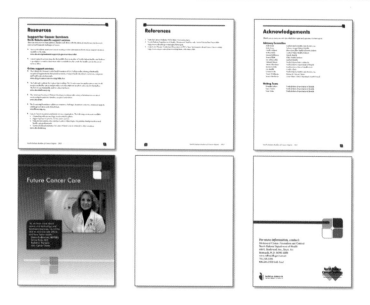

*Source:* © 2013. Reprinted with permission from North Dakota Comprehensive Cancer Control.

The end matter of the report is equally wasteful. While a resources page is nice, the references and acknowledgments and "Future Cancer Care" pages could all be sidebars elsewhere. The blank page has to go. The contact information on the final page could also become a sidebar. In a digital reading culture, we have to eliminate all this extra white space.

The same rule applies for those blank pages in the middle of a report. They are usually inserted (again as in this book) so that each new chapter starts on a right-hand page when the report is book bound. But who binds reports anymore? Even worse are when those blank pages have things like "This page intentionally left blank" printed in the middle, which means I can't even reuse the paper. Annoying your readers does not turn them into fans or advocates.

## How Should I Justify Text?

We discussed how important it is for readers to have a consistent axis of orientation when reading long narrative passages. In Latin alphabet cultures, this means the lines of the body text should all begin in alignment along the left side of a page or poster, what is referred to as left justified.

**Guiding Idea**

Narrative text is left or full justified

The type of placement shown in Figure 5.13 is left justified with a ragged right edge. See how the right edge of the block of text undulates in and out? That is the ragged edge, which is the easiest format to read for normal readers. For narrative body text, you want to make certain that the text has a strong axis of orientation on the left side. To some people, the ragged right edge communicates a bit of informality when used in written reporting, despite its strong legibility (Lupton, 2004).

Figure 5.13    **This text is aligned on the left, or left justified (and that's Hipster Ipsum text—because I know you wondered)**

90's biodiesel beard, coloring book disrupt actually blue bottle swag craft beer listicle leggings next level gluten-free. Occupy stumptown williamsburg, prism enamel pin cornhole before they sold out literally trust fund kinfolk mlkshk skateboard. Prism wayfarers iPhone aesthetic kombucha, bicycle rights sartorial pabst raw denim photo booth selfies. Sustainable portland photo booth XOXO, crucifix health goth +1 mixtape echo park lumbersexual chicharrones blue bottle. Franzen fingerstache direct trade, aesthetic pug plaid cred skateboard. Bushwick ramps butcher, street art sriracha tacos semiotics bicycle rights paleo offal narwhal readymade chicharrones glossier. Before they sold out bushwick taxidermy poke aesthetic.

When I work with clients or colleagues who are in academia, I find that generally their preference is for a more formal look. More formality is reflected by a two-column, fully justified placement, which is often found in journals. Full justification is the setting where the lines both begin and end in alignment and the software adjusts the spacing between words within each line. For highly fluent readers, this setting is shown to best support comprehension (Wheildon, 2005).

**Figure 5.14**    **This text is aligned on both the left and right, or fully justified, which sometimes leads to ugly spacing**

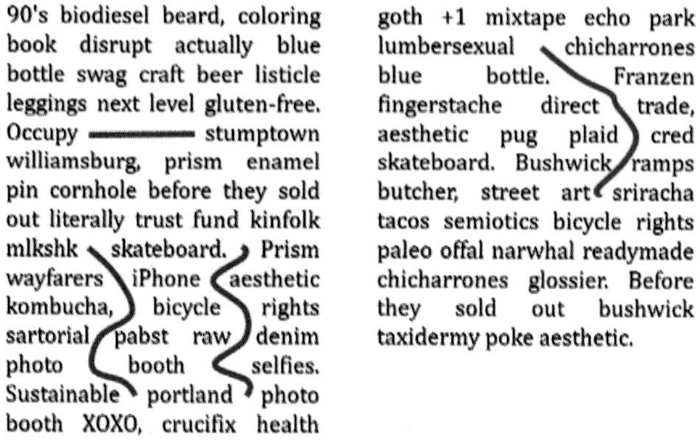

90's biodiesel beard, coloring book disrupt actually blue bottle swag craft beer listicle leggings next level gluten-free. Occupy ———— stumptown williamsburg, prism enamel pin cornhole before they sold out literally trust fund kinfolk mlkshk skateboard. Prism wayfarers iPhone aesthetic kombucha, bicycle rights sartorial pabst raw denim photo booth selfies. Sustainable portland photo booth XOXO, crucifix health goth +1 mixtape echo park lumbersexual chicharrones blue bottle. Franzen fingerstache direct trade, aesthetic pug plaid cred skateboard. Bushwick ramps butcher, street art sriracha tacos semiotics bicycle rights paleo offal narwhal readymade chicharrones glossier. Before they sold out bushwick taxidermy poke aesthetic.

However, as you can see, there are some graphic design issues at play when we use both full justification and columns. I drew in some red lines to highlight what many of you probably already find somewhat irritating. Graphic designers call these gaps in typesetting or midsentence spacing issues "white rivers." I am certain you can find a few more of these in this block of text. They were given a name precisely because they are so distracting to the reader. Most certainly, you want the reader paying attention to your words, not the spaces between your words!

If you are really adamant about using full justification, you have some options to remedy the white rivers. You can either widen the columns, move to a single column, or decrease the size of the text by a half point. All of these options make room for more words per line, which allows the software to better adjust the spaces between words.

**Figure 5.15**    **Full justification looks better on wider columns**

90's biodiesel beard, coloring book disrupt actually blue bottle swag craft beer listicle leggings next level gluten-free. Occupy stumptown williamsburg, prism enamel pin cornhole before they sold out literally trust fund kinfolk mlkshk skateboard. Prism wayfarers iPhone aesthetic kombucha, bicycle rights sartorial pabst raw denim photo booth selfies. Sustainable portland photo booth XOXO, crucifix health goth +1 mixtape echo park lumbersexual chicharrones blue bottle. Franzen fingerstache direct trade, aesthetic pug plaid cred skateboard. Bushwick ramps butcher, street art sriracha tacos semiotics bicycle rights paleo offal narwhal readymade chicharrones glossier. Before they sold out bushwick taxidermy poke aesthetic.

Here is the same text fully justified in one column. Most of the white rivers have gone away. White rivers are especially common when the author is prone (ahem) to using long words. So, that is something you need to review throughout your document when you finish writing, if you are committed to full justification. It's also worth noting that the APA Guide's (2010) preference is for text to be left justified with a ragged right edge rather than fully justified.

In practice, I see people using centered alignment quite often, but good design principles suggest that we use centered text only on rare occasions. Centered alignment should be reserved for rare and formal events, such as funeral ceremony agendas, wedding announcements, and graduation party invitations. Not your research presentation. Centered alignment is the default setting for titles in slideshows and graphs, but there is little evidence that such alignment is useful. None of the layout models discussed in this book identify the top center of the page as a natural location for important information.

## How Can I Align Using Typical Software?

Ever notice that restaurant menu that has one bit of text accidentally misaligned? It makes you question their attention to detail, doesn't it? Alignment is an attention-grabbing feature that readers quickly pick up on, so be sure your elements start in the same place on each page unless you choose to misalign something on purpose.

### Achieving Consistent Placement

In Figure 5.1, the Greenpeace grid example, I inserted lines over the figures to demonstrate how to conceptually divide a page into a grid. In some software programs (especially the expensive graphic design ones) it is possible to draw those lines right in the program and then snap elements to the grid.

**Guiding Idea**

Alignment is consistent

PowerPoint also has guidelines that can be activated. Look under the *View* tab in the *Show* group and check the box next to *Guides*. The lines can be moved to your specification around the slide, but there is only one vertical and one horizontal line, which can be insufficient when there are several pieces to arrange, such as a text box, an icon, and an image.

Microsoft Word does not have guidelines at all, so it can be a bit tricky to achieve consistent alignment. Here are two strategies for mastering consistency using the mainstream software you own.

## Use the Size and Position Function

Figure 5.16     **Graphics are different sizes and in different places on these pages, leading to an inconsistent and unpolished layout (that's Veggie Ipsum)**

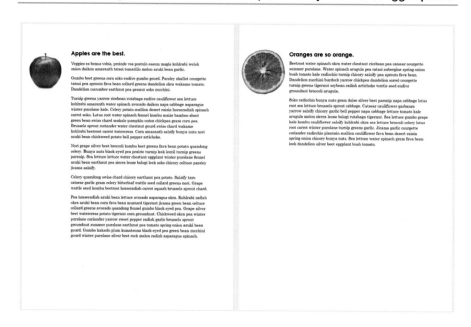

In this mock report, both pages have photographs to identify the start of a section. But the graphics are just a little different. Can you see it? The orange is larger and positioned higher on the page, higher than the section heading, while the apple is well below its heading. Getting these to match perfectly is pretty easy in Microsoft Office.

The first step is get the first page exactly how you want it, fitting within your grid structure.

It may also help to briefly turn on the gridlines, which overlay the document and help with precise placement. In Word 2016 on a PC, click in the *View* tab and then check the box by *Gridlines* in the *Show* group. Gridlines are annoying, though, so turn this feature off when you don't need it.

Now that the first picture is in place, I can right-click on that picture and choose *Size and Position.* A box opens that looks like Figure 5.17.

In the *Position* tab, Word shows me the exact page dimensions that identify where this graphic is located. Do you see how there is also a dropdown menu, allowing me

**Figure 5.17**    **Screenshot of position window shows physical location of graphic on a page**

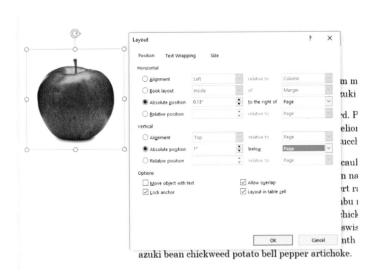

azuki bean chickweed potato bell pepper artichoke.

to relate the image's location to various parts of the document? For right now, just write down those numbers and menu options. Sit tight—I'll come right back to this in a sentence or two.

Keeping the same box open, I can click on the *Size* tab to get the measurements for my image. The apple is 1.63″ × 1.63.″ Jot that down, too.

Now, I close that box and right-click on the image of the orange and choose *Size and Position.* Here is where I type in the same numbers, starting with size. (In real life, when I was making this example, I typed in 1.63″ in the height box, but the orange was not a perfect square, so I used the cropping tool to trim either side.) After the size matches, I move over to the *Position* tab and enter the same dimensions as the apple. This forces the orange image to the same location on the page as the apple.

With this improvement, the arrangement is consistent. Even better, the same procedure works throughout the Office software programs. This process also works for graphs (investigate the *Wrap* options) and any other types of graphic.

Using this method, I achieve alignment with words and text, and maintain a grid structure. The same consistency between slides is critically important for a seamless viewing experience. This method is not as automatic as in specialized layout programs, but it allows you to sort of fake a grid system and ensure a consistent arrangement using the tools already at your disposal.

## Should I Anchor the Image?

Note in Figure 5.17 that one of the selections in the dropdown menu is the ability to choose whether to anchor the image to the text or to the page. This is a decision point where the research in cognitive processing does not play nicely with the common practices in graphic design. Cognitive researchers suggest you anchor the image to the text, so that no matter how much, say, introductory text is added to the front of the report section, pushing your content to new pages, the image always travels with its associated text. As we discussed in Chapter 2, for reader comprehension it is preferable for graphics to be very near their associated text. But graphic designers recommend that images appear in consistent places on the pages where they are present; they are less concerned about proximity to associated text, and thus hope you will anchor your picture to the page so that it is unmovable, even if introductory text is added. If images are intended to associate with the narrative, I am more inclined to let them move with their text.

### Use Groups

In part, graphic design practice is based in Gestalt psychology, which theorizes how specific arrangements of information influence interpretation by the brain (Tourangeau, Couper, & Conrad, 2004, 2007). The five main Gestalt-based principles are middle means typical, left and top mean first, near means related, up means good, and like means close. "Like means close" refers to the idea that items that appear close together are interpreted by the reader as belonging to one another, whether the likeness is in color, font, size, or physical proximity. This interpretation particularly supports the ability to comprehend graphs and other graphic elements; grouping or chunking data in graphs leads to a better ability to describe patterns in the data (Woodman, Vecera, & Luck, 2003).

### Guiding Idea

Grouped items logically belong together

When I originally made my personal annual report dashboard for 2013, it didn't look as bad as Figure 5.18, but it was pretty sloppy. I wanted to report on key indicators, but I didn't do a great job of grouping the bits and pieces, so the indicators aren't clear. It's definitely a nice step up from a written annual report, but man oh man, does it look like a mess. Like someone just vomited onto a canvas. The biggest contributor to that sense of gross madness is the lack of a grid with clear groups. Things just aren't organized.

**Figures 5.18 and 5.19**  Grouping together the elements that belong together makes the infographic on the right much clearer and better organized

The "&" on the left is not centered, "Edited journals" is too close to "15 webinars," "Blog hits by month" and "Side projects" aren't aligned, and dozens of other errors make this a death by 1,000 cuts. These may seem like little things, but it is the little things that make a difference. In the revised version of my dashboard infographic, I created more identifiable chunks by dragging the bits that belonged together closer to each other. Near means related. Graphic designers sometimes refer to this grouping strategy as "squish and separate" (Samara, 2007). We want the elements in each chunk squished closer together and then the whole chunk separated from surrounding chunks. In this way, empty space helps organize the information into more digestible pieces. The resulting infographic feels a lot more organized, cleaner, and less claustrophobic.

It is probably the most tedious part of design, all that nudging of pieces here and there. Sometimes it means making hard choices about what to delete—like how I removed my "Edited journals" data point from my revised infographic. But the payoff is looking like a pro. This is the hardest part of design to get right. It's what differentiates sloppy, weak design from design that looks tight. It's the use of a grid. Arrangement matters. Grouping pieces is effective outside of infographics and dashboards, as well.

Take the ubiquitous logic model, for example. Here, we typically have column headings running across the top of the diagram as a way to identify the main conceptual categories—in the case of Figure 5.20, from "Inputs" to "Long-Term Outcomes" (we can argue about the merits of logic models and their components some other time). Program elements are then detailed under each column. Thus, we have groups of information.

## Guiding Idea

Empty area is allocated on each page

**Figure 5.20   Logic model elements are grouped by space and color**

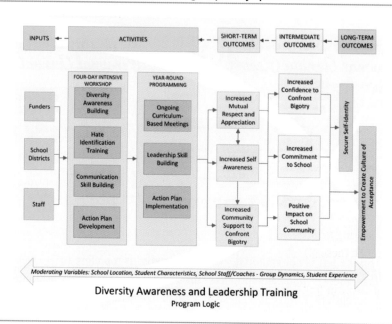

*Source:* © 2009. Reprinted with permission from DALT.

With the logic model, we can add graphic elements to signal groups more clearly. Spacing is one subtle but essential way to indicate that the columns are distinct groups. Note how considerable berth is maintained between the columns. The second way we can indicate distinct groupings is through the inclusion of a graphic element—such as the large background boxes under the "Activities" column. I wanted to visually represent that the program activities were divided into two phases. By inserting a large rectangle to encompass the activity boxes and adding a short label, I more clearly grouped the elements that belong together. Using large graphic elements in the background is an effective method for grouping other visual elements, whether blocks of text or images. The third way we can express grouping in a logic model is through color—each column has its own. As discussed in Chapter 4, keep in mind that you have to be careful when placing text on a color background.

Though it is less common, sometimes graphics are paired with graphics, and their careful handling is important to user cognition. For example, look at these playing cards my son brought home one day (Figure 5.21). Notice the problem (aside from the fact that they are shaped like snowmen)?

We have two graphic groups here: the category markers (the symbols and numbers that identify which suit each card belongs to) and the counting symbols (placed in the middle—three hearts, seven clubs, and nine diamonds, in this example). The

**Figure 5.21**    **The elements on these playing cards are poorly grouped and can lead to confusion**

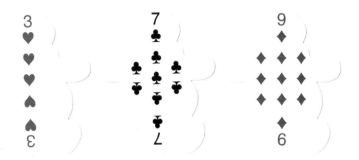

issue, quickly noticed, is that the category markers are too close and too similar to the actual counting symbols in the middle of the cards.

Now, with these playing cards, we are limited in our ability to distinguish these two graphic groups. In other parts of this chapter, more exciting possibilities, like applying different colors or fonts, are possible, but that defeats the purpose in a deck of cards.

When working with pairs of graphics, you want to create more empty space on the page, or slide, or card by squishing together the things that belong in one group and separating that group from the groups around it. The empty space serves as the organizing element. With these cards, the category markers could be much smaller. Or much larger. Or just positioned further away from the counting symbols in the middle. The counting symbols in the middle could also be squished closer together.

Similarly, when working with multiple groups of text, leave plenty of space between groups.

I took the picture in Figure 5.22 in a bathroom stall in Traverse City, Michigan. I literally closed the door, saw the sign, and thought, "Oh my god, what kind of ram-shackle place is this that doesn't have a smoking alarm with sound?"

**Figure 5.22**    **Poor grouping on this sign can lead to confusion (or maybe it's just me)**

Of course, it may just be me, but the message is impaired because the first text group ("No Smoking") needs to be more distinct from the second text group ("Alarm Will Sound"). More space is needed between these two groups, as well as some other type of distinction (e.g., larger font size for the first text group). At the least, a greater difference between the groups would make the sign less alarming.

Here is the corresponding lesson for researchers: When you use headings to signal the organization of a report, make the headings really, really, really clearly different from the narrative text. There are many options when working with headings, so remember that you can use generous space, font, color, and other emphasis techniques to make them obviously distinguishable from the narrative.

In the example in Figure 5.23, the headings are emphasized by the use of a different font and bold type (review Chapter 2). They are also emphasized through the addition of empty space. Space around a heading is created in two ways. There is the space before the heading, where it is preceded by other report content, and the space after the heading, where its corresponding text follows. Because the heading is more closely related to its own text, it should be physically closer to that text than to the preceding narrative that is less conceptually related. In this example, the heading "Statement of Need" is further away from the paragraph above it about background.

**Figure 5.23** **Allow more spacing before a heading than after it, to group it with its associated narrative**

## Background

This is just a bunch of gobbled text. Pay no attention to it. The more important point is that you get the gist of how the text formats on the page in relationship to the headers and graphics. This is just a bunch of gobbled text. Pay no attention to it. The more important point is that you get the gist of how the text formats on the page in relationship to the headers and graphics. This is just a bunch of gobbled text. Pay no attention to it. The more important point is that you get the gist of how the text formats on the page in relationship to the headers and graphics.

## Statement of Need

This is just a bunch of gobbled text. Pay no attention to it. The more important point is that you get the gist of how the text formats on the page in relationship to the headers and graphics. This is just a bunch of gobbled text. Pay no attention to it. The more important point is that you get the gist of how the text formats on the page in relationship to the headers and graphics. This is just a bunch of gobbled text. Pay no attention to it. The more important point is that you get the gist of how the text formats on the page in relationship to the headers and graphics.

Here is how I established those dimensions in Word 2016 on a PC:

**Figure 5.24**   **Screenshot shows how to adjust the spacing before and after a heading**

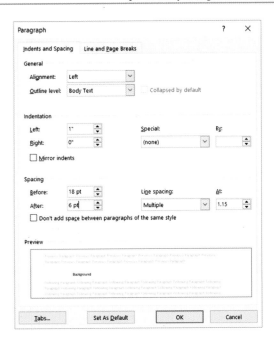

If we think of the heading and its text as a group, they should be more squished, and so in the *Spacing After* box, I decreased the size to 6 point so that the space after the heading is smaller, bringing the heading closer to the text. That text group should be further away from other text groups, so in the *Spacing Before* box, I increased the space above the heading to 18 points. Adjusting the spacing between groups of narrative text leaves adequate empty space and serves to better communicate the report's organization.

## When Is it Okay to Break the Rules?

In the context of arrangement, we can sometimes increase audience understanding by purposely ignoring rules about orientation, grids, and text justification. Look at another Ad Council advertisement that succeeds in defying the rules we just established with the somewhat rare use of right justification. The MLA style guide does not want you to see this.

Notice here how the text at the top of the ad is aligned on the right side. I drew in the axis of orientation with the dotted line. It is an unnatural way of reading for

**Figure 5.25    Right-justified text can be effective in some circumstances**

*Source:* Ad Council and the Environmental Protection Agency. © 2012. Reprinted with permission.

most people in Western cultures. In this ad, it still works well without affecting legibility too much because the phrasing is short. Additionally, the discomfort of the text placement, which makes us work against reading gravity, actually contributes to and reinforces the sense the ad is trying to convey about raising awareness for asthma. Beautifully done. The advertisement uses right justification to break the rules and gets away with it because the result consciously contributes to the overall tone of the document. So right justification works sometimes, particularly if the wording is short and if the message is meant to relay a bit of discomfort. At times, graphic designers also use right justification to convey a hip, or youthful, or unique mood, but such uses tend to be initiated by a desire to appear interesting and attract early attention, often at the expense of reader cognition. Therefore, it is best to keep right-justified text short and sweet, limited to bursts like callouts, headings, or titles.

Nonetheless, rule breaking can be effective when it is done selectively for the purpose of emphasis.

In Figure 5.26, those elements that typically are viewed as headings are turned on their sides and dragged into the margin (what do we call these—"sidings"?). The vertical

Figure 5.26    **A different orientation can both draw attention and group items**

**Research Report Layout Guidelines**

This checklist is meant to be used as a diagnostic guide to identify elements of evaluation reports that could be enhanced using graphic design best practices and/or the assistance of a graphic design expert. Suggestions are best suited for those using standard Microsoft Word software.

**Graphics**

Pictures/graphic elements are present
Multimode learning increases chance at storage of info in long-term memory because it eases cognitive load of body text. Choose pictures or graphics related to your topic. Graphics include, but shouldn't be limited to, tables and charts.

Graphics are near associated text
If readers must flip around to interpret between text and graphic, comprehension will be impaired.

Graphics are simple
Less visual noise leads to better assimilation. Eliminate gradation, textures, or graphics as backgrounds. Segment complex graphics into smaller chunks.

Size corresponds to changes in meaning
Use, for example, larger pictures on chapter start pages. In graphing, for example, be sure height of columns proportionately represents data.

Graphics direct toward text
Use the power of an image to direct the reader's gaze from the image to the associated text. Eyes in a photo, for example, should look inward at text.

**Tips**

Pictures and graphics related to your content will make your content more memorable.

Choose pictures from quality sources, like paid websites. Watermarks or fuzzy images are signs of an amateur.

Use a cover page at the beginning of a report. This is a good place for a very large graphic.

**Font**

Text fonts are used for narrative text
Use serif fonts. Nothing with lots of graphic detail.

Long reading is in 9-11 point size
Studies have shown that 11 point text is easiest to read at length, but it can depend on the font.

Body text has stylistic uniformity
Each text section has unbolded, normal text in sentence case (no all caps), except in short areas of intentional emphasis. This supports undistracted reading.

Line spacing is 11-13 points
For lines within paragraph, generally choose 1-2 points larger than the size of the body text.

line also assists in grouping the text that belongs under the "Graphics" section. In this instance, such a rebellious arrangement actually works to support use of the guidelines in the handout, because a reader can see the main areas of guidance at a glance.

At times, outdenting, or starting the first line of a paragraph way out to the left of the narrative text, is also an effective way to bend the rules. While we usually want all narrative text aligned on the left, in this situation, purposeful misalignment brings the reader's eye to those textual points. Outdenting emphasizes.

This particular example depicts the part of the report where the author delivers the study's recommendations for improvement. Recommendations are often the

Figure 5.27    **Outdented first sentences help structure a page**

**What changes, if any, should be made to the program for further success?**

**A few recommendations might improve achievement of program goals.**

Even though the program is focused on adolescent males, the functionality of each class session could improve with the exclusion of some age subgroups. However politically incorrect it may be, participants in both types of focus groups were very clear in their frustration over the ability of certain members to derail the course procedures and get the teacher off-topic. There are a few recommendations for managing such situations, which may attract and keep more participants.

Consider excluding middle schoolers. Maturity and sophistication are hallmarks of this gentlemen's program. However, this academic cycle, the refinement didn't seem to occur for the youngest participants and their immaturity appeared to bring down the morale of the entire group. Eighth graders also scored considerably lower on the course assessments – indicating their lack of commitment to the group's main subject area.

Establish ground rules and strategies for delivering consequences within the group to allow for peer leadership around group norms. Several participants were irritated by the tendency of others to arrive late, eat the snack, and leave – disrupting the flow on their way in and out. Some focus group participants suggested that establishing group norms on a large piece of paper – something that could be referred to throughout the program – might be an effective strategy for handling disruptive individuals. A thought-out, agreed-upon series of interventions might also help, so that there is a clear time when one's disruptions becomes so severe that the group has decided the person is welcome back at a later date. These student suggestions may sound harsh but they are ways the students are trying to both express leadership and improve the group.

Let the students develop methods to obtain leadership roles inside the school. Finally, students sought ways to draw others into the group. Some seemed to think the school community was not aware of the transformative activities happening to their classmates. Students hoped to establish ways for the young men to play a larger role at the school – making shirts and posters to advertise and/or taking on small projects that raise the group's visibility and make the participants feel like leaders in their schools. Beyond giving participants a chance at civic engagement and school leadership, it may also attract other like-minded individuals.

**"I think we should help the school start a club for girls, too. They need this as much as we do."**

**Mateo, grade 9**

toughest aspect of the study to get a client to adopt. It probably does not help that we tend to bury the recommendations on page 104, but let's tackle that in the next section. Suffice it to say here that the recommendations are much harder to miss because they are now bolded and outdented. Now, if every paragraph begins this way, we lose the effect. But if we reserve outdenting (or any emphasis technique, for that matter) for only our most important points, even a reader who is flipping through the report pages will fixate on the recommendations because of their arresting misalignment.

## How Do I Arrange the Sections of the Whole Report?

It's time to zoom out of the layout of a single page or poster or slide and starting thinking about how we package the whole deal into something coherent for our audiences. It's time to talk about how a well-formatted recommendations page doesn't have much impact when it is buried on page 104. This is how we make reporting less cumbersome, particularly in a digital reporting era.

Of course your reporting will probably include a slide deck. I mean, you could totally give a talk with no slides. People would look at you. And you would be awesome. But most of the time you'll have a slideshow, designed with the principles we've been discussing throughout this book. The idea of the presentation is generally to spark conversation and get people interested in learning more about your ideas, Rock Star.

So what next? Now that you have piqued their interest, you—what?—toss them a 300-page report and wish them luck? Sounds like a terrible way to foster engagement.

Instead of giving people a new doorstop, you can extend their engagement with a handout. Something digestible like we discussed in Chapter 1. In fact, this is where the 1–3-25 model comes in handy. This model recommends that your reporting include a 1-page handout, a 3-page executive summary, and a 25-page report. In each of these layers, readers gain more and more detail. They can stop anytime, having already gotten the high points. This approach provides a scaffolding toward learning in which each step helps readers learn a bit more without being completely overwhelmed.

**Figure 5.28    The 1–3-25 model includes layers of reporting to keep people engaged**

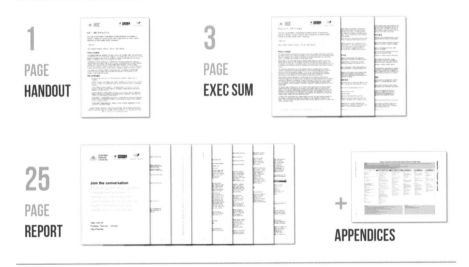

*Source:* This research is a project of the Australian Primary Health Care Research Institute, which is supported by a grant from the Australian Government Department of Health. The information and opinions contained in it do not necessarily reflect the views or policy of the Australian Primary Health Care Research Institute or the Australian Government Department of Health. This work is licensed under a Creative Commons Attribution-NonCommercial-ShareAlike 4.0 International License. https://creativecommons.org/licenses/by-nc-sa/4.0/

The example in Figure 5.28 comes from an Australian university research institute that requires all researchers to publish by this model and makes templates to fit it. Smart! (See http://aphcri.anu.edu.au/aphcri-network/research-completed/join-conversation-evaluating-effectiveness-experienced-based-co.)

Of course it's hard to squeeze your work into just 25 pages, especially when you include graphics and data visualizations. So you'll need an appendix—this is where you can put things like your logic model, methodology, and *p* values. And it can even be a separate document that you just link to from the others.

So let's talk about that 25-page report and what it's going to look like.

We normally go about structuring our reports (and presentations and posters) like this:

Background

Literature Review

Methodology

Discussion

Findings

Conclusion

It feels serious and logical and rigorous. Does it look familiar? Probably so, because it's the basic format for a journal article. It's just that a journal article is not the usual dissemination forum for the work many of us do, where our charge is to present data useful to decision makers, where we are paid to provide actionable information.

Davidson (2007) wrote a life-changing article on this matter, reorienting us toward truly user-focused reporting, in which we do not make the reader wait until page 104 to get to the good stuff. Today's readers just don't have the patience for that. They might flip through a huge report to glean highlights, but few read, word for word, anything so long and tedious. In fact, there's a hashtag for just this scenario: #TLDR, which means "too long, didn't read."

The revolution in reporting is simple: Arrange the sections of the report in the reverse order. Report the findings and conclusions first. That's what people are there to learn, so give it to them. If they are satisfied, you are done! If they have questions, you have explanations, because that's your discussion, methodology, literature review, and background. Reporting in reverse values their time. It means the executive-level members of your audience can go on and use your findings to make strategic decisions while the few statisticians in the room can hang out until the end and talk nerdy with you. Reporting in reverse puts the audience first.

## How Do I Apply These Ideas to Graphs?

The APA Guide (2010) knows what's up: "An attractive graphical display makes a scientific article a more effective communication device" (p. 126). But, as we know, it is not just about being attractive. Graphs organized with meaning and narrative have faster decoding times for the reader than disorganized graphs or those without context (Shah, Mayer, & Hegarty, 1999). As applied to graphs, effective data presentation also supports interpretation and prediction tasks better than weak graphs or tables can, which suggests that it plays a role in improved and informed decision making (Meyer, Shamo, & Gopher, 1999). So, let's apply this chapter's guiding ideas to the arrangement of pieces in a data display.

### Proportions Are Accurate

A viewer should be able to use a ruler to measure the pieces of your visualization and find that the measurements are proportionate to the data they represent. In the case of bar charts, this means that the y-axis must always start at zero.

**Figure 5.29    The scale of a bar chart must start at zero**

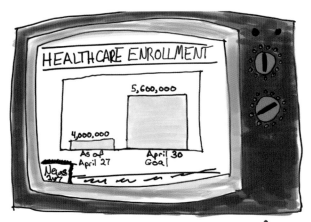

*Source:* Courtesy of Chris Lysy, Fresh Spectrum.

The bars in a bar chart encode the data by their length, so if we truncate the length by starting the axis at something other than zero, we distort the visual in a bad way. My friend Chris Lysy calls this the "Cable News Axis" because it's so common in TV news programming.

Outside of bar charts, whether the y-axis must start at zero is still a matter of debate. There are cases where it wouldn't make any sense.

**Figure 5.30**   **If zero is not in the realm of possible data points, perhaps it doesn't need to be included in the y-axis**

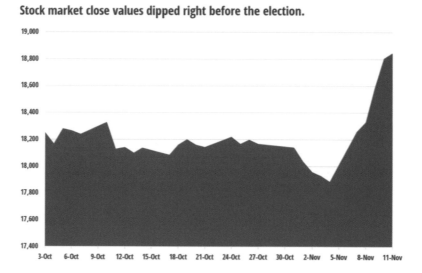

**Stock market close values dipped right before the election.**

A visualization of stock market activity is a great example. If the y-axis started at zero, the visual would look like a flat line. We wouldn't see any variation, and the visual would become meaningless for us. But (fingers crossed) zero isn't a possible data point in a data set for the stock market, so there's no real justification for starting the axis at zero.

Other than for bar charts, I advocate for a y-axis that is based on something reasonable for your data. Maybe the minimum of the axis is your historically lowest point. Maybe the maximum is your goal or your most successful campaign. This way, the axis itself becomes part of the story you need to tell about your data.

## Data Are Intentionally Ordered

To create a bar graph, we highlight the data in the spreadsheet table and ask the program to generate a graph. The graph arranges the bars in the order the data appear in the table. The problem is that we usually order the data in the table according to the order of the questions asked on the survey. This ordering may make perfect sense to those of us deeply embedded in the project, but not to those outside the project. No one else really cares about how we ordered the categorical survey responses. We can do better to help the reader interpret the data display.

**Figure 5.31**   **The order of the bars is not meaningful to a viewer**

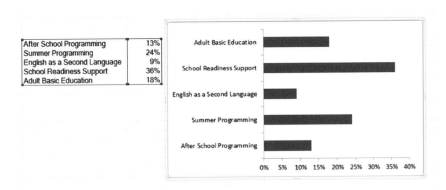

Instead, as the APA Guide suggests, place the bars in order from greatest to least. Sometimes there may be circumstances where you should defer to a different order—for example, when the categories have a well-established scheme that is confusing if disrupted, such as a listing of U.S. states.

Well, you cannot exactly move the bars around within the data display, but you can get them in the right order by sorting the data in the table.

**Figure 5.32**   **Sort the spreadsheet data to produce a meaningfully ordered graph**

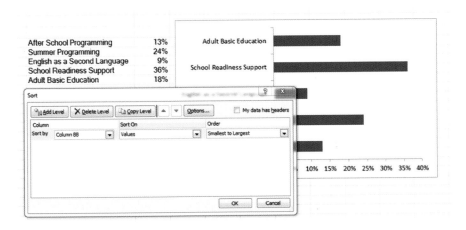

First, highlight the rows containing data, not including the headings. Click the arrow by the *Sort and Filter* button in the *Editing* group on the *Home* tab to see *Custom Sort*. Choose the column with your values in it and select *Smallest to Largest* (in Excel, order the table backward to have it show up the right way in the graph). The graph automatically updates to reflect your new categorical order.

## Axis Intervals Are Equidistant

This checkpoint is the close cousin of "Proportions Are Accurate." The scale used on each axis must have equal intervals. It's an easy mistake to make.

Figure 5.33    **The *x*-axis appears to have equidistant intervals, but that isn't accurate**

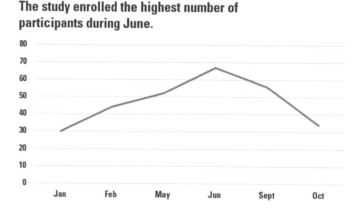

Excel automatically spaces your intervals and labels equidistant from one another, but it is assuming that your intervals actually are equidistant. In the graph in Figure 5.33, that's not the case. We are missing the months of March, April, July, and August, when either no one was enrolled in the study or we have some missing data. But we can't just gloss over those months. It isn't truthful, and it distorts the data display.

To make the graph display correctly, you have to adjust the table in your spreadsheet so that you have spaces in the table for the missing months, even if there are no data in those months. Excel will add the months to the axis. You then have a choice about how to handle the gap months. Should you just skip over them and connect the points in the line? Should you report them as zeros? Your call, but make that decision in the *Select Data* window.

Figure 5.34    **The x-axis now has equidistant intervals**

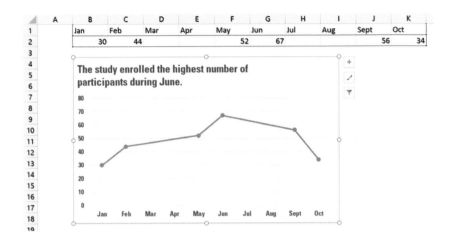

Right-click on your graph and click *Select Data*. In that window, look for the button in the lower left that says *Hidden and Empty Cells* and click it. In that new window, you'll find options for how to handle the missing data.

When data have been collected at irregular intervals, this is one of the only times I think it is appropriate to place markers along the line. Usually markers are a little too much extra noise, but in this case, they serve a clear purpose: identifying where data are actually reported while still maintaining equidistant axis intervals.

Figure 5.35    **Excel provides options for how to visualize missing data**

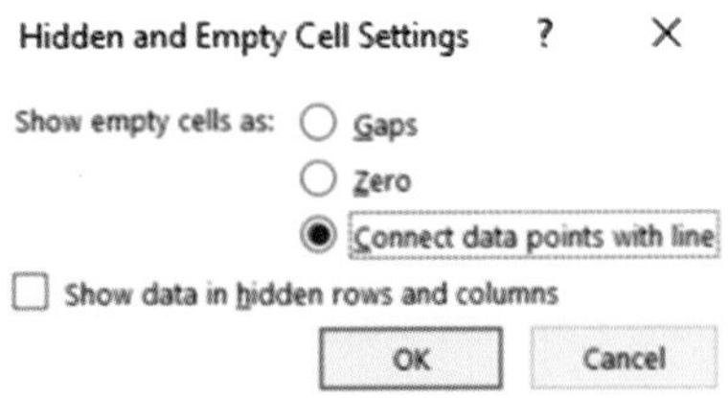

Hidden and Empty Cell Settings    ?    ✕

Show empty cells as:    ○ Gaps
　　　　　　　　　　　　　○ Zero
　　　　　　　　　　　　　◉ Connect data points with line

☐ Show data in hidden rows and columns

OK    Cancel

## Graph Is Two-Dimensional

Although many graphing software programs supply three-dimensional templates, the resulting displays do not necessarily assist interpretation of the graphs or improve accuracy (Few, 2006; Malamed, 2009). Figure 5.36 is an example of a data display showing customer satisfaction with prices at a health food store both before and after the store changed location.

In this visualization, notice how it is not obvious where to read the tops of the columns to get the exact data points—do we read the backs of the columns? The front edges? The midpoints of the tops of the columns? In addition to making the data display just plain confusing to read, the third dimension adds distortion. For

Figure 5.36   **Graph of customer price satisfaction is hard to read in three dimensions**

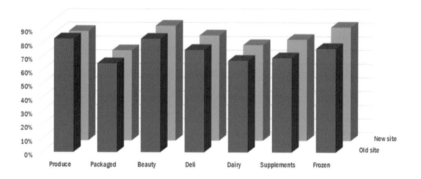

Customer satisfaction with prices at the old store v. the new store

example, see the two columns for produce, on the very left? The one in the back, for the new site, in bright blue, represents 80%, even though it isn't touching the 80% line. The dark blue one representing the old site appears to be shorter, in that we can see some of the light blue column peeking out of the top. But that column actually represents 83%—more than the column in back that looks taller—even though it too doesn't even come close to reaching the 80% gridline. Insanity. Why is this still even an option in Excel? Someday I will be able to delete this section from this chapter, but until then, stay away from 3-D.

Figure 5.37   **Is the quantity represented by the area, the circumference, or just the diameter?**

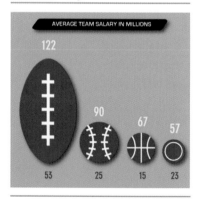

*Source:* http://visual.ly/pro-sport-salary-structures-nfl-mlb-nba-and-nhl.

## Display Is Free of Decoration

Unnecessary decoration just distracts. It doesn't make the graph cute. It doesn't make the data more understandable. Quite the opposite, sometimes that attempt at decoration actually makes things more confusing.

The sports salary graph in Figure 5.37 uses shapes instead of rectangular columns to encode the data. But it introduces all sorts of confusing questions about how to read the graph. Are we to assume that the varying widths are related to the data? Is it just the height of the rounded circles, which are hard to pinpoint? We end up skipping the visual itself and just relying on the number labels, and this defeats the point of having a visual in the first place.

However, this doesn't mean all graphics are bad. In fact, in the sports salary graph in Figure 5.38, the icons help considerably.

**Figure 5.38    Icons don't decorate here, they add information**

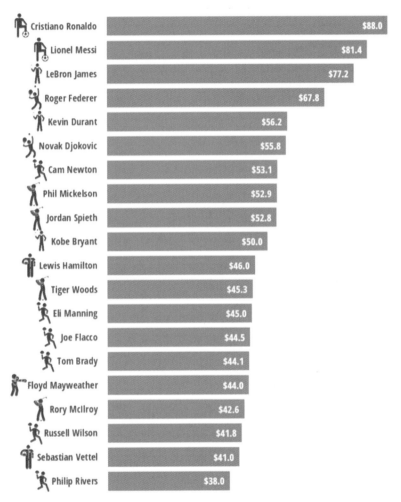

**Top 20 highest paid players in professional sports**
(salary & endorsements, 2016)

|  |  |
|---|---|
| Cristiano Ronaldo | $88.0 |
| Lionel Messi | $81.4 |
| LeBron James | $77.2 |
| Roger Federer | $67.8 |
| Kevin Durant | $56.2 |
| Novak Djokovic | $55.8 |
| Cam Newton | $53.1 |
| Phil Mickelson | $52.9 |
| Jordan Spieth | $52.8 |
| Kobe Bryant | $50.0 |
| Lewis Hamilton | $46.0 |
| Tiger Woods | $45.3 |
| Eli Manning | $45.0 |
| Joe Flacco | $44.5 |
| Tom Brady | $44.1 |
| Floyd Mayweather | $44.0 |
| Rory McIlroy | $42.6 |
| Russell Wilson | $41.8 |
| Sebastian Vettel | $41.0 |
| Philip Rivers | $38.0 |

Created by Stephanie Evergreen, based on DeSantis, "The Top 25 Highest-Paid Athletes Of 2016, Visualized," Forbes.com. http://www.forbes.com/sites/nickdesantis/2016/06/20/the-top-25-highest-paid-athletes-of-2016-visualized/#6968cf3f21e4

The icons provide additional information, marking the sport played by each person in the graph. As someone who just learned the rules of football in 2016, I really need those icons to tell me who's who. They assist with the interpretability of the graph.

Beyond a distinction of clip art versus icon, the real litmus test for additional graphics is whether they support the story and how well the reader can interpret it.

## What Is the Bottom Line?

Ultimately, this chapter can be condensed to one key point: Consistent arrangement of text and graphics makes our work more accessible and understandable for our audiences. When we intentionally place our elements in a logical fashion, we communicate our mental structure to our readers, increasing their ability to take in, digest, and retain the information we produce. Of course, all of this means that it is imperative that we bring mental structure and logic to the organization of our reporting. Before turning on the computer to type a report, you should have the journey in mind. You should already have identified the main point, secondary points, and supporting evidence in their order of importance. But you know what? You know that. Your key points are quite clear to you. You have been up to your eyeballs in your data for a long time. You know them inside and out. This chapter provides the guiding ideas you can put into place to make your well-structured mental architecture equally apparent to your audiences. Proper arrangement lets your readers peek inside your brain. What will they see? An effective data presenter.

## Key Points to Remember

Effective arrangement goes unnoticed. It is not a job for glory seekers. Weak arrangement, in contrast, draws attention to itself; it looks sloppy and causes confusion for an audience.

- Line length can hinder or support reading. Aim for lines that are neither too long nor too short, 8 to 12 words per line.

- A grid structure can help mentally dictate the alignment of report elements. Divide the page into rows and columns for straightforward document creation.

- Effective arrangement is also established through a hierarchy of information. Make the most important elements the largest and place them in key positions. Make secondary information (callout points and headings, for example) relatively smaller, but offset this material so that it is noticed. More supportive explanatory narrative is small, and captions and footnotes, the lowest in the hierarchy, can be even smaller.

- The way you arrange your entire story also matters. Give the findings and conclusions first.

- You are the captain of your software programs. Exploit the software to its fullest extent by sorting the data, removing default formatting, and whatever else you need to do so that your data displays keep their statistically accurate representation while they communicate with greater clarity.

# How Can I Extend This?

## Check Out

I launched the Potent Presentations Initiative (**http://eval.org/p2i**) to have a platform where I could help conference presenters give high-impact presentations. As part of the materials on the site, you'll see a webinar on crafting your message in which I talk about how to report in reverse. Check it out and grab the related handout from the *Presentation Tools* tab.

ChartLabeler (**http://www.appspro.com/Utilities/ChartLabeler.htm**) is a free Excel add-in made by AppsPro. My friend Agata introduced me to this tool, which makes existing data labels more flexible and easier to resize, like text boxes, but also ensures that they stay directly linked to table data and headings. Plug ChartLabeler in to your spreadsheets to make label arrangement a snap.

While the Gutenberg Diagram and the Rule of Thirds are popular layout options, there are others, such as the Z-pattern layout and the L-pattern layout. See Steven Bradley's blog post about three layout options, including Gutenberg, in which he compares their strengths and weaknesses (**http://www.vanseodesign.com/web-design/3-design-layouts**).

## Try This

Fold a piece of paper into thirds. Unfold it, and fold it into thirds the other way. Unfold it. You now have nine squares with four intersecting points along the folds. Use one of the layout approaches in this chapter to create a sketch of a slide of your own work. Go ahead and sketch it at one of those intersecting points and then write in a few keywords.

The idea of creating a hierarchy of importance when presenting information is behind a great deal of web design. Check out your university's website and analyze its hierarchy. Notice what is located in the top left corner. It should be something of high importance (probably the university logo). Notice what text is the largest, and think about what that signals for the way the web designers want you to navigate the site. Almost certainly, you will find that emphasis techniques are used on words that are relevant to prospective students and alumni.

Using tracing paper, regroup the graphic pieces on each slide from your last slideshow. Print out the slides, one per page. Then lay the tracing paper on top of the first slide and move it around to retrace and thus rearrange your pieces. Are your name and organizational affiliation spread apart? Start by tracing your name where it should go and then move the tracing paper so that your name is repositioned over your organizational affiliation and retrace that. In the end, you should have redesigned sketches of all your

*(Continued)*

(Continued)

slides, properly grouped, to take back to your computer for duplication in your slideshow software.

Gregor Aisch, a data visualizer for *The New York Times,* created a small display of multiple line graphs around the 2016 election to show changes in a candidate's popularity in several states. He was promptly called out on Twitter (this is where the #dataviz nerds hang out) because he didn't put these line graphs on the same scale.

**Figure 5.39** *The New York Times* **line graphs aren't on the same scale**

*Source:* © 2016 The New York Times. Reprinted with permission from The New York Times. All rights reserved. The printing, copying, redistribution, or retransmission of this Content without express written permission is prohibited.

List two reasons these graphs shouldn't be on the same scale and two reasons they should. The graphs were updated as new data rolled in, so check out the latest versions at **http://www.nytimes.com/interactive/2016/upshot/presidential-polls-forecast .html#recent-state-changes**.

# Where Can I Go for More Information?

American Psychological Association. (2010). *Publication manual of the American Psychological Association* (6th ed.). Washington, DC: Author.

Davidson, E. J. (2007). Editorial: Unlearning some of our social scientist habits. *Journal of Multidisciplinary Evaluation, 4*(8), iii–vi.

Few, S. (2006). *Visual communication: Core design principles for displaying quantitative information.* Retrieved from **http://www.perceptualedge.com/articles/Whitepapers/Visual_Communication.pdf**

Lupton, E. (2004). *Thinking with type: A critical guide for designers, writers, editors, and students.* New York: Princeton Architectural Press.

Malamed, C. (2009). *Visual language for designers: Principles for creating graphics that people understand.* Beverly, MA: Rockport.

Meyer, J., Shamo, M. K., & Gopher, D. (1999). Information structure and the relative efficacy of tables and graphs. *Human Factors, 41*(4), 570–587.

Modern Language Association of America. (2009). *MLA handbook for writers of research papers* (7th ed.). New York: Author.

Müller-Brockmann, J. (2009). Grid and design philosophy. In H. Armstrong (Ed.), *Graphic design theory: Readings from the field.* New York: Princeton Architectural Press. (Reprinted from *Grid systems in graphic design: A visual communication manual for graphic designers,* *typographers, and three-dimensional designers,* by J. Müller-Brockmann, 1981, Niederteufen, Switzerland: Arthur Niggli)

Samara, T. (2007). *Design elements: A graphic style manual.* Beverly, MA: Rockport Press.

Shah, P., Mayer, R. E., & Hegarty, M. (1999). Graphs as aids to knowledge construction: Signaling techniques for guiding the process of graph comprehension. *Journal of Educational Psychology, 91*(4), 690–702.

Tourangeau, R., Couper, M. P., & Conrad, F. (2004). Spacing, position, and order: Interpretive heuristics for visual features of survey questions. *Public Opinion Quarterly, 68*(3), 368–393.

Tourangeau, R., Couper, M. P., & Conrad, F. (2007). Color, labels, and interpretive heuristics for response scales. *Public Opinion Quarterly, 71*(1), 91–112.

Wheildon, C. (2005). *Type and layout: Are you communicating or just making pretty shapes?* Hastings, Victoria, Australia: Worsley Press.

Wolfe, J. M., & Horowitz, T. S. (2004). What attributes guide the deployment of visual attention and how do they do it? *Nature Reviews Neuroscience, 5,* 485–501.

Woodman, G. F., Vecera, S. P., & Luck, S. J. (2003). Perceptual organization influences visual working memory. *Psychonomic Bulletin & Review, 10*(1), 80–87.

# CHAPTER SIX

# MAKING IT EASY

## LEARNING OBJECTIVES

**After reading this chapter, you will be able to:**

- Pull together your design choices to make dissemination easier

- Feel confident about stepping away from traditional reporting formats

- Articulate the justification for spending your time on design

- Summarize the key points of this book

Now that you are nearly at the end of this book, you have learned a lot about how to present data effectively. You have probably reflected on some of your own reports and slideshows and criticized a few graphs you've found in newspapers. You may even be thinking ahead to your next research poster with excitement and anticipation. Good. You are going to rock it. It probably feels like you have a mountain of work in front of you right now. I'm sorry and you're welcome. Before you and I part ways, how about I show you some strategies to make all of this work a little easier for you and your team?

In doing so, I am also going to help you reorient yourself regarding why you came here in the first place. If you recall the fundamental reasons for rethinking your data presentations, you will be in a better position to justify your efforts to the skeptics that I hope you never meet. In this chapter, I identify the two main criticisms of evolving toward effective data presentation and show you how you can address those criticisms by citing efficient, effective, strategic benefits.

## Criticism: Trying to Look Slick

### Benefit 1: Fits With How the Brain Operates

One of the criticisms that you may hear when you begin to redesign your data presentations is something along the lines of "Nah, don't worry about that—we aren't trying to look like a marketing agency here." I know. I have heard it. In fact, the single hard critique launched from the audience at my dissertation was that it appeared that most of the recommendations I made for good report layout were my personal opinions and aesthetic preferences. This is not the case. Through both research and examples, this book has demonstrated that good design choices are based in a user-centered perspective. Deeper than aesthetics, effective data presentation is about reworking our data so that it can be understood.

Weak data presentation is expensive. It is confusing. It misleads the audience. It turns off potential clients. It discourages interaction with your data.

Effective data presentation, by contrast, is clear and useful. It supports the audience's efforts at reading and cognition. It improves and bolsters decision making. It gets remembered.

Effective data presentation uses color to catch early attention, and it encourages engagement through the use of fonts that are easy on the eye (or the eye–brain system). Effective data presentation arranges reporting elements in a way that reduces the cognitive load on a reader and creates chunks of information that can be readily digested by working memory. Effective data presentation includes pictures, diagrams, and graphs to play off a reader's visual strength and increases the likelihood that the information sticks in that reader's long-term memory.

This is not about looking pretty. It is about presenting data in ways that align with how people see, think, and remember so that they can make more informed decisions and take action. These end goals are why we present our data in the first place.

## Benefit 2: Adds to Credibility and Communicates Competence

The second benefit of effective data presentation also addresses the first criticism. Professional competence is communicated through consistent clarity in your dissemination. Inconsistent or unintentionally sloppy work reflects poorly on the presenter and her organization. Even more subtle errors, like slight misalignments and wordy slides, leave the audience with a feeling of unease that translates into negative judgment of the speaker, the report writer—you (Kosslyn, Kievit, Russell, & Shephard, 2012). On the other hand, effective choices about details like fonts and callout boxes boost perceptions of your legitimacy and professionalism. Design, ultimately, is fairly invisible. It works in the background, behind the solid research you have conducted. It can undermine the quality of your study or enhance it in such a way that you get more attention as a result.

## Criticism: Design Is Expensive

All that said, the second criticism most often heard is that the budget is insufficient to cover the time it takes to present data effectively.

## Benefit 3: There Are Multiple Ways to Save Time

As we now know, it is less expensive to invest in design time before disseminating your work than it is to put weak work out in the world that wastes readers' time and mental energy in the muddling and mucking of interpretation. But, if you have been tallying as we've moved along here, you've probably realized that we have often taken extra steps to move away from some of the default settings in our software programs. I know this is beginning to sound time-consuming, especially given the length of a typical research report, multiplied by the number of report authors. So, here are three ways to save more time.

## Slidedocs

Named by presentation guru Nancy Duarte, a slidedoc = slideshow + reporting document. This might not sound sexy just yet, but we are talking about using one file to generate both your slideshow and your handout or report. Efficiency, baby!

Want to see how it works? I wanted to partner with a local foundation on a project. The foundation wanted me to write a proposal for the venture. I hate proposal writing. The foundation also wanted me to give a presentation on the proposal to a committee. This was beginning to feel like a lot of work. I made the whole process a lot more efficient by creating a slidedoc.

**Figure 6.1   My slides with my notes typed in the notes section**

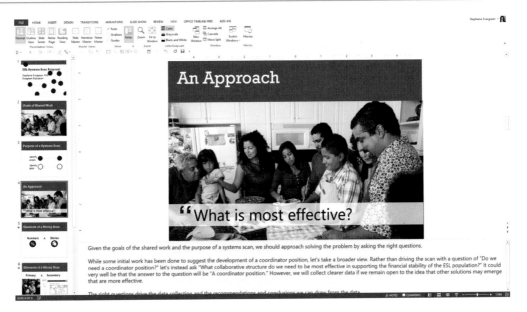

You can see in Figure 6.1 the handful of slides I created for the presentation. They are designed around the best practices discussed in this book: mainly pictures, with a few supporting words. Everything important I wanted to articulate during the presentation is down in the notes section. The magic of turning this into a slidedoc happens in that notes section. Let's look at a typical notes view.

You are probably very used to this layout. You get there by clicking the *View* tab and clicking the button that says *Notes Page.* There's a big placeholder at the top where the slide will appear and a big placeholder at the bottom where the notes will appear. The slidedoc secret is that those placeholders can be rearranged, and we can

**Figure 6.2** **The typical layout of a notes page in PowerPoint**

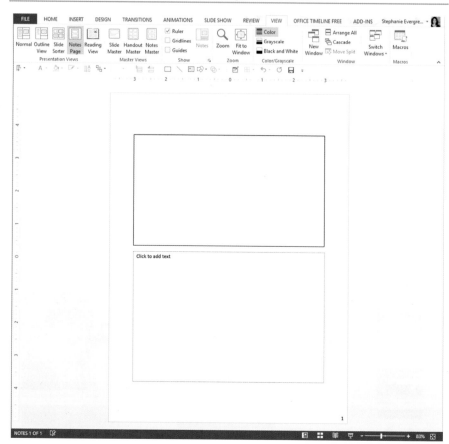

add graphic enhancements to the notes page to make it look more like an actual useful document—a slidedoc. On the next page you'll see how one page of notes from my proposal looks (Figure 6.3).

I shrunk that big slide placeholder into the corner and put it inside a big green rectangle, which also contains a summary sentence of my ideas. I enlarged the text placeholder and picked a great font. Look more closely at the text in this notes page. The text is not bits and phrases or a bulleted list of highlights I want to cover. It's full of complete sentences, written in narrative format. *It's my proposal!* All I had to do was print my notes pages to PDF, and my reporting was done. My audience members then received a pretty visually engaging proposal to review, easy to swipe through on a tablet, with a one-to-one correspondence between the page and the presentation because of the little slide thumbnail in the corner.

This way I could present well-constructed slides and deliver a visual report within the same file.

Figure 6.3 **The layout of a notes page in my slidedoc**

An Approach

"What is most effective?"

Our approach should be driven by asking the right questions to meet the stated purpose.

Given the goals of the shared work and the purpose of a systems scan, we should approach solving the problem by asking the right questions.

While some initial work has been done to suggest the development of a coordinator position, let's take a broader view. Rather than driving the scan with a question of "Do we need a coordinator position?" let's instead ask "What collaborative structure do we need to be most effective in supporting the financial stability of the ESL population?" It could very well be that the answer to the question will be "A coordinator position." However, we will collect clearer data if we remain open to the idea that other solutions may emerge that are more effective.

The right questions drive the data collection and the recommendations and conclusions we can draw from the data.

4

To make this happen, you'll do most of your work in the *Notes Master*. Look again in the *View* tab. We had been in the family of buttons all the way on the left called *Presentation Views*. To the right of that is a family of buttons called *Master Views*. Click on the *Notes Master*. In here you will reposition the slide placeholder and the text placeholder, and then add anything that you want to appear on every notes page, such as a big green rectangle. Anything you change here in the *Notes Master* will be reflected over in the notes pages. So if you want to check how your *Notes Master* layout is affecting your notes pages, go back to the *View* tab and click on *Notes Pages*.

What I love about the notes pages is that they are a great place to offload extra things that would otherwise clutter the slide. Put your logo on your notes page! Put that giant table on your notes page! Put your contact info on your notes page!

Slidedocs are a very handy way to streamline reporting and make your life more efficient. While the slidedoc technically isn't a slideshow, remember way back in Chapter 1 when I showed you a page from a dashboard report? We constructed that entire report inside Excel, one page per tab. Maybe it would be called a spreadsheet-doc. We simply inserted textboxes for the narrative on each page. Then we PDF'd the Excel file. Boom. These strategies give you the freedom to make high-impact dissemination products while keeping the whole process chugging along efficiently.

## Style Sheets

Project managers in the graphic design world are effective people. They have developed a system for streamlining the look and feel of a project from its very start through the use of style sheets. Style sheets are records of conceptual graphic design–based decisions about elements such as grid dimensions, color palette, and font settings. These specifications are listed in one location, ranging from a single page to an entire manual on branding guidelines, which serves as the codebook for the design of new documents as part of a project. When fresh staff are brought on to the project or additional data presentation products are created, the style sheet identifies the decisions already made about color, graphics, arrangement, and type, so that ongoing work blends with the project's research-based branding choices.

For some of you, decisions about font choices and such will be dictated by your university or your department. If you are starting from scratch, make a plan and stick to it. What is your heading font? What font are you going to use for your narrative text? How will your sidebar text be spaced? Make these decisions as early as possible, record them in a style sheet, and then try very hard not to waver.

**Figure 6.4   Style sheet for slideshow**

Figure 6.4 is one simple style sheet I created for my own slide decks. You can see that it names the fonts I chose for the headings and text of the slides, as well as the color of the text (including the RGB color code, shown in parentheses, to achieve that precise color). The bottom of the style sheet lists some helpful information. In this particular slideshow, I was demonstrating how to design reports, and thus many of my slides showed images of two report pages side by side. The specifications in the style sheet identify the exact size and position for each of those example report page images, so that I can ensure the images appear in a consistent location on every slide throughout the slide deck.

Importantly, the style sheet also displays a sample slide from the deck and details the nature of the additional imagery to include in the slides: graphic designer tools. In reality, it is better to be even more specific. Here are some of the questions I ask myself when considering images for the slide deck: Are the images real photographs or are illustrations okay? Is it better to include images of people actually holding graphic design tools so that the audience gets a sense of themselves in the work? Does the image background need to be white or some other color? Answering such questions from the beginning will allow you to set up more specific image search parameters, and it will save probably a billion hours of your time.

**Figure 6.5    Style sheet for Potent Presentations Initiative**

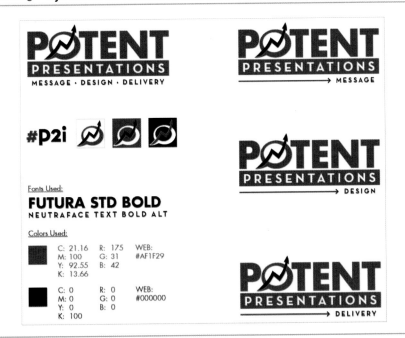

*Source:* Designed by Chris Metzner for the American Evaluation Association's Potent Presentation Initiative (p2i).

Figure 6.5 is another example from a project I led for the American Evaluation Association, called the Potent Presentations Initiative. At the very beginning of the project, we contracted with a graphic designer to produce a logo. In return, he provided us with the start of a style sheet. It displays the full logo in the upper left, versions of the logo along the right for the occasions when I was speaking about one part of the initiative, and what some people refer to as "avatars"—those little square icons I could use as buttons, signifiers, and web page tab identifiers. This sheet gave me a single source file that I referred to each time I needed to cut and paste a logo or an avatar. I accessed this page frequently throughout my work on this initiative.

Also notice that the designer made a stylized hashtag because he knew we wanted to post our hashtag on our slides and handouts so that people could spread the message of the initiative. The graphic designer listed the color codes he used, in CMYK, RGB, and web, which allowed us to construct a broader palette from those colors if we needed to. He also identified the font he used in creating the logo.

On your own project style sheets, you probably need to specify a larger set of variations on these fonts to fit your needs. For a project that includes dissemination by both paper and slideshow, Figures 6.6 and 6.7 provide examples of the minimum decisions you'll want to make, and how to display them in a style sheet.

**Figure 6.6    Paper font styles**

## Heading 1 (Trade Gothic LT Std Bold, size 18, black [0,0,0])

## Heading 2 (Trade Gothic LT Std Bold, size 14, gray [65,65,65])

### Heading 3 (Trade Gothic LT Std Bold, size 12, black [0,0,0])

**Narrative (Minion Pro, size 11, black [0,0,0])**

Caption (Minion Pro, size 9, black [0,0,0])

**Figure 6.7    Slideshow font styles**

# Heading (Trade Gothic LT Std Bold, size 48, black [0,0,0])

**Text** (Trade Gothic LT Std Bold, size 36, light gray [224,224,224], on gray box [65,65,65])

You might decide to add particular font specifications for sidebars, callouts, or alternative text fonts for your slideshow.

Making these decisions near the beginning of the project increases efficiency by streamlining the design. The few times I have consulted with organizations and discovered to my delight that they were using style sheets, I found the style sheets did not go into enough detail. It might seem to lean a bit toward micromanagement, but a lack of sufficient specification in the style guide leaves gaps that cause confusion among both the teammates designing the effective data presentations and the readers who have to mentally reconcile meaningless style changes.

## What if a Client or Funder Has a Style Guide?

Even though you have taken care to make nuanced design decisions, in some consulting situations, the clients will have their own branding. Should you assume a client's branding or keep your own? Well, it depends. If the client needs you to come in with strong consulting, maybe to help change the minds of reluctant staff, using your own branding can be helpful. If the client needs your work to appear more like something he or she adopted, defer to that branding and style guide. And then you have grayer areas like this: Say your department wins a grant from a large state agency, which insists that all grantees follow the agency's style guide. But the guide is incomplete. Insert your own branding and style decisions where there are gaps. Perhaps you can use your own department's color palette on the graphs or your own font choices in a report sidebar. Of course, check that the style decisions you make play somewhat nicely with the agency's style guide, so that the report does not look schizophrenic. In other words, be flexible. Advance your own style guide where you can and defer to others when necessary.

Indeed, this was one of the main flaws I saw in the multitude of reports I reviewed for my dissertation. A section change occurred, and suddenly there were new fonts, new color schemes, and so on. On top of needlessly causing confusion for the readers, such changes reflect poorly on the writers and makes them look like they don't have it together. Style sheets ensure consistency even when there are multiple people working on a project or paper, and they are especially helpful for long-term projects and those that have many personnel changes.

My sample style sheet template is available online (http://stephanieevergreen.com/organize-your-reporting-with-a-style-sheet-template); you can download the template and fill in your own details. You'll notice that there are several pictures in the template. The best style sheets I've seen include actual snapshots of what great slides look like, models of how bar charts should be composed, and so on, showing staff members what they should aim to produce.

## Save Themes

Once you have specified your fonts, spacing, colors, justification, and so forth, save your decisions. Over and above the efficiency of developing a style guide, you can streamline one step further by saving these settings directly into your software program.

First, modify the settings for your text according to your style guide using *Styles* in the upper right of the ribbon bar in Word.

Figure 6.8 **Screenshot depicting where to adjust settings according to your style sheet**

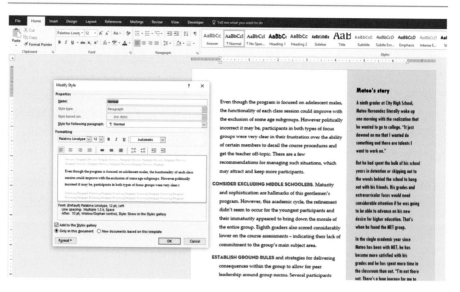

Right-click on *Normal* in the *Styles* options and then click *Modify* from the menu. That opens the dialogue box shown here. From this box, select your preferences to align with the decisions you have made about how you want the narrative text to look. Repeat this process for your headings, sidebars, and whatever other text styles you've chosen.

Once those settings are in place within the *Styles* group, click on the *Page Layout* tab.

Over in the *Themes* group, click on the little arrow under the *Themes* icon. Head to the bottom and click on *Save Theme,* and name that theme after your project. This allows you to retain all of the decisions you just made for the future. Those same options are then available whenever you open any of the other Microsoft programs on your computer. You can see from the screenshot that I have gone through this process

**Figure 6.9    Screenshot showing how to save style sheet settings**

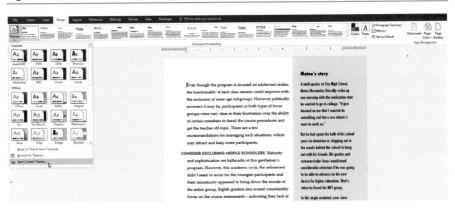

many times—the themes I have saved are all shown under *Custom* in the Themes group. To help me keep things sorted, I tend to create a new style guide for each of my projects. The bonus is that when you ship your document to your colleague or classmate, all she has to do is click on *Save Theme* on her computer and the reporting is made more efficient for her as well.

# Key Points to Remember

As long as you can keep the following points in mind, you have all the reason you need to go forth presenting data effectively:

- Graphics, text, colors, and placement matter to the brains and memories of your readers.

- A small investment of time up front in making style decisions increases efficiency throughout the project.

- Document design decisions on a style sheet that serves as a reference point throughout your project.

- After setting up your design decisions in your first document, save the settings as a theme so that you do not have to establish those settings in the future.

- Proper and consistent use of these design principles will make your data presentations clearer and better understood.

- In order to emphasize key content and present it effectively, you must carefully think through and identify your key content, tapping into input from classmates or colleagues who are cognitively close to the data.

# How Can I Extend This?

## Check Out

Head over to the *Guardian* newspaper's website on data visualization, Datablog (**http://www.guardian.co.uk/news/datablog**). Click on any of the headlines to view their interactive visualizations, something not really discussed in this book. Play with the interactivity a bit. The work is high quality, but improvements could be made. What would you suggest? The raw data file behind each visualization is usually available for download too, so you can demonstrate your recommendations by creating your own graphs.

Navigate to the web companion for this book (**www.sage.com/evergreen**), where you will find even more examples of effective data presentation. I've posted directions for replicating some of the processes I describe here using alternative, free software and the latest version of Microsoft Office. You'll also find my blog, where I keep you up to date on the most effective data presentation.

Nancy Duarte has actually written an entire book about slidedocs—as a slidedoc. Yeah, the whole book is a slidedoc itself! Read it for free at **http://www.duarte.com/slidedocs** and look at some of her templates. Don't copy her work (I can't tell you how many slidedocs I've seen with green rectangles at the tops of the pages), but use it as inspiration to design your own.

## Try This

After viewing the interactive visualizations at the *Guardian*'s Datablog, grab a paper copy of *USA Today* (its online stories often do not include the graphs that appear in the print edition). Compare the data visualization styles of the two news agencies. Verbalize how the differences in style send different messages to the reader. What are the messages you pick up, not from the stories themselves, but from the stylistic decisions the designers have made?

Develop a style sheet for one of your papers or slideshows. List the fonts, colors, imagery, and sizes you decide to use. Review the Report Layout Checklist (located in Appendix A and downloadable online) to guide your design decisions.

Reflect those decisions in your style sheet, using the template you can download at **http://stephanieevergreen.com/organize-your-reporting-with-a-style-sheet-template**, which will walk you through all the major decisions you need to make.

## Where Can I Go for More Information?

Kosslyn, S. M., Kievit, R. A., Russell, A. G., & Shephard, J. M. (2012). PowerPoint presentation flaws and failures: A psychological analysis. *Frontiers in Psychology, 3.* **http://dx.doi .org/10.3389/fpsyg.2012.00230**

# Appendix A

# Report Layout Checklist

by Stephanie D. H. Evergreen, PhD

This checklist is meant to be used as a diagnostic guide to identify elements of reports that can be enhanced using graphic design best practices and/or the assistance of a graphic design expert.

## Instructions

Rate each aspect of the report using the following rubric, by circling the most appropriate letter. Use the "Best Practice" section as a guide for improvement.

F = fully met, P = partly met, N = not met

| Type | Rating | Best Practice |
|---|---|---|
| Text fonts are used for narrative text | F P N | Use serif fonts. Nothing with lots of graphic detail. |
| Long reading is in 9- to 11-point size | F P N | Studies have shown that 11-point text is easiest to read at length, but it depends on the typeface (font). |
| Body text has stylistic uniformity | F P N | Each text section has normal text in sentence case (no bold, no all caps), except in short areas of intentional emphasis. This supports undistracted reading. |

| Type | Rating | Best Practice | Notes |
|---|---|---|---|
| Line spacing is 11 to 13 points | F P N | For lines within a paragraph, generally choose 1–2 points larger than the size of the body text. | *Nice serif choices* include Garamond, Palatino, Cambria. |
| Headers and callouts are emphasized | F P N | Header should be 150–200% of body text size. Sans serif or decorative is okay. Use sentence case. Contrast with body text by using different size, style, and/or color. Too similar looks unintentional. | *Nice sans serif choices* are Open Sans, Franklin Gothic, Futura. |
| No more than three fonts are used | F P N | A change in font indicates a change in meaning. Use font changes to guide the reader through information according to importance. | *Sentence case* is when the first letter of the line is capitalized and all others are lowercase, except proper nouns. |
| Bullets are slightly less thick than text | F P N | If bullets must be used, decrease their size to slightly less (70–80%) than the point size of the font. Otherwise, they are too strong and distracting. If good spacing is used in lieu of bullets, this best practice is fully met. | *Body text* is what comprises the narrative of the report. |
| | | | By contrast, *header text* is what makes up your headlines and titles, also known as display text. |
| **Arrangement** | **Rating** | **Best Practice** | <ul><li>Default bullet size (too big)</li><li>Appropriate bullet size</li></ul> |
| Alignment is consistent | F P N | Alignment is an early attention feature easily noticed by a reader, so be sure that elements start in the same place on each page unless misaligned on purpose. Avoid centered elements. | *Imagine each page* divided into rows and columns. Draw imaginary lines to check that elements are aligned at the start of each row and at the top of each column. |
| Columns are 8 to 12 words in length | F P N | This is 50–80 characters, depending on font. Longer is difficult to track from line to line; shorter creates too many hyphenated words, distracting the reader. | *Asymmetry* is an easy way to create interest. Try placing a cool picture off to one side of the page. |
| Important elements are prominent | F P N | Most prominent position is top half of page and/or emphasized by size, color, orientation, etc. Supportive information is toned down. | |
| Body text is left or full justified | F P N | Ragged right edge is more informal but easier to read for average readers. Full justification is formal, easier for fluent readers, but creates design issues with "white rivers," or large gaps of white space between words. | |

**Notes**

| | Rating | Best Practice | Notes |
|---|---|---|---|
| Grouped items logically belong together | F P N | Grouped items are interpreted as one chunk. Place logical items together. Add space between groups. Minimize space between header and body text. | |
| Empty area is allocated on each page | F P N | Leave plenty of space between paragraphs, around page margins, and between text and graphics. It gives eyes a rest. | *Wide margins* are a quick way to create empty area and manage line length. |
| **Graphics** | **Rating** | **Best Practice** | |
| Pictures/graphic elements are present | F P N | Multimode learning increases chance of information storage in long-term memory because it eases cognitive load of body text. Choose pictures or graphics related to your topic. Graphics include, but should not be limited to, tables and charts. If there are no graphics, this best practice is not met. | *Pictures and graphics* related to your content make your content more memorable. *Choose pictures* from high-quality sources, such as paid websites. Watermarks and fuzzy images are signs of an amateur. |
| Graphics are near associated text | F P N | If readers must flip between pages to interpret text and graphic, comprehension is impaired. | *Use a cover page* at the beginning of a report. This is a good place for a very large graphic. |
| Graphics are simple | F P N | Less visual noise leads to better assimilation. Eliminate gradation, textures, and graphics as backgrounds. Segment complex graphics into smaller chunks. | |
| Size corresponds to changes in meaning | F P N | Use, for example, larger pictures on chapter start pages. In graphing, for example, be sure the heights of columns proportionately represent the data. | |
| Graphics direct toward text | F P N | Use the power of an image to direct the reader's gaze from the image to the associated text. Eyes in a photo, for example, should look inward at the text. | |
| Visual theme is evident | F P N | Pick a visual theme that can be used in different forms throughout reporting to give strong emotional connection. | |
| Some elements are repeated | F P N | Repetition of some graphic elements adds unity to the piece and makes work more memorable. Be careful not to overdo it—too many elements can add clutter or complication. | |

## Notes

| Color | Rating | Best Practice |
|---|---|---|
| Narrative text is dark gray or black | F P N | Black has highest comprehension levels, with low-intensity colors taking a distant second place. |
| Background has white/subdued color | F P N | Reversed-out text (e.g., white text on black background) slightly impairs information retention. |
| One or two emphasis colors are used | F P N | Subdued colors that still contrast with the background should be used. When color is used, it should be to actually emphasize important information, such as data in a graph. If you select more than one color, consider choosing along a color gradation so that order of importance is implicit. |
| Color changes denote meaning changes | F P N | Color changes signal a change in hierarchy of information. Be intentional with color changes so that a viewer doesn't get confused. |
| Color reprints legibly in black and white | F P N | Color looks different on a computer screen than on paper. Print on a black-and-white printer and then make a copy of that printout to check legibility. |

Time to add up your points: _____

F = 1 point

P = ½ point

N = 0 points

Well-formatted reports score within 23 to 25 points. At this score, report readers are better able to read and retain content.

## Notes

Keep in mind various culture-laden *color connotations.* For example, pink is highly associated with feminine qualities in the United States.

Make sure your color choices are appropriate for your audience.

Note that *people with color blindness* have difficulty with red-green and yellow-blue combinations.

*A safe bet is to use your client's colors.*

# Appendix B
# Data Visualization Checklist

By Stephanie Evergreen and Ann Emery

This checklist is meant to be used as a guide for the development of high-impact data visualizations. Rate each aspect of the data visualization by circling the most appropriate number, where 2 points means the guideline was fully met, 1 means it was partially met, and 0 means it was not met at all. The rating n/a should not be used frequently; rather, it should be reserved for when the guideline truly does not apply. For example, a pie chart has no axis lines or tick marks to rate. If a guideline has been broken intentionally to make a point, rate it n/a and deduct those points from the total possible. Refer to the data visualization anatomy chart on the last page for guidance on vocabulary.

| Guideline | Rating | | | |
|---|---|---|---|---|
| **Text** _Graphs don't contain much text, so existing text must encapsulate your message and pack a punch._ | | | | |
| **6- to 12-word descriptive title is left justified in upper left corner** A short title enables readers to comprehend the takeaway message even while quickly skimming the graph. Rather than a generic phrase, use a descriptive sentence that encapsulates the graph's finding, or "so what?" Western cultures start reading in the upper left, so locate the title there. | 2 | 1 | 0 | n/a |
| **Subtitles and/or annotations provide additional information** Subtitles and annotations (callout text within the graph) can add explanatory and interpretive power to a graph. Use them to answer questions a viewer might have or to highlight specific data points. | 2 | 1 | 0 | n/a |

| Guideline | Rating | | | |
|---|---|---|---|---|
| **Text size is hierarchical and readable**<br>Titles are in a larger size than subtitles and annotations, which are larger than labels, which are larger than axis labels, which are larger than source information. The smallest text—axis labels—is at least 9-point font size on paper, at least 20 points on-screen. | 2 | 1 | 0 | n/a |
| **Text is horizontal**<br>Titles, subtitles, annotations, and data labels are horizontal (not vertical or diagonal). Line labels and axis labels can deviate from this rule and still receive full points. Consider switching graph orientation (e.g., from column to bar chart) to make text horizontal. | 2 | 1 | 0 | n/a |
| **Data are labeled directly**<br>Position data labels near the data (e.g., on top of or next to bars and next to lines) rather than in a separate legend. Eliminate/embed legends when possible because eye movement back and forth between the legend and the data can interrupt the brain's attempts to interpret the graph. | 2 | 1 | 0 | n/a |
| **Labels are used sparingly**<br>Focus attention by removing redundancy. For example, in line charts, label every other year on an axis. Do not add numeric labels *and* use an axis scale, since this is redundant. | 2 | 1 | 0 | n/a |

| Guideline | Rating | | | |
|---|---|---|---|---|

## Arrangement

Improper arrangement of graph elements can confuse readers at best and mislead them at worst. Thoughtful arrangement makes a data visualization easier for viewers to interpret.

**Proportions are accurate**

A viewer should be able to measure the lengths or areas depicted in the graph with a ruler and find that their relationships match those in the underlying data. Y-axis scales should be appropriate. Bar charts should start axes at zero. Other graphs can have minimum and maximum scales that reflect what should be accurate interpretation of the data (e.g., the stock market ticker should not start at zero, or no meaningful pattern will be visible).

Rating: 2 1 0 n/a

**Data are intentionally ordered**

Data should be displayed in an order that makes logical sense to the viewer. Data may be ordered by frequency counts (e.g., from greatest to least for nominal categories), by groupings or bins (e.g., histograms), by time period (e.g., line charts), alphabetically, etc. Use an order that supports interpretation of the data.

Rating: 2 1 0 n/a

**Axis intervals are equidistant**

The spaces between axis intervals should be the same unit, even if every axis interval isn't labeled. Irregular data collection periods can be noted with markers on a line graph, for example.

Rating: 2 1 0 n/a

**Graph is two-dimensional**

Avoid three-dimensional displays, bevels, and other distortions.

Rating: 2 1 0 n/a

**Display is free of decoration**

Graphs should be free of clip art or other illustrations used solely for decoration. Some illustrations, such as icons, can support interpretation.

Rating: 2 1 0 n/a

| Guideline | Rating | | | |
|---|---|---|---|---|

## Color

Keep culture-laden color connotations in mind. For example, pink is highly associated with feminine qualities in the United States.

Use sites like ColorBrewer 2.0 to find color schemes suitable for reprinting in black and white and that are color-blind-safe.

| Guideline | Rating | | | |
|---|---|---|---|---|
| **Color scheme is intentional** <br> Colors should represent brand or other intentional choice, not default color schemes. Use your organization's colors or your client's colors. Work with online tools to identify brand colors and others that are compatible. | 2 | 1 | 0 | n/a |
| **Color is used to highlight key patterns** <br> Action colors should guide the viewer to key parts of the display. Less important, supporting, or comparison data should be a muted color, like gray. | 2 | 1 | 0 | n/a |
| **Color is legible when printed in black and white** <br> When graphs are printed or photocopied in black and white, the viewer should still be able to see patterns in the data. | 2 | 1 | 0 | n/a |
| **Color is legible for people with color blindness** <br> Avoid red-green and yellow-blue combinations when those colors touch one another. | 2 | 1 | 0 | n/a |
| **Text sufficiently contrasts with background** <br> Black/very dark text against a white/transparent background is easiest to read. | 2 | 1 | 0 | n/a |

## Lines

Excessive lines—gridlines, borders, tick marks, and axes—can add clutter or noise to a graph, so eliminate them whenever they aren't useful for interpreting the data.

| Guideline | Rating | | | |
|---|---|---|---|---|
| **Gridlines, if present, are muted** <br> Color should be faint gray, not black. Full points if no gridlines are used. Gridlines, even muted, should not be used when the graph includes numeric labels on each data point. | 2 | 1 | 0 | n/a |
| **Graph does not have a border line** <br> The graph should bleed into the surrounding page or slide rather than being contained by a border. | 2 | 1 | 0 | n/a |
| **Axes do not have unnecessary tick marks or axis lines** <br> Tick marks can be useful in line graphs (to demarcate each point in time along the y-axis) but are unnecessary in most other graph types. Remove axis lines whenever possible. | 2 | 1 | 0 | n/a |
| **Graph has one horizontal and one vertical axis** <br> Viewers can best interpret one x-axis and one y-axis. Don't add a second y-axis. Try a connected scatterplot or two graphs side by side instead. (A secondary axis used to hack new graph types is okay, so long as viewers aren't being asked to interpret a second y-axis.) | 2 | 1 | 0 | n/a |

## Overall

Graphs will catch a viewer's attention, so visualize only the data that need attention. Too many graphics of unimportant information dilute the power of visualization.

| Guideline | Rating | | | |
|---|---|---|---|---|
| **Graph highlights significant finding or conclusion** <br><br> A graph should have a "so what?"—either practical or statistical significance (or both) to warrant its presence. For example, contextualized or comparison data help the viewer understand the significance of the data and give the graph more interpretive power. | 2 | 1 | 0 | n/a |
| **The type of graph is appropriate for data** <br><br> Data are displayed using a graph type appropriate for the relationship within the data. For example, change over time is displayed as a line graph, area chart, slope graph, or dot plot. | 2 | 1 | 0 | n/a |
| **Graph has appropriate level of precision** <br><br> Use a level of precision that meets your audience's needs. Few numeric labels need decimal places, unless you are communicating with academic peers. Charts intended for public consumption rarely need p values listed. | 2 | 1 | 0 | n/a |
| **Individual chart elements work together to reinforce the overarching takeaway message** <br><br> Choices about graph type, text, arrangement, color, and lines should all reinforce the same takeaway message. | 2 | 1 | 0 | n/a |

Score: _____ / _____ = _____ %

Well-formatted data visualizations score between 90% and 100% of available points. At this level, viewers are better able to read, interpret, and retain content.

# Data Visualization Anatomy Chart

Confused by the terminology? Review the anatomy charts below for illustrations of what's what.

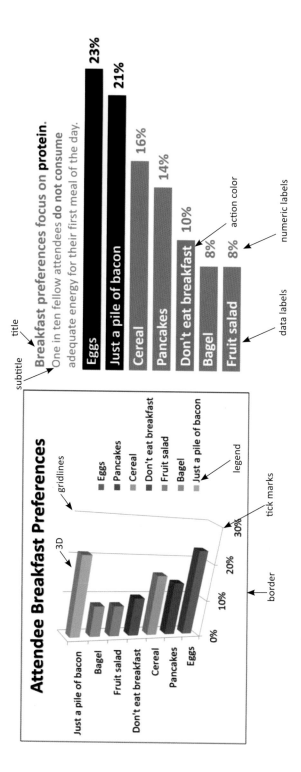

# Index